England

A prolific, confessedly compulsive poet and playwright, Maureen Duffy published her first novel, *That's How It Was*, in 1962. Since then she has written many novels including *Love Child*, *Gor Saga*, *Londoners*, *Illuminations* (1991), *Occam's Razor* (1993) and most recently, *Restitution* (1998). Her non-fiction work includes *The Erotic World of Faery*, *The Passionate Shepherdess* and *Purcell*.

Other books by Maureen Duffy

Novels

That's How it Was
The Single Eye
The Microcosm
The Paradox Players
Wounds
Love Child
I Want to go to Moscow
Capital
Housespy
Gor Saga
Scarborough Fear
Londoners
Change
Illuminations
Occam's Razor
Restitution

Non-Fiction

The Erotic World of Faery
The Passionate Shepherdess — A Biography of Aphra Behn
Inherit the Earth
Men and Beasts
A Thousand Capricious Chances — Methuen 1889–1989
Purcell — A Biography of Henry Purcell

England

The Making of the Myth
from Stonehenge to Albert Square

Maureen Duffy

FOURTH ESTATE • *London*

This paperback edition first published in 2002
First published in Great Britain in 2001 by
Fourth Estate
77–85 Fulham Palace Road
London W6 8JB
www.4thestate.co.uk

Copyright © Maureen Duffy 2001

10 9 8 7 6 5 4 3 2

The right of Maureen Duffy to be identified as the author of this
work has been asserted by her in accordance with the Copyright,
Designs and Patents Act 1988

A catalogue record for this book is available from the
British Library

ISBN 1–84115–167–X

Typeset by Rowland Phototypesetting Limited,
Bury St Edmunds, Suffolk.
Printed in Great Britain by
Clays Ltd. St Ives plc

Contents

'He that is mad and sent into England.

Ay, marry, why was he sent into England?

Why, because 'a was mad, 'a shall recover his wits there;
or if 'a do not, 'tis no great matter there.

Why?

'Twill not be seen in him there: there the men are all as
mad as he.'

HAMLET

Introduction

I WAS BORN and brought up English in spite of having an absent Irish father and an Irish name. My mother's family had lived in Essex since the Conquest as yeomen under Elizabeth and paupers under Victoria, until they moved to the East End of London when agriculture collapsed in the 1870s. My first fictional impressions after Robert Louis Stevenson's Treasure Island of English eccentrics, Squire Trelawney and the Doctor, Long John Silver and Ben Gunn, came from Kipling, and his celebration of English history and myth in *Puck of Pook's Hill* and its sequel, *Rewards and Fairies*. Dan and Una, the child protagonists of the two books, are taken by Puck on a trip through English history as it might have happened in their part of Sussex, in a series of imaginative fictions that supplemented what we learnt at school about kings and queens and battles, and the everyday lives of Roman soldiers or mediaeval monks.

Myth is a late term in our language, dating from the 1840s when, under the influence of German scholars, we were taking a Grimm interest in Teutonic languages and fairy tales as belonging to our common ancestors, and introducing the study of Anglo-Saxon into the university curriculum. The *Oxford English Dictionary* has two basic definitions of myth: 'a purely fictitious narrative usually involving supernatural persons, actions or events and embodying some popular idea, concerning natural or historical phenomena' and, as a secondary meaning, 'a fictitious or imaginary person or object'. Both apply to the fictional narrative nation states tell about themselves in establishing an identity. England is both a real place, part of a small island once joined to that land mass known as Europe, and an imagined icon, almost, indeed, a person as embodied in 'motherland'. Where other nations speak of a male state, a fatherland, ours, like France, is always female. She is, in the words of 'Land of Hope and Glory', written at the beginning of the twentieth century, 'mother of the free'.

Kipling's version addresses her directly:

> Land of our birth, our faith, our pride,
> For whose dear sake our fathers died;
> Oh, Motherland, we pledge to thee
> Head, heart and hand through the years to be!

The British Empire's heyday was fittingly presided over by an empress, Victoria. (Nobody seriously thinks of Edward VII, George V and Edward VIII as emperors.) England is also a supernatural person, Britannia, a kind of sea goddess, from our long addiction to the sea and our island status. Like the Christian Church England has always been capable of absorbing, or making over the attributes and territories of others, especially those who were here before like the Britons, Picts and Scots. Britannia herself should embody Britain but the concept of England has for centuries swallowed up the identities of the other parts of the island, and taken over with them what should be properly a goddess of the Celtic fringe who existed as an icon before the English even arrived.

Today our image of ourselves, our identity, is under threat, or at least we seem to feel it so. Scotland and Wales have no difficulty with their myths; they have had several hundred years of opposition and reluctant integration in which to polish them. We, the English, on the other hand had always believed deep down that the union was indissoluble, that the Scots and Welsh didn't really mean it in spite of the example of Ireland. Now devolution has actually happened and they have assemblies, flags, control over their own affairs. We feel aggrieved, abandoned, and find it hard to accept the outcome of what we have done. We argue over whether 'they' should have the right to sit in 'our' parliament and vote on 'our' affairs. We have always secretly regarded our confederates as children, as we did the rest of the empire, even though they are historically our predecessors. Nanny knew best for over two hundred years and Westminster ruled okay.

The myth of England and the English is based on the stories we have told ourselves over the centuries, stories that make a montage of what we want to believe about us, and of how we wish to present ourselves to each other and the outside world. Some stories become an instant thread in the mythical tapestry, others are seemingly forgotten but can be revived when the myth needs a different thread to adapt to changing circumstances. Sometimes we need the victorious Henry V at Agincourt to cheer us on; at other times we need Scott of the Antarctic to teach us the gentlemanly endurance of the stiff upper lip. These heroic figures and their stories have been passing into our mythology since at least the time of 'England's darling', Alfred the Great. Historians and archaeologists unearth new facts to debunk them and try to reshape their legends, but they don't affect their place in the myth and the attributes they embody, that make up our picture of ourselves as seen by us and 'the foreigner'.

The myth has always thrived best when we were at loggerheads with Spain, France or Germany and under threat of invasion of our sacred soil, our island fortress. Now we no longer have an enemy to face. Instead we're being advised to beat our swords into ploughshares and lie down, a rather mangy British lion, with the smart Euro-lambs, all of whom of course have their own national myths, the cultural expressions of tribalism that they have no intention of surrendering. Nevertheless our feeling of separation, of being different, is strong from the very facts of being at once an island and sometime a world power, an empire in the long list of failed empires that stud history like collapsing supernovae.

Because a myth is a work of art, 'a fictitious narrative', it changes with the teller, and with the popular idea 'concerning natural or historical phenomena'. We look in the distorting mirror of time and adjust our clothes and expressions. But an image remains that is recognizably us. We aren't, or needn't be, simply the victims of our own cultural history. We can choose to emphasize or reject certain facets of ourselves. We can throw out the baby with the bathwater as nations do in times of violent revolution, when they reject all that has gone into the making of their identity in search of something entirely new, as first the French and then the Russians tried to do with their revolutions, or we can take a more traditional English way and cherry-pick among our national characteristics. The danger is that we may come up with a handful of stones: militarism, intolerance, xenophobia, that our travelling hooligans choose to express their Englishness.

Now we, the English, together with the Welsh, Scots and Northern Irish, are being invited by history and our continental cousins to join in putting together a harmony in diversity, a European union, with the aim of ensuring that the brutal tribalism of the twentieth century won't be repeated. Already our attempts have failed in the former Yugoslavian states, with bitter and degrading results for everyone involved. We're also being offered the chance, if we support the idea of maintaining our European diversity, of providing a humane counterbalance to robotic globalization which can, of its very nature, take no account of those it tramples in its march, much like the European conquerors of the Americas.

Since unrecorded time we have been myth makers; indeed, that and cooking may be the only skills that separate us from the other animals. We exist not just for economics, finance, trade or pure politics but for culture, which informs everything we do and say. The myths we tell ourselves are as important as the facts. Nobody ever won a war or resisted a defeat on *materiel* alone. Propaganda is at least as important as guns. That's why when our self-image seems to be at its weakest it also seems most important to examine the making of that image, its icons and imaginative components, and see what options we have among them to clothe the body of England in the twenty-first century.

1

Before

Before the Roman came to Rye or out to Severn strode,
The rolling English drunkard made the rolling English road.
A reeling road, a rolling road, that rambles round the shire,
And after him the parson ran, the sexton and the squire;
A merry road, a mazy road, and such as we did tread
The night we went to Birmingham by way of Beachy Head.

IT MIGHT BE thought that a poem written in 1912 by G. K. Chesterton, most famous for his priest–detective Father Brown, to fill up a corner in an obscure magazine, would have little to say to the England of the millennium. Immensely popular in its time, incorporated into his novel *The Flying Inn*, published six months before Europe plunged into the Great War, the poem encapsulates several of the most persistent elements of the myth of England and Englishness, as that the English are the aboriginals of this island, that drunken disorder is a manly virtue, and foreigners are there to be bashed, elements that often provide the most virulent tabloid headlines, and inform the ethos of the most vociferous occupants of the football stands where our beleaguered and obsolescent working class enacts its fantasies of national power and identity.

Chesterton himself, of course, knew perfectly well that in the actual chronology of these islands Britons preceded Romans, who came before the English. He chose the mythical history over the real because of its innate popular appeal to his audience, of which he himself was the first member. The poem's inclusion in so many anthologies, and canonization by the *Oxford Book of English Verse*, shows how right he was.

The myth that the English were the original inhabitants of this island is still, I suspect, believed by many English people, as a poll of the nearest bus queue or shopping mall would demonstrate. This belief sanctifies the status quo. The 'real' natives of Britain are the English. Anyone else is somehow a foreigner, a Taff, a Jock or Mick. So universal is this perception and so powerful that real foreigners, those from beyond the sea, themselves use 'British' and 'English' as interchangeable; most of their languages have some form of 'Anglo', Anglais, Inglese, Englisch, to describe the inhabitants of Great Britain, otherwise known on official forms as the United Kingdom, a bow towards the Ulster loyalists with the inclusion of Northern Ireland. I can't think of another state that has so many recognized versions of its name, in itself an indication of a confused identify that seems to need reinforcement by the highly centralized form of government of the last three centuries and the repeated affirmation of the national myths. Behind the mask of English phlegm, often seen as a form of arrogance, must lie a deep uncertainty about who we are. Recent moves towards devolution and the terror of absorption into a federal European state have only highlighted our insecurity and increased our dependence on the myth of olde England.

'Did the French build Stonehenge?' a 1998 newspaper headline cries in terror. The terms of the question are absurd but revealing. Hidden in them are the Napoleonic wars and the unease of the *entente cordiale*. Could France, our old enemy and recent friend, rival for the leadership of Europe together with our old friend and recent enemy Germany, take the credit for what is, along with

Shakespeare, arguably our greatest national monument? No one wrote in to point out that when Stonehenge was first built there was no more a France than an England, that as far as archaeology has been able to show, a Bronze Age civilization stretched from Ireland to the fringes of Asia, exchanging goods and ideas, like how to build chambered tombs, trioliths and barrows, with regional variations to suit climate and geography.

At some unrecorded point, which new archaeological finds are constantly pushing back in time, the inhabitants of this island moved from the Stone Age to the Bronze, from hunter-gathering to agriculture when the idea of growing corn reached us with a bag of emmer, which had been cultivated for several millennia in more hospitable parts of the earth than our dark, dank northern forests. We began to clear the trees and plant fields. Meanwhile the Babylonians had invented writing for stock control of the imperial granaries and slaves. India, Egypt and China used the wealth of the new agriculture to produce artefacts that still make us catch our breath at their intricacy, utility and sheer beauty. Even Europe started to catch up around the warm seas of the Mediterranean where the painted palaces of Knossos and Mycenae began to rival those of the older civilizations.

The great Bronze Age merchants and travellers were the Phoenicians. They seem to have been the first to bring these islands to the attention of the evolving classical world, as the place for tin, needed to turn soft copper into harder bronze that made a better cutting edge. As far as classical civilization was concerned Britain was the limit of the known world. Beyond it were only the grey wastes of the farthest seas.

Iron succeeded bronze as the new technology, making it easier to cut down trees and turn the heavier northern earth. Whether the way to smelt iron was discovered spontaneously in these islands or brought by a new influx of immigrants no one yet knows. As agriculture improved and populations expanded, the pressure for new land increased. The first-century Roman historian Tacitus says that some of these groups, known generically as Celts, crossed the seas from the Continent in two main waves: the Goidelic and the Brythonic. The Goidels were thought to be ancestors of the Gaels of Scotland and Ireland, and the Brythons of all the inhabitants of the rest of the islands, now particularly the North Welsh and the Cornish. This simple division was soon disrupted. Nobody stayed put for long. More Gallic Celts crossed the Channel. Gaels further colonized South Wales and Scotland. Eventually some of these 'Britons' would migrate to the Breton peninsula, only to return with the invading Normans.

The position is also complicated by the Irish being known at this time as the Scots, and the Scots as the Picts, while all the rest were called Britons. There wasn't an Englishman in sight unless you crossed over to northern Germany and the Frisian Islands, close to the Danish borders, and tracked down to modern Angeln, the home of the Angles, in Schleswig-Holstein, which was also the land of the better-known Saxones and Teutones.

In the time of Alexander the Great, Pytheas, a navigator from Marseilles, which was then a Greek colony, sailed along the length of Europe, taking in Britain and leaving an account of his travels. Then in 220 BC, these islands were given further recognition by the known world. Another Greek, a mathematician and keeper of the great library at Alexandria, Eratosthenes, was keen on measuring things. He measured the earth to within fifty miles of its agreed modern circumference, and he mapped it out as best he could, including for the first time the name Brettania, attached to a right-angled triangle of an island, beside its sister, Hibernia, whose name suggests the land of winter, off the coast of Spain.

That the longer of the two islands was already known as Brettania, the land of the Britons, argues that the inhabitants had a sense of themselves as one people and were thought of as one people by the ancient world, although divided into the many small

4

princedoms, each with a name like a modern European football team: Iceni, Brigantes, Coritani, Catuvellauni. The Romans, when they began to take notice of these islanders, thought of them as barbarian tribes, but although at each others' throats most of the time the Britons had developed a civilization comparable to that of the northern part of the Continent, principally with that part of it known as Gaul where many of the names show that they had close links. They traded for domestic and military wares, and they shared a religion with a mythology very like that of Greece and Rome, as far as can be judged from the limited Irish and Welsh records written down much later. They had a trained priesthood, the Druids, who also kept up links with the Continent as it increasingly fell under the domination of the Roman Empire.

Rome began on her policy of expansion after gaining her independence from the Etruscans and founding the Republic in the fifth century before Christ. She fought the Phoenicians for mastery of the Mediterranean and then the Greeks. Now she was ready to turn her attention west and north. In a series of brilliant campaigns, Julius Caesar set about bringing the continental Celts under Roman control.

By 56 BC he believed he had been largely successful, in either defeating or pacifying most of Gaul (modern France, Belgium and Holland) and had driven the Germans back across the Rhine, but while he was wintering in Illyria, now Albania, war broke out again with a seafaring tribe, the Veneti, who lived in the Breton peninsula and largely controlled trade with Britain. Caesar finally defeated them by destroying their ships. He then went on to attack the Germans to discourage them from crossing into Gaul as soon as his back was turned again.

The Veneti had given him an excuse for invading Britain by involving British allies in the conflict, and now he looked across the Channel. Britain was said to be a prosperous land of full granaries, though the people of course were mere savages. It was even rumoured that they went into battle naked and painted blue.

In 55 BC Caesar set sail to reconnoitre before attempting a full-scale invasion.

He had not even been able to find out whether Britain was indeed an island, or if the known part facing the Continent was merely a peninsula. In late summer Caesar got together a fleet of eighty transports and sailed by night in favourable weather, reaching Britain about nine o'clock in the morning by the shortest crossing, to find the Britons manning the hills and armed with javelins. They had been warned by traders that the Romans were intending to invade and, while some had sent envoys to Caesar to sue for peace, accepting Roman dominion, others had prepared for war.

Realizing that the narrow beach he had anchored on was quite unsuitable for a landing, he sailed a further seven miles along the coast and ran his ships aground on a sloping beach close to Deal. In spite of this the water was still too deep for the soldiers to disembark easily and they were fiercely attacked by the Britons in their two-wheeled, two-horse chariots. It looked as if Caesar was in for an unaccustomed defeat until the standard bearer of the tenth legion jumped down into the water, calling on the rest of the soldiers to follow or see their eagle captured.

Meanwhile, as Caesar tells it, he ordered the flatter-bottomed warships to come in close to shore so that they could use the artillery, slings, bows and catapults against the enemy chariots. These two actions enabled Caesar to concentrate the infantry and charge the Britons who fled, returning as soon as they had recovered to ask for peace.

All this time Caesar had been expecting the arrival of his cavalry who had sailed in eighteen transports from a more northern port, but a violent storm drove them back to the Continent when they were in sight of the camp. The same storm, combined with a very high tide, severely damaged the transports and warships riding at anchor so that the whole expedition was in danger of being stranded in Britain without provisions, and with the winter coming on. Not surprisingly, the Britons decided that this was an opportunity to get rid of the Romans for good. While Caesar was occupied in repairing his ships, using bronze and timber from those worst damaged to make the rest seaworthy, the seventh legion was sent out to cut corn in case the whole troop was forced to overwinter in Britain. The natives attacked them with cavalry and chariots, as they were perfectly entitled to do in defence of their own harvest. Their tactics clearly impressed Caesar. 'By daily training and practice they attain such proficiency that even on a steep incline they are able to control the horses at full gallop, and check and turn them in an instant. They can run along the chariot pole, stand on the yoke and get back into the chariot as quick as lightning.' Caesar arrived like the US cavalry in the nick of time to save the badly shaken seventh legion, and they were able to withdraw to the camp when the natives ran off.

Several days of bad weather followed, which prevented any further action. Meanwhile the Britons gathered themselves together for a last assault, and as soon as the weather improved they advanced their infantry and cavalry. The Romans had managed to get thirty horsemen from a Gallic collaborator and a long, fierce battle took place, which the Romans won, pursuing the enemy as far as they could run, and then laying waste everything in reach. Again the Britons sued for peace, agreed to send hostages and Caesar, let off the hook of a winter campaign, was able to set sail with great relief, only to find rebellion had broken out again in Gaul.

His first expedition to Britain had almost been a costly failure but he was given a public thanksgiving of twenty days. For his next attempt the following year he made much more elaborate preparations, with specially designed ships suited to the British coastal conditions. During the winter his soldiers managed to build six hundred of the new craft, and twenty-eight warships. In these he embarked with five legions, a maximum of thirty thousand infantry and two thousand cavalry, a sight that caused the Britons

7

to take to the forests. Yet once again success eluded him. Another violent storm destroyed forty of the new ships and severely damaged the rest, and the Britons had managed to find a leader, Cassivellaunus, the king of a people centred on the St Albans area. Caesar crossed the Thames to attack Cassivellaunus in his home stronghold and even though the river bed was mined with sharp stakes, he succeeded in getting enough troops across to defeat the British prince, who gave up any further hope of winning a pitched battle against the Romans and took to harassing them with all the skills of his charioteers instead.

Caesar managed to capture his stronghold, a typical Iron Age camp, in a densely wooded place protected with a rampart and a ditch, but found only some cattle left behind. Cassivellaunus, like the Indians, had melted away but the other Britons began to desert him and their princes yet again to sue for peace individually.

All this had taken time and Caesar decided to cut his losses and return to Gaul before the winter set in. He hadn't succeeded in establishing Roman rule in Britain and he was never to return, but he left valuable first descriptions of the place and people, which would eventually whet the appetite of Claudius, nearly a hundred years later, to send Vespasian in AD 43 to succeed where Caesar had failed.

Caesar relied mainly on Belgic informants in Gaul for some of his information about the Brits, which makes its accuracy suspect as third-party testimony. He himself would have seen the blue woad markings on the troops that opposed him but his claim that the Britons were polygamous, sharing wives between the male members of the family, seems like malicious hearsay. He acknowledged that those he did come into contact with, mainly in Kent, differed very little from the people of Gaul. He noted that they were already using small coins and iron ingots for money, something he would himself have experienced in his dealings with the British princes. There were, he was told, two sorts of people: those who claimed to be aboriginal, and later settlers from Gaul, related to the same Belgae, who lived along the south coast where most of the corn was grown. He thought those in the interior ate only milk and meat, and dressed in skins. He knew about the Isle of Man and had heard rumours of other islands from writers lost to us. He didn't know about the highlands of Scotland but thought the island ended where Edinburgh is now, slicing off the whole of the western coast, north of Wales.

Caesar's account was studied by generations of English schoolboys. By osmosis, in the minds of the schoolboys, one empire was substituted for another: British, or rather English, for Roman. The Celtic fringe were the naked blue-painted savages of Caesar's memoir as the parodic version of Men of Harlech makes clear:

> *March up Snowdon with your woad on.*
> *Never mind if you get rained or blowed on,*
> *Never need a button sewed on . . .*

His account also brought Britain its first recorded literary mention, in Virgil's *Eclogues: Et penitos totos divisos orbe Britannos* – 'and the Britons completely cut off from the whole World'. This isolation ended when Vespasian conquered the south of Britain, including the Isle of Wight, and established a Roman province with the full panoply of Roman law, education and administration. For a time Caractacus, King of the Catuvellauni, held out in the Welsh borders but he was betrayed by the wicked Queen of the Brigantes, who ruled what is now Yorkshire, when he asked her for asylum, and was taken in chains to Rome in AD 51. Brought before the Emperor Claudius, he spoke so nobly in his own defence that he was pardoned, beginning the Welsh reputation for 'the lovely gift of the gab', or Welsh windbags as perceived by the English.

Caractacus was our second named British hero to pass into literature, in John Fletcher's play, *Bonduca*, adapted from Holinshed's *Chronicles*, the great sourcebook for Jacobean dramatists which Shakespeare drew on for *Cymbeline*, his version of the story of Cunobelinus the father of Caractacus, otherwise known to history as the Welsh Caradoc. They in turn were descended from Caesar's opponent Cassivellaunus. As the very Welshness of the name Caradoc implies, this British dynasty didn't become part of the myth of England. To Shakespeare and his contemporaries the Britons were the romantic, mythical equivalent of archaic, pre-classical Greek statuary or the Arthurian legends for Tennyson. But their successor among British rebels against the Romans did.

Boudicca, later known as Boadicea, who is also Fletcher's *Bonduca*, has been truly taken over into the myth of England. The Roman historian Tacitus, both in his annals and his biography of his father-in-law, Agricola (who governed and subdued Britain between AD 70 and 84, with breaks as governor of Aquitaine and consul in Rome), tells the story of her rebellion in 61 against the governor of Britain, Suetonius Paulinus. While he was attacking the island of Anglesey, the refuge and holy place of the Druids who, the Romans, perhaps rightly, believed were always inciting the Celts to rebellion, Boudicca seized the chance to strike back.

She was ruling the kingdom of the Iceni, a tribe based in East Anglia, after the death of her husband Prasutagus. Technically it had been left jointly to the Emperor Nero, as the custom was, and to Boudicca's two daughters. The Roman authorities refused to accept women as legitimate and satisfactory heirs for a client state, and arrogant underlings tried to seize the territory and its treasury, raped her daughters and flogged the queen. In revenge she united all the British, according to Tacitus, and at the head of the Iceni and Trinovantes, she sacked and burned Colchester, St Albans and finally the newly flourishing city of London. Famously she led from her chariot with her daughters beside her. Her statue stands at the entrance to Westminster Bridge, and a round barrow, called Boudicca's Mound, is said to be the site of her burial on Parliament Hill, after she was defeated at Battle Bridge, now King's Cross. This, however, seems to be Londoners fancifully trying to claim her for their own. In reality she not only burnt the city but, judging by the number of skulls found by archaeologists excavating the Walbrook, in the City by Cannon Street, ordered the massacre and beheading of its citizens before turning north up Watling Street in pursuit of Paulinus, who had left the citizens of London and St Albans to their fate. Somewhere to the north he chose a site for battle where her chariots would be least effective. The struggle lasted all day until the British were defeated by a counter-attack that left many thousands of them dead. The queen herself took poison rather than suffer the humiliation of capture. She was given a lavish funeral by her followers at an unknown place.

Both Cowper and Tennyson wrote poems about her. By AD 161 she was appearing with her shield on coins of the peace-loving emperor Antonnius Pius, the adopted son of Hadrian, famous of course for one of our greatest tourist attractions, Hadrian's Wall, which he had built to keep back the Picts. Britannia in her Boudicca manifestation as warrior queen was given a new lease of life in 1665 when Charles II's then mistress, Frances Stewart, provided the model for her representation on a copper coin.

Tacitus said of the original Boudicca that 'the Britons make no distinction of sex in their appointment of commanders', an observation borne out by the number of strong female icons in the fragments of Irish and Welsh mythology still preserved. Part queen, part goddess, these proto-Britannias have the power to command, like the Celtic goddess of death and battles, the Morigu, who surfaces later in Arthurian legend as Morgan LeFay.

The image of Britannia herself is so thoroughly Anglicized away from her Celtic original that she can be seen behind the popular perception of strong English queens like Elizabeth I and Victoria, and even in the aggressively handbag-swinging Margaret Thatcher. But her most truly English manifestation is presiding over the last night of the Proms in the resounding chorus of 'Rule Britannia', where the image projected has nothing to do with a Celtic queen, who should more properly, as a Briton, be an emblem of Wales which has long since given up any claim to her. Instead she encapsulates a *Boy's Own*, end of empire symbol, requiring bowler hats, soft toys and Union Jack shirts.

After Agricola a series of generals, Hadrian, Antoninus Pius and Severus in 208, used the further conquest of Britain to advance their careers, with varying degrees of success. All attempts to subdue Caledonia, the land of mists in the far north of the island, failed, as the series of walls designed to protect the southern part from their attacks shows. Effectively Britain became two islands, three if Ireland is included to make up the British Isles, for Roman rule never extended there either but there was constant toing and froing between the different parts. Southern Britain was thoroughly Romanized as Britannia Romana, while the Caledonians became known as the Picts, whose meaning may be 'the painted people', or derive from a tribal name like the continental Pictores. They may have been the Irish Scots who crossed the sea in their curraghs and settled in large numbers in South Wales and lowland Scotland, but their own tradition said that they were Scythians, known to the classical world as the fierce horsemen of the Russian steppes. DNA testing may prove or disprove this myth, as too the Irish legend that they themselves were originally from the Iberian peninsula.

By the time the Emperor Constantius Chlorus died in York in 306 on an expedition against the Picts, cities had sprung up around the original Roman forts linked to each other by a network of roads. Villas, baths, theatres, temples and administrative buildings were built. Some, like that at Lullingstone, could be compared in comfort and even luxury to those on the Continent. Britain's economy had developed rapidly through increased trade with the rest of the empire. Gravestones recorded the deaths of soldiers and civil servants from all over the Roman world, as well as those of the British who now took on Latin approximations of their names. The standard classical education turned them into scholars, administrators and orators for whom Latin was a second language like English in the India of the Raj. Raw materials of corn, skins and honey were traded for all the consumer desirables, from glazed red Samian ware to fine jewellery, that now fill the showcases of our museums. Britons became Roman citizens, indistinguishable under the law from Africans, Spaniards or even Italians. Once again, as with Caesar's account, retrospective mythologizing suppresses these cultivated native Roman citizens from the island story, leaving only the hairy naked tribesmen.

Along with the material imports came the immaterial: philosophy and religion. The official religion was centred on the emperor but extended to the major gods of the Roman pantheon, both male and female. A wax tablet recovered from the Walbrook, dated by the emperor's name to between 84 and 96, begins by invoking Jupiter the Best and Greatest, then Mars, and finally the 'Gods of the fatherland' whoever they might be. Some time in the second century the mystery cults of Isis, Mithras and Jesus also reached Britain. According to a legend retold by William of Malmesbury in the thirteenth century, Joseph of Arimathea, having left Mary Magdalene in Marseilles, first brought Christianity to Britain, along with the Holy Grail, the spear with which Longinus the centurion wounded Christ, and his own staff which, struck into the earth, flowered as the Glastonbury thorn.

The less romantic truth must be that legionaries from the eastern empire, where Paul had first set up congregations on his missionary journeys, had helped to carry the new religion throughout the Roman jurisdiction. By the end of the second century the first Christian writings in Latin began to appear, where previously they had all been in Greek. They came from one Tertullian of Carthage in North Africa and, remarkably, in the course of them he mentions the Britons, suggesting that Christianity had reached even the farthest corner of Roman jurisdiction.

The first known British historian, Gildas, about whom more later, writing in the second half of the sixth century, suggested that Christianity reached Britain in the time of the Emperor Tiberius, which would almost fit the Joseph of Arimathea story. A much more serious claim is made in the 700s in the work of the first English historian, Bede, who says that a British High King called Lucius sent to Rome in 156 asking to be made a Christian. Orthodox historians have generally dismissed this, referring to Lucius as 'legendary', but the name itself is a perfectly acceptable Latinization of a common Celtic root meaning 'light' as in Llew. If such a king was converted at that time it would make sense of Tertullian's comment in about 200. According to Bede, many of the lesser princes followed Lucius's example.

What is certain is that by the time of the Emperor Diocletian there were enough Christians in Britain to produce several martyrs to his persecution, the most famous being St Alban in about 305. Alban was a rich young pagan who sheltered a Christian priest fleeing from persecution. He was so impressed by the priest's piety that when the soldiers came to arrest him, Alban dressed in his guest's cloak and gave himself up in his place. Ordered by the judge to return to his duty and sacrifice to the official gods he refused, and was at once sentenced to be beheaded. When he was led out to execution the huge crowd that had come to watch blocked the bridge so that Alban was unable to cross over to his place of death until, by a miracle, the waters divided. His would-be executioner was so impressed that he threw himself at Alban's feet in instant conversion and was beheaded along with the saint. Even the judge was now won over and changed his policy towards the Christians.

Bede reports that two citizens of Caerleon were also martyred, as well as many others, but it was Alban's story, first told by Gildas, that spread throughout the Western Church. Once the persecution was over, Bede says, the churches that had been destroyed were rebuilt, implying that there were already churches in the main

British cities. Other authorities list at least twenty-eight such cities, giving some idea of the penetration of Roman civilization. Many of these can still be recognized from their 'chester' endings as having been the site of Roman forts, but others such as Bath and St Albans and London itself are less obvious. Increasingly, archaeological finds from towns and villas include examples of Christian motifs and typical east–west aligned burials. The movement was given a further boost by the conversion of Constantine who had been proclaimed emperor at York after the death of his father there. Constantine had been brought up a Christian by his mother, Helena, who was later credited with finding three buried crosses in Jerusalem, one of which performed miracles. A nail from this cross formed part of the crown of the Emperor Charlemagne.

The Church in Britain was sufficiently established to send three bishops to the Council of Arles in 314, including Restitutus, Bishop of London. Late in the century Saint Jerome wrote of the 'travelling Briton who sundered from our world . . . seeks a place known to him only by fame and the narrative of the scripture'. The religious package tour had begun. From then on British priests might turn up anywhere and houses in the swiftly growing monastic network were obliged to give them lodging. Until, that is, the British blotted their copybook with a native heresy that threatened the jurisdiction of the Roman Church: Pelagianism.

St Jerome called Pelagius its originator, an Irishman – 'Scottus' – but it seems most likely that he was a British monk who had studied law in Rome. His heresy, which spread rapidly in Britain, has a pragmatic 'English' character to it, rather than what is usually thought of as Celtic mysticism. He said, quite simply, that since God had given mankind free will they could choose between good and evil, and were capable of perfection by the exercise of choice. Pelagianisim was a kind of proto existentialism, which denied the existence of original sin by emphasizing individual decision.

The whole Church became involved in the great debate: divine grace against free will, with the solid mass of St Augustine upholding the traditional view, which underpinned the structure of the Church as it had evolved. It was for the Church, as the conduit of divine grace, to bind or loose through its ceremonies and institutions. But many distinguished writers and theologians argued for the dignity and freedom of man against the strait-jacket of predestination. Pelagianism would return again and again, as would predestination and original sin, often in the later guise of English puritanism with its emphasis on that fatalism that forms part of our myth of endurance, of the bullet that has your number on it, and that at its most extreme leads to apathy and pessimism, a shrug of the shoulders, and 'better the devil you know . . .'

The traditionalists won and Pelagianism was condemned in 418. But it had made such advances in Britain that ten years later the then Pope, Celestine, thought it necessary to send two distinguished bishops, Germanus of Auxerre and Lupus of Troyes, to bring the British Church back into the fold. According to Germanus's biographer, writing after his death, the Pelagians came out 'flaunting their wealth in dazzling robes before huge crowds, and made long empty speeches which the Gallic bishops rebutted with floods of eloquence'. By this time the Roman Empire was collapsing under external attack and internal corruption. The Christian Church was concerned to preserve its own entity as the last resort of order and morality against barbarism. It couldn't afford to allow itself to be fragmented more than it had been already by the split between East and West, between Greek-speaking and Latin-speaking, Orthodox and Catholic, the fundamental division that still exists, with the added complication since the Reformation of the vernacular Protestant third way.

Gildas hysterically documents the decline and fall of Roman Britain, blaming the British themselves for their wickedness and their failure to unite. Gildas was a northerner from Strathclyde, which had been Christianized by St Ninian around the end of the fifth century. Fifty years earlier, missionaries had reached Ireland, notably a young Briton who had been captured by Irish raiders and sold into slavery for six years. After his escape he returned to his father's estate in the west but was haunted by a vision of his pagan captors begging him to come back and teach them. St Patrick returned: his mission must have been to the north and west of the island, since the same Pope Celestine who sent St Germanus to Britain to root out Pelagianism also dispatched one Palladius to 'the Irish believing in Christ', but it was Patrick who got the credit.

The final collapse of the Roman Empire itself had begun while Britain was enjoying a period of relative peace and prosperity. A terse paragraph from the last of the great Roman historians, Ammianus Marcellinus, gives a more accurate description of Britain's invasion. 'A barbarian alliance brought Britain to her knees. Nectaridus, Count of the Coastal Defence, was killed, the general Fullofundes ambushed . . . The Picts plundered at will, as did the warlike Attacotti and the Irish. . . . The Franks and their neighbours the Saxons raided the coast that faces Gaul . . .'

Count Theodosius was sent by the Emperor Valentinian to restore order, wintering in London, now called Augusta, in 368, but although he managed to drive out the barbarians from the rest of the country London itself began to decline. The Channel crossing was no longer safe for trade and the centre of power began to shift west, to Winchester and its port of Southampton. The death of Valentinian in 374 seemed a signal to the barbarians to attack the empire from every side. Huns poured in from Asia, forcing the eastern Goths across the Danube where they in their turn overran the eastern empire, threatening Constantinople. A Spaniard, Magnus Maximus, was proclaimed emperor in Britain, ruled for a time in York and London before crossing to the Continent, taking British legions with him, and was eventually defeated by Theodosius, the eastern emperor.

Meanwhile the Picts, Irish and Saxons had renewed their attacks on the Britons who sent a plea to Rome for money and troops. At that moment Alaric, the leader of another barbarian tribe in western Germania, the Visigoths, captured Rome. He stayed for only a fortnight before leaving with great booty of gold and silver, and hostages, including the emperor's sister. Not surprisingly the western emperor, by now Honorius, the son of Theodosius, who was the last to rule the whole of the Roman Empire alone, replied that there was nothing he could do. The Britons were on their own and must look to their own defence, an answer that legalized whatever system of government they might elect. The problem was that they had been part of an empire for roughly four hundred years, equivalent to the period from the accession of James I to the second millennium. They were used to a ruler, however weak and distant. Now they had to choose among themselves.

They chose Vortigern, meaning British 'top ruler', who seems to have come from the Gloucester area. At first he was very successful, subduing the Irish invaders and making peace with the Irish High King. As part of the deal, Christian missionaries were to be allowed to operate freely in Ireland. Then Vortigern made the mistake of enlisting mercenary forces against the Picts who were attacking by sea down the east coast. Vortigern called in a troop of Germanic seafarers under the captaincy of a Dane, Hengist, along with his brother Horsa. The mercenaries under their command were known as Saxons to the Romans but they were made up of several groups living around the mouth of the Elbe, and though at first they may not have acknowledged it, they were in need of a new place to settle. A warm climatic phase was raising the sea level and drowning their lands. The same phenomenon was noted by Gildas, quoting a letter from the British to the Roman consul Aëtius, although he dates it wrongly to the 430s instead of 446: 'The barbarians push us back to the sea, the sea pushes us back to the barbarians; between these two kinds of death, we are either drowned or slaughtered.' The Thames rose. On the east coast silt buried earlier Roman villas, creating the fens. Worst of all, the English were about to arrive.

2

The Coming of the English

THE STORY OF the coming of the English is comfortably shrouded for many of us in the mists of time. That's because it doesn't sit easily with that part of the myth that says 'There'll always be an England', implying that there always has been. Queasily some of us will admit to believing that we came from Germany, a kinship both Hitler and Goebbels were keen to exploit at different stages of World War Two. The fact that the English arrival wasn't even a proper invasion and conquest, like the Norman one, but a higgledy-piggledy takeover by wandering groups of mercenaries and freebooters, is undignified. The hero of these events isn't even English. He is the British Arthur, holding out against these marauders, us, and, courtesy of later versions of his story, exhibiting all the supposed virtues of an English gentleman: good manners, aloofness combined with clubabbleness, the restrained exercise of power, a disinclination to sex and an ambiguous defeat from which he pulls a kind of victory. Myths take to themselves the heroes they need and cut the facts to fit them out in heroic costume. Fact and fiction interweave to give us the stuff of our dreams.

★   ★   ★

The original story of how the English first came to Britain was told by Gildas some hundred years after the event. Three shiploads came first, captained by Hengist and Horsa, who were given the Isle of Thanet to settle in. At first they did what they were paid for and took on the marauding Picts. Bede is the first to name them and to specify the three tribes of Saxons, Angles and Jutes, and the places they eventually settled in. He calls them 'the three most formidable races of Germany'. By now Germanic peoples had overrun the whole of north-western Europe, setting up kingdoms of the Franks, the Goths, the Longobards and the Burgundians. They intermarried with local people and were integrated into the declining empire, until in 476 western emperors ceased to be appointed in Italy. Only the eastern emperor reigned in Constantinople as nominal head of the whole empire.

Bede doesn't tell the story of the deliberate seduction of the British ruler Vortigern by Hengist's daughter. If he knew it he would have thought it too unseemly, and not conducive to the image of the Saxons as brave, though pagan, warriors that he wanted to put over. After their initial success the mercenaries sent word home that the land was flowing with milk and honey, and that others should come and join them. First came sixteen ships and then another forty. Vortigern, besotted with Hengist's daughter, gave them Kent and then lands in the north around Hadrian's Wall. Soon, so many of them had sailed for Britain that Schleswig-Holstein was completely depopulated. Now sure of their own strength, the Anglo-Saxons demanded more payment for their services and when Vortigern refused, they allied themselves with the Picts and began to sack the cities and lay waste the countryside.

Meanwhile St Germanus had been recalled from Gaul to stamp out Pelagianism, which had reared its head again. This time he seems to have been effective in uniting the British Church with continental Catholicism, which may have been a factor helping the Britons to fight back against the invaders. At first they were successful, reclaiming Kent from Hengist. But after a further battle, fought to a standstill with neither side the winner, Hengist tricked the British. Three hundred unarmed senior Britons agreed to meet a similar number of Hengist's men, also unarmed, for a peace negotiation. The Anglo-Saxons, though, concealed their daggers in their shoes and at a given signal massacred the British, keeping only Vortigern himself alive, the first example of that part of the myth our continental neighbours dub 'perfidious Albion', a term first translated from French in 1841. Albion had been an early alternative to Britain for both Celts and Romans from the root 'albus', meaning white, presumably because of the White Cliffs of Dover. With their leaders dead the Britons were easy prey. Thousands fled overseas to populate Britannia Minora, Bretony, in northern France.

At last a commander arose among the Britons to lead the fight back. Ambrosius Aurelianus was said to be the last of the Romans and of noble blood. He fought a cavalry war against an enemy who had only infantry and it lasted for thirty years. The English held most of the south coast and East Anglia. And then came the mythical Arthur. Scholars are still divided about whether he ever existed except in legend. Bede doesn't mention him and neither does Gildas, though they both give an account of Ambrosius Aurelianus's struggle against the English. The first mentions of Arthur are in the later British historian Nennius, who wrote roughly a hundred years after Bede, and in some Welsh annals of uncertain date. Arthur finally beat a combined English army at the battle of Mount Badon near Bath but the result was a stalemate with the country divided into small independent kingdoms of ethnic British or English who continued to fight each other. It was nearly another century before the Britons were finally defeated. Legend and the Welsh annals record Arthur's defeat and death at the Battle of Camlan in 537.

Gildas describes the disorder of his own times: petty princes fighting against each other, the decay of the cities, and the collapse of the infrastructure which had been revived after the uneasy restoration of Arthur's time, and his victories over the English in the north, Midlands and west, and the Irish in South Wales. Although Gildas doesn't specifically speak of Arthur, something or someone has to be missing from the historical record that would explain why it took the English until the second half of the sixth century to accomplish what the Franks had done in half the time: taking over a former Roman province and becoming converted to Christianity.

Bede himself begins the real myth of England by settling the name. If the Saxons had never come to Britain we would still be the British. If the Saxons or the Jutes had produced a writer and historian of the stature of Bede we might now be living in Saxland or Jutland and be Saxish or Jutish. Bede was an Angle living in the Angle Kingdom of Northumbria at Jarrow, in its northern province called Bernicia, under the 'most glorious King Coelwulf', to whom he dedicates his *Historia Ecclesiastica Gentis Anglorum*, which established the name of the country and its people. Tacitus had included the Angli in a list of the German tribes defeated by his father-in-law Agricola. They managed to populate the whole of East Anglia, the Midlands, then called Mercia, and the north-eastern half of Britain up to the Scottish border. The south belonged to the Saxons and Jutes while the Britons still held the west, including Devon and Dorset. Ironically for the myth, the *echt* Englishman comes not from the shires but from Coventry or Newcastle, unless contaminated by the later Viking invasions. Geordie could probably claim to be the nearest we have to a true English accent.

One of Bede's chief complaints against the British is that they made no attempt to Christianize their conquerors. Bede, writing out of his own natural bias, two hundred years after the events he describes, can't really be expected to be impartial. Defeated and embittered, the British withdrew into their religion. After all, if God and Christ were supposed to be the greatest, and on their side, where was the sense in sharing this advantage with the enemy?

As long as the invaders remained pagans the issues were clear. And for a time the heathen English were held in check.

Christianity continued to flourish in Ireland, and Wales where there was a great monastic school at Llantwit Major in Glamorgan, founded by St Illtyd. His most famous pupils were Samson, who interested himself in Cornwall and Brittany, and was a politician as well as a teacher, and Dubricius who is said to have crowned King Arthur. Meanwhile Ireland produced one of the best-known saints in these islands: Columba, who founded his monastery at Iona in 563 and continued the mission to the Picts begun by St Ninian. In the next generation another Irishman, Colombanus, took on the missionizing of the descendants of the German tribes of Switzerland, southern Germany, and north Italy, founding among others the great monasteries of Luxeuil, St Gall and Bobbio. Yet still the English clung to their ancestral gods, familiar to us from the names of the days of the week, Tiew, Woden, Thor and Freya, and as the protagonists of Wagner's *Ring* cycle.

By the end of the sixth century Arthur was dead, betrayed according to legend by his own son and nephew Medraut, and the British had been devastated by a plague, which seemed like divine punishment for the sins Gildas describes. Chastity and monasticism spread throughout Ireland, Wales and Brittany, now a religion of isolated communities of devotion where once British Christianity had been an urban cult, organized into bishoprics based in the now wasted cities.

The continental Church was well aware of the situation in Britain. The most powerful English king in the south, Ethelbert of Kent, was married to a Frankish princess, Bertha, herself a Christian. Part of the marriage contract had been that she was to be allowed to practise her religion. She had brought her own chaplain with her and restored the earlier British church of St Martin at Canterbury. When Pope Gregory decided to send Augustine with his forty monks to convert the English, Kent was the obvious place to start.

Even Bede is cautious about the charming story which is said to explain Gregory's interest in the English but he tells it with obvious pride, and in doing so adds another strand to the development of the myth. According to Bede, Gregory was once shopping in the marketplace, which clearly included a slave market, when he was taken by the sight of three beautiful boys for sale: 'with fair complexions, fine features and noble heads of hair'. They came from Deira, the southern province of Northumbria, and were therefore Angles as the pope was told, causing him to pun 'Not Angles but angels', in the most famous version of the story. He also made play with Deira saying they should be delivered *de ira*, from wrath. He asked if they were Christians and when he was told no he said how sad it was that such faces of light, such gracious features, should belong to the author of darkness and conceal minds empty of grace. The physical stereotype of the fair-haired clean-cut English, which found its apotheosis in the female version as 'the English rose' and the male in Leslie Howard, who wasn't English at all, had been given its first literary airing. From now on foreigners were dark; dagos, wops, ultimately and with the empire, wogs, beginning, of course, with the original inhabitants, the Welsh, as they came to be called by the English from a word meaning 'stranger', while the Britons called the English 'Garmans', Germans.

Charged with truly converting Angles to angels, Augustine and his companions baulked. They were appalled at 'the idea of going to a barbarous, fierce and pagan nation, of whose very language they were ignorant'. Gregory refused to let them off the hook. He supplied them with Frankish translators and the Bishop of Arles as a go-between. In 597 they landed in the Isle of Thanet, and King Ethelbert allowed them to settle in Canterbury and begin their mission. The prototype of the Christian English gentleman was about to be formed for transmission to the nineteenth century and Tom Brown's schooldays.

For a time the mission was successful. Ethelbert was converted. In turn his daughter Ethelburga was given in marriage to Edwin,

King of Northumbria, with the same condition in the marriage contract as her mother had had, that she should be allowed to practise her religion. The chaplain she took with her to the north was the dark-haired, aquiline-featured Italian, Paulinus, sent by Pope Gregory in 601, along with several other clergy, to help Augustine. By the time of this marriage, Augustine himself was long dead and so was his royal convert. It looked as if the young Church wouldn't survive the loss of this first generation. The old gods were reinstated and the priests sent by Gregory, now bishops of London and Rochester, retired to France. Laurence, Augustine's successor at Canterbury, was about to join them when a scourging from St Peter in a dream recalled him to his duty. The bishops returned. Kent was reconverted but London, now the capital of the East Saxons and still, according to Bede, 'a trading centre for many nations who visit it by land and sea', refused to accept their bishop, Mellitus, back again. Instead he got Canterbury, in more than compensation, when Laurence died.

The new religion had an initial success in Bede's Northumbria, producing incidentally one of the most beautiful metaphors for the human condition in our literature. It comes, surprisingly to some scholars, not from an educated Christian mouth but from an anonymous pagan adviser to the king. Edwin, the prototype of the noble pagan, had called his council together to discuss the question of which religion they should follow. First to speak was Coifi, the high priest, who put forward the utilitarian argument that the old gods had done nothing to advance him in the king's favour, even though he had served them zealously, and they must therefore be powerless.

Then comes the speech by one of the king's councillors, that provides a vignette of contemporary life, and is also a profound reflection on it. It must have been spoken, and handed down, in English. Bede translates it into Latin for the purpose of his history. King Alfred will have it translated back into English a century and a half later.

When we compare the present life of man on earth with that time of which we have no knowledge, it seems to me like the swift flight of a single sparrow through the banqueting hall where you, your majesty, are sitting on a winter's day at dinner among your thanes and ministers. Inside there is a bright fire in the middle to warm you while outside winter storms of rain and snow are raging. The sparrow flies swiftly in through one door and out at the other. While he's inside the winter storms can't touch him but after this little moment of calm he flies out into the wintry world again and your eyes lose sight of him. Even so man's life appears. We know nothing of what came before it or what follows after.

The speech is very close in tone to the poetry that survives from this period and once again it brings Wagner's *Ring* to mind, the fatalism of the defeat of the old gods with the fall of Valhalla. It's these words, which seem to embody the brevity of man's life and its end in darkness and oblivion, and foreshadow a constant strand in modern English belief. It isn't the high priest's pragmatism which converts the King and his ministers but that the new religion offers the comfort of a loving father and brother, and the hope of heaven. Not to be outdone, Coifi rushes off to destroy the pagan altars and shrines.

The death of Edwin in a fiercely fought battle at Hatfield Chase, where he was defeated by the last great British king, as Bede still calls him, Cadwalla, a Christian in alliance with the pagan Englishman, Penda of Mercia, Northumbria's southern neighbour, caused Christianity to lapse for a time until St Oswald, the first Anglo-Saxon king to be canonized, killed Cadwalla in turn and became Bretwalda, ruler of Britain. This title, like the High King of Ireland, meant that for the time being the warlord of one of the petty kingdoms was acknowledged as supremo. After three Northumbrian kings it passed to the Mercians and then eventually to the West Saxons and Alfred.

English society was still in its heroic phase, very like that of ancient Greece as described by Homer. The Britons too, after four hundred years of romanization, had reverted to a condition, which also obtained among the Irish, of warring petty princedoms. The duty of a king was to extend his lands by making war on his neighbours and carrying off enough booty to reward his warband. Christianity began to introduce new elements into this world view by providing an alternative way of life based on contemplation rather than action. But the process of conversion was slow, subject to backslidings and reversals. It took the combined efforts of Irish monks and Roman priesthood a hundred years before the last of the English, the South Saxons, whose name today gives us Sussex, one of the last shire bastions of the Church of England, finally succumbed to the firebrand St Wilfred of Northumbria.

Northumbria owed its second stab at conversion to the community of Iona. At the request of King Oswald, the Irish sent Aidan to take up where Paulinus had been forced to leave off. The Irish and the British Christians still celebrated Easter according to the eastern rather than the Roman date and the Northumbrians naturally followed suit. Augustine had first tried to make the British Church conform to Roman practice but without success. By the time of King Oswy (brother of Oswald) the difference in the dating of Easter had become an acute symbol of the division among Christians: the queen who followed Roman rule had only reached Palm Sunday when the king was keeping Easter, according to Irish custom. Matters came to a head when the king called a meeting at Whitby to settle the date. Whitby was a double monastery of some six hundred men and women under the governance of the remarkable abbess, Hilda, its founder, who was renowned for her wisdom. The Irish were represented by the forceful Colman; the Romans by Wilfred. The argument was fierce and pulled no punches. Wilfred in particular, who had visited Rome, accused the Irish of arrogance. 'The only people who stupidly contend against the whole world are these Scots [Irish] and their partners in obstinacy the Picts and the Britons, who inhabit only a portion of these the two uttermost islands of the ocean.'

With this tirade Wilfred adds a new element to the myth of England: our perception of ourselves as islanders, apart from the Continent, in a word, our insularity. Now, since the discovery of the Americas by Europeans, we are no longer at the end of the world but a bridge, as we see it, between old and new. The notion of ourselves as distinct and apart has had a profound effect on our psychology and political development. We have made a virtue out of this accident of geography, now undermined by the Channel tunnel, which so many English people feared would signify the beginning of our national end. It would be interesting to know whether St Wilfred was particularly struck by the island syndrome, which he attributes to the Celtic fringe, because he had himself travelled as far as Rome. By Shakespeare's time the insular image would be firmly attached not to Britain and the native inhabitants, but to England, 'bound in by the triumphant sea', the 'sceptred isle'.

Colman retired defeated back to Ireland and Wilfred went to France to be consecrated a bishop. Bede himself had been educated at his monastery of Jarrow from the age of seven and speaks with admiration of the Irish monks who had been responsible for reconverting Northumbria. His attitude to the Britons, however, is, for a man of peace, aggressively hostile. It's almost as if he is foreshadowing the contempt still felt by many English people for the Welsh, as if it had got into the bloodstream at this very early date and was still being carried over a millennium later. I have heard it seriously maintained by some people that they could never vote for x or y 'because they are Welsh'. Where the Scots are often admired for their hardiness, engineering skills and canniness, and the Irish are treated with affection as stupid children, the Welsh are regarded as untrustworthy windbags.

The Whitby decision in favour of Roman rule, which Bede designates 'Catholic' and which included such arcane matters as the shape of a monk's tonsure, isolated the British and their Church still further, while strengthening the English links to the Continent. The British had been part of the Roman Empire while the Angles and Saxons were still untutored pagans in their forest clearings. Now the positions were reversed. Once the matter of its allegiance had been settled and the conversion of England completed, English priests were free to travel and take their new-found convictions back to the lands they had come from where they still spoke the same Germanic dialects.

Unlike romanized parts of the Continent, France and Spain in particular, the English and British continued to speak their own languages, which must have further underlined their separation. The Germanic tribes of Franks and Visigoths who had taken over France and Spain quickly adopted a romance dialect based on Latin. For the English, Latin was a second, written language. Their own poetry and traditions were oral and only gradually converted into written texts. Bede's death hymn, however, was preserved in English and he recounts in his history the tale of the first English poet with a known name, Caedmon.

Caedmon is the prototype of the people's poet. He was attached to Hilda's monastery of Whitby as a layman working with the animals. The English had preserved the custom of passing round the harp during a feast so that everyone took it in turns to sing one of the old songs, tales of battles and monster slaying as well as more reflective pieces, but all essentially pre-Christian in spirit. When Caedmon saw the harp coming his way, he would slip out of the hall and go back to his hut. On one such night, instead of going home, he went to the stable because it was his turn to guard the animals. He lay down to sleep. Suddenly he heard his name called. A man was standing beside him. 'Caedmon, sing me something.' Caedmon explained his difficulty and why he was always obliged to leave the feast early. 'Nevertheless sing me something.'

'What shall I sing you?'

'Sing me the creation of the world.'

So Caedmon did and when he awoke he could remember every-thing from his dream and was even able to add more verses. Bede has an interesting aside at this point. Translating Caedmon's verse into Latin he adds: 'This is the general sense but not the actual words that Caedmon sang in his dream; for verses however mas-terly cannot be translated literally from one language into another without losing much of their beauty and dignity.' The English version has been inserted in at least four manuscript versions of this story, in the margin or at the foot of the relevant page.

In the morning Caedmon went to his superior, the reeve, and told him what had happened. He was taken before Hilda who was careful to investigate this phenomenon fully. Learned men were gathered to assess the quality and authenticity of the verse. Caed-mon, who was illiterate, was read passages of scripture and doctrine, which he was required to versify. Hilda was convinced by his performance, which must have had something of the nature of a modern rap or dub poet. She made a monk of him and took him into Whitby. Bede says he was already well advanced in years when all this happened to him in 680. The wise woman Hilda realized that in Caedmon's English verse she had a medium for converting the ordinary people, for whom Latin meant nothing but ritual repeated. Only his first effort has survived but, according to Bede, Caedmon turned not only the whole of Genesis and Exodus but also the New Testament into English verse, and composed many poems on 'the joys of heaven, the pains of hell and the last judgment', pre-dating in words by several centuries the paintings that were to fulfil the same purpose of instruction on the walls of mediaeval churches.

Contact with the Continent also put the English in touch with Roman building techniques. Learning how to make mortar and glass meant they could start to replace the first wood and thatch churches with stone ones like those they had seen on their visits to Arles and Rome. Cantors were sent from the pope to teach the priests to sing in the Roman style, fulfilling the promise of

Augustine's arrival with his forty singing companions a century before. The late seventh and early eighth centuries would come to be seen like a golden age that was not to last, an early example of our tendency as part of the myth to hark back to the good old days. In 787 the first three Viking ships arrived on the Dorset coast. A local official went down to the harbour to ask them in the king's name who they were and their business. Whereupon they killed him and his companions. His death signalled the end of that peace and progress.

One version of the *Anglo-Saxon Chronicle* says that the raiders were from Hardanger Fjord in West Norway, although most of the subsequent invaders would be Danes. It was Norsemen, though, who destroyed Bede's Northumbria before sailing on via the Orkneys to capture Dublin and set up a kingdom there. The last paragraphs of Bede's history show a land at peace. Overlordship of Britain had passed to Mercia, and the Northumbrians were entering monasteries in droves, preferring prosperity to the arts of war, which Bede, in a letter to a friend, Bishop Egbert, reported with some concern, questioning their motives. To enter a monastery was a way of avoiding taxes, and civil and military duties, and religious houses often became family affairs that could be handed on from one generation to the next. The abandonment of arms was perhaps one of the reasons why Northumbria in particular was so devastated by Viking attacks.

Bede had died fifty years before the Viking raids began but his reputation as teacher and author was carried both by copies of his books and the word of mouth of his pupils and theirs throughout Christian Europe. His true successor was Alcuin of York who became the finest scholar of his day and was eventually given the civilizing of his court and people by the Emperor Charlemagne. Educated himself at York under Bede's friend Egbert, he helped to build a magnificent new church at York in the Romanesque style with twisted columns, marble inlay and thirty altars decorated with precious metals and gemstones, and dedicated to Santa Sophia,

Holy Wisdom, like the cathedral at Byzantium. While refining the Frankish court, Alcuin carried on the development of Bede's concept of the English people. In a long poem about the history of York he speaks of Edwin, King of Northumbria, as having the imperium over all the people of this long island, 'Saxons, Picts, Irish and Britons'. He also speaks of the English as 'God's destined race' as if they were the children of Israel, as indeed he saw them. The Britons had forfeited God's grace through heresy and a failure to convert and accept the English. Therefore the promised land had been taken away from them and was now given to God's new people. It also gave the English the right and the duty to proselytize among the pagans, an idea that would leap a thousand years to resurface as the British Empire and 'the heathen in his blindness'.

English identity had first developed in opposition to the British. The tribalism that is the genetic root of nationalism needs a 'them and us' to define and strengthen it. With the exile of the British to the western and northern extremities it seemed as if God's care for his new people was irrefutable. The arrival of the first long ship on the Dorset coast threw this new-won confidence into doubt. If the English had been rewarded by God before, why were we now being punished? What were our sins? The tendency to beat the breast and to look back to a golden age of stability and shared values in times of reversal has been constantly repeated throughout our history until it has become ingrained.

The 'sins' included political corruption, going soft, and sexual misdemeanours, often hinted at as too unspeakable to be fully expressed. It could be argued that the whole tendency to self-blame had been started by the British historian, Gildas, in the catalogue of his people's failings that had led to their defeat, but the English certainly took it over and improved on it, until today any politician can get a round of applause, or a newspaper increase its circulation, by a tirade against contemporary evil that the Anglo-Saxon polemicist would have recognized at once. In our contemporary version of the myth centred on a return to so-called 'family values', against all the historical and statistical evidence, things were always better in the past when we respected 'moral values'.

Not that there weren't evils that could be pointed to as the cause of God's punishment. Power struggles between members of the same ruling family, as well as constant warfare between the petty kingdoms, made the raiders' incursions easy against small war bands and untrained levies. Their method at first was to descend from the sea on some lonely coast where a rich monastery was sited, sack and then burn. Loot of gold, silver, jewels, vestments was what they came for. They obviously knew where the richest pickings were to be found. First to go in Britain were Lindisfarne from where the monks fled, carrying off St Cuthbert's bones to the safety of Durham. Then Bede's Jarrow was sacked. But Ireland suffered worst of all and many of the holy furnishings from Irish monasteries ended up in Norwegian graves, and the monks and lay people in Norse slave markets. The list of houses destroyed reads like a tourist guide.

The *Anglo-Saxon Chronicle*, an historical record that was first put together by order of King Alfred based on pre-existing material including Bede's history, reports the first shiploads of Danes in the early 830s. From then on they came again and again, at first to plunder and go home for the winter, then for the first time in 850 they stayed in the Isle of Thanet where the first English had settled. The Vikings also used their seafaring skills to take them as far as Italy, and to carve out a chunk of Charlemagne's Frankish territories that became Normandy, the land of the northerners.

The year after their first winter stay, a further three hundred and fifty Danish ships came up the Thames, stormed Canterbury and London, and were only stopped from conquering the whole of Southern England by King Aethelwulf with an army drawn from all of Wessex, which now stretched from Dorset to Essex. Fifteen years and the death of three kings later in 865, a huge army led by two sons of Ragnar Lothbrok, Ivor the Boneless and Halfdan, all of whom sound like characters out of a computer game, took East Anglia. Leaving their ships, they commandeered all the horses in the area and sent out raiding parties to devastate the countryside until the locals were forced to buy peace with Danegold. Then they set out for York, which they occupied for four months before the divided Northumbrians could get together an army to try to dislodge them. The English were badly defeated, their kings and leaders killed. The survivors bought peace. The Danes set up a puppet king and moved on to Nottingham.

The collapse of Northumbria and the Viking settlement of York profoundly altered our historical topography. Until that event it was more than likely that York would have emerged as the capital of Britain, and the whole political and economic tilt would have been to the north rather than to the south as it now became, and has remained. All was changed by the rise of Wessex and the dominance of the great trading port of London.

3

England's Darling

NOTTINGHAM WAS PART of the kingdom of Mercia whose king had married the sister of Aethelwulf of Wessex, and of his more famous brother, Alfred. When Aethelwulf died Alfred took over Wessex and became the leader of the English, who were still resisting the Danes. For seven years he fought back against the Viking armies, sometimes successful, often defeated. The low point came in 878 when he was forced to withdraw to his island fortress at Athelney in Somerset. It's to those weeks around Easter that the story belongs of his burning the old woman's cakes, which he'd been told to watch. He had been too preoccupied trying to work out a strategy to notice the smoke rising from them.

The event is probably apocryphal and doesn't appear in the contemporary biography of him by the Welshman he made bishop of Sherborne, Asser. Asser's biography was written during Alfred's lifetime, when the king was forty-five, probably for the priests back home at St Davids. It's a work of love and therefore suspect, but the figure of the king that emerges justifies the subsequent perception of Alfred as probably the greatest of English kings, the one we would all wish for if there's to be a monarchy at all. Clearly Asser loved him. No one else except Charlemagne had such a loving biographer but perhaps no one else deserved it. Asser is responsible for the account of Alfred's boyhood and of his two journeys to Rome before he was seven. On the second of these journeys he was made a consul by the pope, who could bestow such purely emblematic honours from a vanished empire, and this came to be seen as Alfred's anointing as future king. According to Asser, Alfred's education was neglected because of the continuing war and a lack of teachers in Wessex, and he was unable to write, even in English, until he was twelve. A similar story is told of the great educator Charlemagne who was said to have had difficulty forming his letters all his life, and to have kept a writing tablet under his pillow so that when he had a sleepless night he could practise them.

After seven weeks of sending out raiding parties from Athelney, Alfred felt strong enough to leave his fortress in the marshes. Reinforced by all the fighting men of Somerset, Wiltshire and Hampshire, he fought a great battle at Eddington, which ended with the defeat of the Danes and the conversion of their King Guthrum. The festivities attending his baptism lasted for twelve days. Traditionally the white horse on the downs above Westbury marks this victory.

After Eddington Alfred enjoyed a decade of relative peace, in which he pushed his kingdom to the north by treaties and marriage, and then retook London from the Danes at his second attempt. He built fortresses, reorganized the administration and set out to provide the English with an education and a literature, with translations of Bede, Orosius, Boethius and Gregory's *Pastoral Care*. And he was an inventor. Worried about timing his ration of hours between God and secular affairs, Alfred invented the horn lantern, a series of candles marked in hours, to cover the whole day and night. When he found that because of draughts the candles burnt unevenly, he enclosed them in lanterns made of very finely shaved horn, instead of glass, that let through the light but shut out the wind. Asser also gives a touching picture of him at this period –

37

busy at his books in an unkingly way, recalling a story from Alfred's childhood of his learning a whole volume of English poems off by heart, that his mother had promised to whichever of her sons was first able to understand it. His own eldest daughter and son were both carefully educated at home by the best tutors.

This time of peace wasn't to last. War broke out again in the 890s when an army that had been ravaging France crossed to England where they were joined by Danes from Northumbria and East Anglia. Alfred designed new, bigger warships, which defeated the Danes on the coast. The war ranged over the whole country, with Alfred and his provincial governors pursuing and defeating the enemy until the raiding armies either withdrew or bought land in the Danish part of the island with the loot they had collected.

Alfred died, after two peaceful years, in 899. The *Chronicle* says he was 'King of all the English apart from those under Danish control, and ruled for twenty-eight years'. He left the continued expansion of his kingdom to his son, Edward the Elder, and his daughter Ethelfleda, a widow, who ruled Mercia in her own right, constructed fortresses and successfully commanded her armies in the field, in the tradition of the long dead Boudicca. By the middle of the tenth century, building on Alfred's strategy and achievements, his descendant, Eadred, could truly be called King of England.

It can be argued that these later successes were greater than Alfred's own but only he is called 'the Great', and England's darling, and the person on the Clapham bus would be hard put to it to name any of these successors. Alfred's distinction is to have furthered the English myth. Many stories were told about him which don't appear in Asser's official biography but which must have circulated in lost songs and mini-epics. There's the tale of him reconnoitring the Danish camp disguised as a minstrel, rather like Robin Hood, as well as the cake-burning episode, both written down within a hundred years of his death. His military career reads like a mediaeval pre-run of World War Two. Alfred has that ability to hold on, not admitting defeat, until he can make a spectacular comeback, which informs both our myth and our modern national epic. He has his lowest hour, his Dunkirk, when he is forced to retire to Athelney after his first defeat, then the raiding parties which are his Battle of Britain, and finally Eddington which is his D-Day.

Yet, as in an Ealing studio comedy, there is something unheroic, rather *Dad's Army*, about Alfred, with his piles, being ticked off by the swineherd's wife, or strumming through the enemy camp, and this too is part of the English tradition of irony, eccentricity and muddling through. Victory has to appear almost a bit of luck, brought about by amateurs. A long-cherished belief of historians, now under convincing attack, was that Alfred's army was the *wyrd*, a free patriotic association of English peasants against the wild yet highly professional Viking warriors, like the civilian recruits and conscripts, the Tommies of 1939–45. The truth is almost certainly that both forces were made up of, in a sense, mercenary professionals. The Vikings, like the Saxons of Roman times, turn up in the pay of the Frankish emperors and German princes, while part of an English king's obligation was to maintain his trusted war band, the housecarls, and those of his provincial governors who were often related to him by blood or marriage.

Alfred achieved his final, though partial, victory by building forts and warships and by the setting up of governors whom he could trust to defend their own patch or to assemble with a trained force if he called on them to defend the English race, 'the Angelcynn' of his own writings, when the attack was on a broader, national front.

The Viking threat receded as the Northmen settled down, bought farms, became Christians and intermarried with the local people, already a mixture of Britons and English throughout the major part of the island. *Englisc*, as it appears as an adjective in Alfred's section of the *Anglo-Saxon Chronicle*, became the universal language with an increasingly rich written and spoken literature.

It was eighty years after Alfred's death before serious Viking raiding began again. The intervening kings read like the cast list of *King Lear*: Edward, Athelstan, Edmund, Eadred, Eadwig, Edgar.

When the last king, Edgar, died suddenly in 975 his sphere of influence covered, as overlord, Kenneth King of the Scots, Iago of Gwyneth, Dunmail of Strathclyde, Malcolm of Cumbria as well as his own English provinces, and the Danelaw in the east. His death left two underage princes, Edward and Aethelred, by two different wives. Edward, the heir, was duly crowned, and seemed to enjoy friendly relations with his half-brother and stepmother, Aelfryth, but on an informal visit, only two years into his reign, he was brutally murdered by their retainers at Corfe Castle. They had come out to meet him with every sign of respect. Before he had time to dismount they took hold of his hands and stabbed him. He was buried without any honours.

The *Chronicle* described his murder as 'the worst deed for the English race . . . since they first sought out the land of Britain'. Edward became a martyr, although he had been known in his youth for his hot temper. A year after his death his body was brought from its obscure grave to the abbey at Shaftesbury and miracles began to happen at his tomb. 'Men murdered him, but God exalted him. . . . Those who earlier would not bow to his living body, now bow their knee to his bones.' His young half-brother, known to posterity as Aethelred the Unready, 'without counsel', was crowned king, but a portent of a bloody cloud of fire was seen several times in the night sky, and the next year Southampton, Thanet and Cheshire were all attacked by raiders.

Year after year they came, often under the leadership of Olaf Tryggvason, later King of Norway, whose victory at Maldon in Essex was bewailed in one of the most striking epics in Old English, *The Battle of Maldon*, written of course from the viewpoint of the defeated but heroic English and their leader Byrhtnoth. 'Mind shall be harder, heart the braver, courage the more as our strength lessens . . .' the ageing warrior exhorts his men, after allowing the

Vikings to cross the river, in an act of foolhardy chivalry. The language is almost Churchillian: 'We shall fight them on the beaches . . .'

After this defeat, which allowed the Vikings access to the east of the country and finally to London itself, the sum of sixteen thousand pounds in Danegold was collected to buy them off. Olaf went back to become King of Norway but his brother, Swein Forkbeard, broke his word and returned to ravage the country again. All attempts to contain or destroy the invaders were defeated. 'All these misfortunes befell us through lack of decision,' the anonymous writer of this part of the *Anglo-Saxon Chronicle* says, 'in that they were not offered tax in time, but when they had done great evil, then a truce and peace was made with them. And nonetheless for all this truce and peace and tax, they travelled about everywhere in bands and raided and roped up and killed our wretched people.' This phase culminated in the capture and murder of the Archbishop of Canterbury, and the sack of the city by Thorkell the Tall in 1012. Archbishop Alfeath was publicly pelted with bones and stones, and finally struck on the head with the butt of an axe by the drunken raiders, because he'd refused to allow any ransom to be paid for his own freedom.

The following year Swein Forkbeard, by now King of both Denmark and Norway, landed at Sandwich. He marched north to Danish Northumbria, which submitted to him, followed by the Midlands. With his army horsed and provisioned, he went south and besieged London where Aethelred was imprisoned with Thorkell the Tall, who had now thrown in his lot with the English king. Many of Swein's warriors were drowned trying to ford the Thames. The Londoners fought back fiercely and he was forced to turn west, where he overran Wessex itself whose governors surrendered to him. Aethelred took refuge in a ship on the Thames while his wife Emma, sister of Richard, Duke of Normandy, fled to her brother for safety. Aethelred retreated to the Isle of Wight for the winter, sending his two sons, the Princes Edward and

Alfred, to their mother in Normandy where he joined them a few months later. Swein was de facto King of England. His reign lasted less than a year.

On Swein's death it was agreed, by all councillors, 'both ordained and lay', that Aethelred 'their natural lord' should be asked to return to England on condition that he mended his ways and governed them more justly than he had before. Danish kings were outlawed from England for ever as the *Chronicle* reports. Meanwhile the Danish army had chosen Cnut, Swein's son, as leader, and he had taken an English wife, perhaps with his eye to the future. As soon as he arrived, Aethelred set out after Cnut, who was in East Anglia trying to equip his army, and caught him unprepared with a savage attack during which he captured, burnt and killed 'all human kind that could be got at'. Cnut retreated to his ships, sailed down to Sandwich and put ashore the hostages that had been given to his father, with their hands, ears and noses cut off. He was very young and it was his first and last defeat.

He was back the following year with a new force, to be opposed by a new player in this game of battles and scorched earth, King Aethelred's son, Edmund Ironside, who had married, against his father's will, the widow of a governor of the five Danish boroughs of eastern England which had then accepted him as their lord. When Aethelred died unlamented on St George's day 1016, London and the surrounding area chose Edmund as king while the rest of the country, who weren't prepared to rely on any descendant of Aethelred for good governance, chose Cnut. The two kings fought each other five times over the next six months until a truce was declared that gave Edmund Wessex and the rest of England to Cnut. How this would have worked out in practice can never be known for Edmund himself died in November and the whole country submitted to Cnut. England was now ruled by a Dane, who was shortly to become King of Denmark, and then Norway as well. Yet in 1014, in a fiery sermon from Wufstan, Archbishop of York, there is the strongest expression of English nationalism, of this 'people', in a word 'theode' that is also the close relative of the word for a king, language and, as a verb, to join. This people is the 'Engle'.

Cnut's marriage to Aelfgithu of Northampton didn't stop him marrying Aethelred's widow, Emma of Normandy, to pacify her brother who was still supporting the two young princes, the real heirs to the English throne now that their half-brother Edmund was dead. Somehow Cnut must have squared the fiery Bishop Wulfstan who, in our long tradition of polemical priests and prelates, had castigated the English for their lax ways and said that the Danish invasion was a judgement on them. By his first wife, whom he continued to keep as consort, Cnut had two sons: Harold, who became King of England for four years after Cnut's death, and Swein whom he tried to make regent of Norway. By Emma, whose English name was also confusingly Aelfgifu, he had Harthacnut who lasted as King for only two years after Harold. Cnut reigned for nearly twenty years, basing himself in England. As far as English mythology is concerned there's only one story that has come down to us but it supports the impression of a wise ruler. This is the tale of 'Canute' standing on the shore with the tide coming in, and refusing to accept the sycophantic advice of his courtiers that he could command the waves to go back.

Not all his decisions were wise. The Norwegians refused the English Aelfgifu and her son Swein as regents. Cnut also failed to secure the English succession of Emma's son Harthacnut, who was regarded as his legitimate heir. The prince lingered too long in Denmark after his father's death and his half-brother, Harold, gained the support of the most powerful men of England but not of Earl Godwine, who had been made the chief noble of the kingdom in about 1025, above Cnut's own compatriots, and married to the king's sister's sister-in-law. The English acceptance of an astute foreign king had given us a period of stability, free from Viking raids. But his influence on the course of English history was slight. Perhaps his potentially most important act was the elevation of Godwine and the replacement of the English word ealdorman for a great noble, with the Danish *earl*. Cnut's immediate successors, unlike their father, treated the country as a source of Danegold, imposing a tax for the payment of their own ships' crews of eight marks a rowlock, which when levied for Harthacnut's sixty-two vessels caused a rebellion in Worcestershire.

Harthacnut, who finally succeeded Harold, and 'never did anything kingly for as long as he ruled', died of convulsions as he was standing 'at his drink', as the account says, suggesting someone on his feet throwing back bumper after bumper rather than leaning on the bar. His half-brother Edward, son of Aethelred the Unready and Emma of Normandy, was already in England. Harthacnut seems to have offered him joint kingship, though it's hard to see why. Emma herself had been forced by Harold to seek refuge at the court of Baldwin of Flanders where she had lived with Edward after the death of her other son, Alfred, who had unwisely tried to visit his mother while she was still in Winchester. He had been taken prisoner, blinded and his companions massacred, some said by Earl Godwine who was afraid he might replace Harthacnut in the succession.

Although he had probably murdered Edward's brother, Godwine now threw his immense power and wealth behind the new king. After the disastrous sons of Cnut, the country was prepared to overlook its suspicion of Aethelred's offspring and restore the English royal line, descended from Alfred and the kings of Wessex. Edward's unpromising first act was to demand all his mother's gold, silver, lands and 'untold things' because 'she had kept it from him too firmly'.

Perhaps Godwine already saw in this vacillating king, who could alternately dither and punish rebellion with surprising cruelty, an opportunity for his own dynasty to succeed to the throne. His daughter Edith was married to Edward but the marriage, if ever consummated, was one only in name. What is referred to by historians as the king's 'asceticism' must obscure some grave sexual problem. It was after all the first duty of a king to secure the succession and provide an heir in the interests of political stability, and so he would have been advised. Great men and women might retire to monasteries after first fulfilling their secular duties, which included procreation. Edward seems to have been unable to comply, preferring to live the life of a monk while still retaining the crown and a semblance of marriage for twenty years.

Nevertheless Edith was his queen and the rise of Godwine's dynasty, like an eleventh-century Kennedy clan, continued. As well as Edith there was another daughter, Gunhild, who was a nun in St Omer, and six sons. The eldest, Swein, named after his Danish mother's royal relative, was given an earldom in the Welsh Marches. His subsequent behaviour would nowadays probably be dubbed sociopathic. On the way back from attacking the south Welsh, in company with Gruffydd, King of Gywnedd and Powys, 'he commanded the abbess of Leominster to be fetched to him, and kept her as long as it suited him' and then sent her back. It was a crime calculated to draw down Edward's loathing. Swein took refuge with his Danish cousin, another Swein. He tried to make a comeback three years later but his own family refused to help him. Finally he persuaded his Danish cousin Beorn, who had an earldom in the Midlands, to go with him to where King Edward was aboard ship at Sandwich with a fleet assembled against a raiding party. They rode out first to Bosham where Swein had left his seven ships. Beorn, relying on their kinship, had taken only three companies with him. He was bound by Swein's sailors, taken on board ship and murdered. Swein was forced to flee to Count Baldwin in Bruges whose half-sister was married to another of Godwine's sons and who always seemed to be willing to provide a refuge for English exiles.

Swein was reconciled with King Edward the next year but then the whole Godwine family fell from grace. Eustace, Count of Boulogne and Edward's brother-in-law, returning home from a visit to the king, stopped at Dover and demanded lodgings in the town. When one of the householders refused he was killed, whereupon the townspeople turned against the count's men and a pitched battle took place with several killed on either side. Finally Eustace fled from the angry citizens back to the king who ordered Godwine to take a force and punish the townspeople severely.

Kent was part of Godwine's own earldom of Wessex and he was unwilling to ravage his own lands. He and two of his sons, Swein and Harold, who was Earl of East Anglia and Essex, gathered an army to force the king to give up Eustace and a party of Frenchmen who had taken over a castle, which some chronicles say was in Dover and others in Swein's territory of Herefordshire. At first Edward was ready to give in but the northern earls gathered an army and marched to his defence. Civil war seemed inevitable but Godwine's supporters began to desert him. The king called his council. Godwine and all his sons were outlawed and the queen, deprived of all her land and treasure, was sent to a nunnery. Harold and his younger brother Leofwine went to the court of Diarmaid, King of Leinster and Dublin, while the others went off to Bruges and Baldwin.

After wintering in exile, the following year they set sail in June, Harold from Ireland and his father from Bruges, for an invasion of England. Edward, meanwhile, who had redistributed their lands among his French friends, gathered his forces and the two armies met at London. Once again the fear of civil war and how it might be exploited by enemies abroad brought about a reconciliation. The Godwines were restored to their lands and the queen given back her property. Swein, who had set out on a pilgrimage to Jerusalem in barefoot penance for the murder of Beorn, died at Constantinople on his way home and a few months later Godwine himself fell off his seat with a stroke while dining with the king in Winchester. Drinking and dining carried serious health risks in old England. Speechless and helpless, he lingered a few days. Harold was made Earl of Wessex on his father's death.

Two years later his brother Tostig was given the earldom of

Northumbria. At first all went well. Tostig set up a friendship with Malcolm, King of the Scots. He had succeeded to the throne when Siward, the previous Earl of Northumbria, defeated Macbeth who had killed Malcolm's father Duncan in battle not, as Shakespeare retells it, by cold-blooded murder. The Godwine clan were now at the height of their power and two younger brothers, Leofwine and Gyrth, were also found earldoms.

It was as well that Tostig was able to take the young King of Scots under his protection and keep Scotland quiet, for at the same time Gruffydd, King of Gwynedd and Powys, who had managed to bring the southern Welsh under his overlordship, decided to invade England. He was accompanied by the disaffected and out-lawed Aelfgar, Earl of East Anglia, with a force from Ireland.

The militia of all England was called out under Harold's com-mand, and a settlement finally reached, with Gruffydd swearing allegiance to Edward, and to keep the peace. It lasted four years. Then Harold and Tostig attacked the Welsh king's stronghold and put him to flight. He was killed by his own people who were sick of war, and his severed head brought to Harold, ending the last attempt at a united Wales.

It had become clear that Edward would die childless. The blood heir to the throne was therefore the surviving son of Edmund Ironside, who had been taken to Hungary when Cnut became king, beyond the reach of a potentially murderous royal hand. Known as Edward the Aetheling, the prince had married into the family of the Holy Roman Emperor, Henry III, and been royally treated. In 1054 Bishop Aldred of Worcester was sent by Edward to Cologne to negotiate the Aetheling's return. It took the prince two years to make his way to England, where he died in London shortly after his arrival, without even meeting his cousin Edward. 'Alas that was a cruel fate,' the Worcester version of the *Anglo-Saxon Chronicle* says, 'and harmful to all this nation.'

Tostig's attempt to govern Northumberland ended in a rebellion of the North in 1065. He was seen as a southerner and only a half-Dane. The people demanded a return to the Danelaw of Cnut and one of their own as earl. Harold had to negotiate his own brother's removal to prevent a more serious uprising. Northumbria was given what it asked and Tostig went into exile, of course with Baldwin of Bruges. Edward's chief concern now was the completion of the magnificent abbey he was building at Westminster.

There were several candidates for the throne. By blood it should have been the Aetheling's son, Edgar, but he was still a child. Then Harald Hardrada, 'the ruthless', King of Norway, thought he might have a claim through his ancestor Cnut. And William the Bastard, Duke of Normandy, alleged that King Edward had promised the throne to him during his earlier visit to the English court. The people's choice as expressed by the king's council, and ultimately by the king himself, was for a strong warrior who had shown himself capable of raising and leading a force in the field. Invasion was expected daily from several quarters. Their choice was for Harold Godwineson. Only the Earl of Northumbria opposed it, even though Harold had restored his earldom to him at the expense of his own brother Tostig. It took a visit from Harold, accompanied by the still fiery Bishop Wulfstan, to convince the Northumbrians that Harold was their best bet against invasion.

Duke William and his Normans were to make much of the story that Harold had compromised his right to accept the throne on a voyage to the Continent, when he had been shipwrecked, captured by Guy, Count of Ponthieu, and then sent to William. Harold was said to have sworn an oath of loyalty to the duke, and helped him in an attack on Brittany where William gave him arms, making him technically William's man, under the Teutonic traditions of fealty to one's lord.

At the time, which seems to have been about eighteen months before Edward's death, the succession was still unclear. If the whole episode isn't a later invention by the Normans to justify their invasion, and Harold was William's prisoner, he must have felt that his life was almost certainly at risk if he didn't swear. Later on his return to England, when he was offered the crown he would have considered an oath taken under duress, in quite other circumstances, when he was a captive and not able to make a free choice, as not binding upon him. What's also interesting is the pragmatic, elective element in the English monarchy as there had been in the choice of Cnut. It could be argued that this power of the Old English *witan*, the council of wise men who in effect approved if not quite elected the king, has passed down to Parliament, or at the very least, to today's Privy Council, which could still have a say in the succession, perhaps replacing Charles with Anne or William as 'the people's choice'. The beginnings of constitutional monarchy in England can be found before the Norman conquest. There has always been an implied contract between monarch and people, something the Stuarts never understood, with such disastrous consequences.

Edward the Confessor, 'pure and mild' as an elegy calls him, was too ill to attend the consecration of his beloved abbey at Westminster in December, and died on the eve of Twelfth Night, to be buried there next day. Harold was also crowned in the abbey the same day. He was to reign for forty weeks. At once 'he began to abolish unjust laws and make good ones', and try to put the country on readiness to resist invasion. He wasn't helped by the abolition of the ship tax, one of Edward's only popular measures, which had left the king without a navy. In April Halley's comet appeared over England, shining for a whole week. With hindsight it became an omen of what was to come.

The closing months of Harold's reign read like nothing less than the Trojan War. A few weeks after the fateful comet, Tostig invaded Northumbria with a Flemish force from his brother-in-law, Count Baldwin. They were beaten by the Northumbrians and Tostig retired for the summer to his friends in Scotland. Meanwhile Duke William in Normandy had been making his invasion plans, which included getting the Church's blessing on the enterprise in the form of a banner from the pope. He had recruited landless knights from as far as the Norman colonies in southern Italy, as well as from the territories bordering on the dukedom. The Normans themselves were descended from Vikings who had either invaded the French coast and settled, or been given land after serving as mercenaries. Now the duchy was too small for them, and for William's ambition.

Both opponents were busy assembling their fleets and armies. The English were first. The land forces were stationed along the coast while Harold waited all summer with the fleet at the Isle of Wight. By September there were no more provisions to maintain such a large force, or money to pay the crews. The militia were allowed to go home and the ships to sail for London, but many were lost at sea. The Norwegian claimant to the throne, Harald Hardrada, chose this strategic moment to make his move. A fleet of three hundred ships sailed into the Tyne, where it was joined by the fleet Tostig had been raising in Scotland.

They set sail for York. The Earls of Northumbria and Mercia caught up with them and a great battle took place outside the city. The English earls were beaten although they did inflict great losses. A formula like those apologetic war bulletins from the Ministry of Defence was always used in the *Chronicle* to embody the unhappy outcome of such a battle. Even though the English had been presented during the course of it as seeming to win, in the end it had to be admitted that 'the Norwegians had possession of the place of slaughter'. The myth requires that we shall at least go down fighting, usually against 'superior forces'. The English cover-up or face saver has a long and undistinguished history. Hearing the news, Harold force-marched his army north, caught the victors by surprise at Stamford Bridge and massively defeated them. Tostig and Hardrada were both killed but Harold was magnanimous in victory, allowing Olaf, Hardrada's son, and his bishop, and the Earl of Orkney to return home with twenty-four ships, after swearing allegiance. Two days later William landed at Pevensey.

His first act, following Norman military custom, was to build a castle at Hastings. Harold, still recovering from the fight at Stamford Bridge, was forced to march south again as soon as he heard of the new invasion, trying to gather fresh forces on the way. Some of these reinforcements hadn't reached him, and he had no real chance to organize those troops he had, before joining battle with William who had had a fortnight to rest and regroup. Harold drew up his army at 'the grey apple tree'. What has come to be called the Battle of Hastings was about to begin. William attacked continental style, with archers, crossbowmen and cavalry. The English fought in the old heroic way with battleaxe and double-handed sword.

At first they had the advantage, forcing back the Bretons and other auxiliaries on the Norman left. They fell back to be joined by the centre and right of the line. The invaders' retreat was only checked when William himself appeared in front of them and stopped what threatened to become a rout. Those English who had followed up the retreat now found themselves cut off and cut down. This tactic was to be used again, twice more.

All day the English centre still held, exhausted and dwindling where the King fought among his housecarls, the warrior band. Then Harold himself fell, as tradition has it, shot through the eye by a stray arrow. His two younger brothers had already been killed. The house of Godwine had fallen like the house of Atreus; Harold like Hector before the walls of Troy. The last English King of England was dead.

4

Mother Tongue

WHEN HAROLD FELL, four Norman knights rushed forward to
finish off the dying king. Some accounts say his leg was gashed,
others that it was completely severed, for which William had the
perpetrator banished. One story has it that Harold's body was so
mutilated that his common-law wife, and mother of his many
children, Edith Swanneck, had to be brought onto the battlefield
to identify it by certain secret marks which only she knew. He
was taken for burial to Waltham Holy Cross, the abbey in Essex
which he had founded. Another version says he was first buried
by the seashore by William's command and that Harold's mother
was forced to beg for the right to bury him. A final twist has him
escaping from the battlefield and living out his days as a hermit
blind in one eye.

Any pretence that the myth of England has ethnic reality has
to be abandoned in the face of Harold's death and William's victory. The original English, Bede's Angles, had been largely overrun
by the Danes. The old Britons survived in Cumbria, Devon and
Cornwall, while the mantle of England had passed with Alfred to
the Saxons. Welsh and Scottish princes still held the West and
North. Nevertheless, in spite of long periods of warfare and foreign

occupation of part of the island, English culture had been pre-eminent for some five hundred years. Now that was over. There was a Frenchified Viking on the throne, supported by his Breton and Viking allies from all over Christendom, ruling this polyglot, multi-ethnic state, 'this dear land of England' as the *Chronicle* had called it on the death of Edward the Confessor. The myth of England itself would be under threat for the next century and a half as the Norman barons fought each other for territory and power in England and France.

William rested his army for five days at Hastings, perhaps expecting that the remaining English leaders would come in to him. Then he set out on a leisurely march towards London, subduing Romney, Canterbury and Dover, and leaving a string of fortifications behind him. Edith, Edward the Confessor's widow, sent him the keys of Winchester, which she was holding. He reached Southwark and the southern end of London Bridge. Inside the city a party had formed in support of Edgar the Aetheling who had the strongest claim by birth, as the *Chronicle* says, led by Archbishops Stigand and Ealdred, the Earls of Northumbria and Mercia, Morcar and Edwin, the chief men of London and the Bishops of Worcester and Hereford. William's answer was to burn Southwark and lay waste on both banks of the Thames, effectively cutting off the city, a strategy that caused the collapse of the Aetheling's party, all of whom submitted to the duke and swore fealty at Berkhamstead. Just to make sure, he ravaged all the country between there and London, some twenty-five miles.

William was crowned king in Edward's abbey of Westminster on Christmas Day. Like the English kings before him he swore to rule his people justly, but it was felt necessary to have him not merely crowned but acclaimed by the congregation. The question was put by the bishops in English and French, and the shouting that followed caused his men outside to think the new king was being attacked and to set fire to the surrounding buildings. His first acts as king were to build the forerunner of the Tower of

London to keep the citizens in no doubt who was ruler, and to impose a heavy new tax on the whole country. Those who had shown themselves unfriendly to him had to ransom their estates, while the lands of those who had fallen in the battle were forfeit and bestowed on William's landless knights as their reward. Edgar, the Aetheling, found shelter in Scotland where his sister Margaret had married the king. He would eventually join a rebellion in Normandy against William, be taken prisoner, then pardoned and disappear from the *Anglo-Saxon Chronicle* in 1106.

When William set out to visit Normandy at the end of March he divided responsibility for the kingdom between William Fitz-Osbern, now Earl of Hereford, and his own half-brother, the militant Odo, Bishop of Bayeux and Earl of Kent. By the time William returned, the repressive measures of these two had alienated everyone they had dealings with. Exeter and the West, still strongly British and known as the West Welsh, held out against William's force for eighteen days and were then able to strike a better deal than most.

This was only one of a series of rebellions. The most serious was an attempt to replace one foreign ruler with another: Swein Estrithson, King of Denmark, a descendant of Cnut. A mixed fleet of Norwegians and Danes, some two hundred and forty ships, joined forces with the English leaders at York, which the Normans then set on fire. While this was going on Edric the Wild led a rebellion in Herefordshire, calling in the Welsh as allies. William marched to crush them, then turned back to deal with the Danes whom he bought off. With this threat safely out of the way he set out to punish the North for its rebellions, laying waste the countryside of Yorkshire, Cheshire, Shropshire, Staffordshire and Derbyshire so that they could never trouble him again.

The most romantic of the revolts, which has become legend, is that of Hereward the Wake, or the watchful, a thegn, a lesser noble of modest rank, from Lincolnshire. The Danes made another landing in 1070, and joined with Hereward and the other English rebels in the Isle of Ely where they were protected by the marshes. Hereward took Peterborough but once again William bought off the Danes. When they withdrew to their ships Hereward became the leader of the English resistance on Ely and was joined by Morcar of Northumbria and many others. William besieged the island by land and water, forcing the garrison to surrender, except for Hereward who cut his way out with a few friends. He disappears from history after, some say, actually joining William in a later campaign on the Continent, but he is part of a mainstream of English rebels which includes Robin Hood and Dick Turpin.

William's hold on the country was tightened by the building of castles, the gift of land and titles to his supporters, and the replacement of the more easygoing English Church, with its modest buildings, by the stricter continental organization based on monasteries, opulent cathedrals and churches. In spite of a threat of invasion by a new Cnut of Denmark, nearly twenty years after the Battle of Hastings, William by the end of his reign was secure on the throne. The year of his death was filled with disasters. London and many other towns burnt down. There was famine and plague, which William perhaps caught before sailing with an army to France where he set fire to the town of Nantes with all its churches, and those who had sought sanctuary in them.

He died in Normandy, robbed by his attendants and left almost naked on the floor, to be buried by a country knight, out of compassion. Accounts of his death varied even within fifty years. Some said he went too near the flames of the burning city while urging his men to add more fuel; others that the pommel of his saddle ruptured his great belly while he was leaping a ditch. He had been an almost superhuman figure that contemporaries found hard to judge. Pot-bellied, so that there were jokes about his being pregnant, with receding hair, not very tall but so immensely strong that he could shoot from horseback using a bow no one else could even draw, he was admired in a fearful way rather than loved. It was said of England under his rule that you could travel safely from end to end with a bosom full of gold and not be molested. For commoners, the punishment for rape was full castration.

His greed was notorious and he farmed out his royal manors to the highest bidder, on the toughest terms. Only the monks, if they behaved themselves, were treated less than harshly. Even his half-brother Odo, bishop and earl, eventually fell from favour and was imprisoned. Large tracts of the country were set aside for his hunting, and the game laws included blinding as a punishment. The elegy on him in the Peterborough version of the *Chronicle* says satirically:

> *he loved the stags so very much*
> *as if he were their father;*
> *also he decreed for the hares that they might go free.*
> *The rich complained and the poor lamented,*
> *but he was too relentless to care though all might hate him,*
> *and they were compelled, if they wanted*
> *to keep their lives and their lands*
> *and their goods and the favour of the king,*
> *to submit themselves wholly to his will.*
> *Alas that any man should bear himself so proudly*
> *and deem himself exalted above all other men.*

As an instrument of control he instituted the Domesday Survey, sending investigators into every corner of England to record every person, every hide of land, every ox, cow or pig: 'it is shameful to tell – but it seemed no shame to him to do it.' The result is one of the most detailed and fascinating historical records, designed to ensure that no one escaped the payment of taxes.

> *He was fallen into avarice*
> *and loved greediness above all.*

Before his death he lamented bitterly that he was dying with no time to reform his life as he had always intended, and made a last-minute bid for salvation by ordering his treasure to be distributed among the churches and freeing his prisoners. His other possessions he reluctantly divided among his three sons. William, nicknamed Rufus for his red hair, got England and set out to take over the throne even before his father was dead. Robert was given Normandy. The youngest son Henry had to be content with five thousand pounds in silver.

William Rufus began promisingly, bringing out his father's treasure, accumulated over so many years, from its secret hoard in Winchester; some to be distributed to every monastery, every parish church and every county in accordance with William's dying wishes. This liberality soon turned to profligacy. Rufus was forced, by the rebellion of a group of Norman barons led by Odo, his bishop uncle, in favour of his brother Robert's claim to England, to buy the loyalty and services of the few remaining English lords. Odo was captured in his castle at Pevensey and agreed to leave England. On his way to the coast, however, he was rescued by his supporters in Rochester.

The king called on his Englishmen to lay siege to the city on pain of the greatest shame of being called a 'nithing', without honour. Odo was recaptured and this time left England for good. In the following years Rufus fought sometimes against his brothers, sometimes with them against the Welsh and the Scots. Men came from all over Europe to take service with the king whose whole income was wasted on keeping his troops. The historian monk William, librarian of Malmesbury Abbey, says: 'There was no man rich but the money changer; no clerk unless he was a lawyer; no priest unless he was a farmer . . . the halter was loosed from the robber's neck if he could promise any money to the King.'

There were other worries too. The king was extravagant in his dress. Hearing that his new boots had only cost three shillings, he sent them away, demanding a pair costing at least a mark of silver.

His chamberlain brought him an even cheaper pair but pretended they had cost what the king ordered. 'Yes,' William said as they were drawn on, 'these are fit for majesty.' From then on the chamberlain charged him whatever he pleased. The king's example encouraged luxury in his court. 'Then was their flowing hair and extravagant dress, and then was invented the fashion for shoes with curved points. The model for young men was to rival women in delicacy of person, to mince their gait and to walk with loose gesture and half naked.' The unmarried king, if not homosexual himself, although the implication is very strong, certainly surrounded himself with such camp followers, as too did his brother Robert in Normandy. 'Enervated and effeminate, they unwillingly remained what nature had made them.' Prostitutes of both sexes followed the court. The Archbishop of Canterbury, Anselm, left the country in disgust, having failed to reform what the Church saw as the obscene behaviour of William's entourage.

His reign lasted thirteen years, with the king becoming increasingly unpopular as he continued his father's policy of harsh game laws and heavy taxation. When his brother Robert decided to go on the first crusade, he sold William Normandy for ten thousand marks, which William raised by a tax that even forced the clergy to melt down the church plate and furnishings to pay it. His death remains a mystery. According to William of Malmesbury, the king dined and drank heavily before going out to hunt with a few attendants, who soon became dispersed through the forest, except for one, Sir Walter Tirel, who stayed with him. The king let fly an arrow and wounded a stag, which ran on. William followed it with his eyes, holding up a hand to shield them from the sun. Tirel, attempting to shoot at another stag, accidentally, it seems, shot the king instead. Without saying a word William broke off the shaft and fell upon his breast, deliberately forcing the arrow deeper into his body. He seemed already dead when Tirel reached him so there was nothing for the knight to do but escape as quickly as he could.

Rufus was taken, still dripping blood, in a cart to Winchester, and buried in the cathedral under the tower, which fell down the next year. His youngest brother Henry was now elected king, rather than the feeble Robert. At once the new king began reversing the abuses of the old regime, setting up the Court of Exchequer to reform the collection of taxes. Sheriffs were appointed as the king's local representatives. Henry kept his barons under control and the country at peace for thirty-five years. His greatest struggle was over the question of who should appoint bishops: the king or the pope. Henry may be said to have won. The pope gave the spiritual authority with staff and ring to the king's candidate. The bishop did homage as a feudal baron to the king; a relic of this still survives in the bishops' seats in the House of Lords.

Henry spent much of his reign in Normandy protecting his interests there against the King of France and the French barons under his sovereignty. While he was away England was effectively governed by Roger, Bishop of Salisbury, his chief minister. The great tragedy for Henry was the loss of his sons, William his heir, and Richard his favourite bastard, in the wreck of the *White Ship*.

The king was returning to England after four years in Normandy and set sail in November 1120, leaving his sons to follow him in the finest, fastest ship in the fleet. The accounts of its loss with all the gilded youth on board read like a preview for the sinking of the *Titanic*. According to William of Malmesbury the sailors were drunk when they put to sea at night in an attempt to overtake the ship that had already sailed. They had hardly left harbour when the ship ran aground on a rock. All attempts with oars and boathooks to get it off failed and the water rushed in. Some were washed overboard, some drowned below decks. A skiff was launched with the eldest prince, and presumably others on board, but he went back for his illegitimate sister, the Countess of Perche, and the little boat was swamped by the number of people jumping into it.

Only one person escaped, a butcher, by clinging to the mast. One account says that one hundred and fifty soldiers, fifty sailors and three captains, as well as all the royal entourage perished. The king's treasure was washed up on the sands next day but none of the bodies was found to be buried. 'Delicate as they were they became food for the monsters of the deep.' They included 'almost every person of consequence about court, whether knight, or chaplain, or young noblemen training up to arms. For . . . they eagerly hastened from all quarters, expecting no small addition to their reputation, if they could either amuse or show their devotion to the young prince.'

Henry fainted when he heard the news 'but soon, hiding his grief, he resumed his royal courage, as in scorn of fate', says Simeon of Durham in his version of events. The king had remained a widower since the death of his queen, Matilda, but now he quickly remarried in hope of an heir. But his hope wasn't to be fulfilled and he died without a legitimate son, fifteen years later in Normandy. His body was brought back to England to be buried in his own abbey of Reading. 'Then this land immediately grew dark because every man who could, immediately robbed another.'

He had tried to provide for a peaceful succession eight years before his death by getting his chief men, lay and clerical, to swear England and Normandy after his death to his daughter who, confusingly, was called Matilda, Maud or Adelaide at different times. These included David, the new King of the Scots, his brother-in-law, who owed allegiance to Henry. However, when Henry died his nephew Stephen, his sister's son, was in England and the people of London had him crowned probably thinking, wrongly as it turned out, that a man would be better at keeping the peace. Twenty years of anarchy followed. Its description forms one of the most famous pieces of English prose just as the *Anglo-Saxon Chronicle*, begun by King Alfred, is coming to an end, with its last entry written by a monk at Peterborough in 1154.

I do not know nor can I tell all the horrors nor all the tortures that they did to wretched men in this land . . . they laid a tax upon the villages time and time again. Then when the wretched men had no more to give they robbed and burned all the villages that you could well go a whole day's journey and never find anyone occupying a village or land tilled . . . they greatly oppressed the wretched men of the land with building castles and when the castles were made they filled them with devils and evil men. Then by both night and by day they seized those people who they imagined had any wealth, common men and women, and put them in prison to get their gold and silver and tortured them with unspeakable tortures . . . it was said openly that Christ and his saints slept.

Stephen was a French king; his rival Matilda a would-be French queen. Their successor, her son Henry II, the first Plantagenet, was lord of Normandy, Brittany, Anjou and Aquitaine. The kingdom of the English had become an appendage to the king's concerns in France.

By the end of Henry's reign the takeover, indeed the makeover, of England was complete. French was the language of the court and the Norman aristocracy, Latin of scholarship, law and religion, English of the peasants, and significantly of women. Many of the Norman knights had taken English wives. Their children must have been bilingual as often happens with second-generation immigrants. English survived as the mother tongue, although driven underground, among the *villeins* and *serfs*, so called by their French masters, and in the nursery. Its survival and eventual re-emergence is against the grain both of the English myth of Norman superiority and linguistic history where, as for example in the Americas North and South, the conqueror's language usually replaces the original tongue.

It was long accepted wisdom that, in the words of *1066 and All That*, the Norman conquest was 'a good thing' and the correct stance was pro-Norman. By the conquest, it was taught, the backward English were brought into the mainstream of continental civilization. Architecture improved, that is, it became more grandiose and its achievements are still visible. At one time it was even doubted whether the pre-conquest natives could build in stone at all. But the Norman cathedrals replaced existing English stone structures at a cost. They were funded by heavy taxation, the spoils of war and the imposition of greater servitude. The freemen of the English South and the Scandinavian North were absorbed into the three-tier Norman feudal system and effectively suppressed. A similar process would obliterate the Tudor freeholders and their franchise during the eighteenth century, reducing them first to tenants, then to disenfranchised, illiterate agricultural labourers.

By an irony of fate, among William the Conqueror's knights rewarded with land and titles were several Bretons, descendants of the British who had fled the Anglo-Saxons but who now became Anglo-Normans. The English earldoms, the sub-kingdoms like Wessex and Mercia with their great lords, were broken up and apportioned to roughly two hundred of the new barons, but often not all the lands were together so that it was more difficult for any one lord to raise a whole region against the royal authority. This system of scattered properties has continued and the aristocratic title may now have little to do with the actual seat.

The royal grants of the Norman kings laid down the pattern of an aristocracy that still pertains. It remains de rigueur for the upper classes to be able to claim Norman ancestry and the historical fact is reflected in their surnames which can, in many instances, be traced back to the French originals with, of course, some exceptions. Even six hundred years later the Stuart kings found it necessary to invent Norman surnames for their illegitimate children: Fitzcharles, Fitzjames and Fitzroy. Not all the Normans were knights, even if they were landless. Some must have been merely attendants and foot soldiers whose names would by intermarriage have seeped into the English peasantry.

William of Malmesbury, who claimed to be of both English and Norman descent, makes an interesting contrast between the two. He alleges that the 'desire after literature and religion had decayed for several years' before the arrival of the Normans. 'The clergy, contented with a very slight degree of learning, could scarcely stammer out the words of the sacraments; and a person who understood grammar was an object of wonder and astonishment.' William of Malmesbury means Latin grammar and it suits him, as a monk, to criticize the English Church, which was based on a secular clergy, rather than the continental monastic rule, although monasticism was developing fast in England even before the conquest. The struggle between the two systems came to a head in the battle over the appointment of a new archbishop of Canterbury in Henry I's reign, when the secular bishops held out for one of their own while the monks of Canterbury, backed by the pope, fought for one of theirs.

The English are also accused by William of Malmesbury of drunkenness and gluttony, compared with the Normans who are 'particular in their dress and delicate in their food but not to excess'. The Norman's home is his castle unlike the Englishman's, which is a pub: 'They were more inclined to revelling than to the accumulation of wealth. Drinking in parties was an universal practice, in which occupation they passed entire nights as well as days. They consumed their whole substance in mean and despicable houses unlike the Normans and French who in noble and splendid mansions live with frugality.'

There's a downside to this refinement. The Normans were 'so bred to war that they can hardly live without it'. Polite and quick to take offence, they 'envy their equals, wish to excel their superiors and plunder their subjects. . . . They weigh treachery by its chance of success and change their sentiments with money.' William also says that the English corrupted their conquerors to drunkenness while adopting their manners. The residents of Spanish holiday resorts and the organizers of football matches would testify to the ongoing English interest in alcohol, and if it's true that this has a genetic component, then it's one of the few ethic Englishnesses that has survived most significantly among the descendants of that suppressed majority that formed the 'lower orders', the English villeins and serfs.

The castles of the Norman barons were eventually translated into the country houses and stately homes of later centuries as the need for real castles receded, but the concept of exclusivity, of worlds apart, remained. The baronage intermarried. Its children became pages and handmaidens in each others' establishments as part of their education. Both customs continue in a modified but recognizable form today, with boarding schools having replaced the castle apprenticeship to gentility but with the exclusivity remaining. The language of the court and the upper classes was French; their love songs those of the aristocratic troubadours like Robert d'Estouteville, captured by Henry I in his French wars and imprisoned in England for many years.

When Eleanor of Aquitaine married Henry II in 1153 she brought the refinements of Provence to the Anglo–Norman court. Her grandfather had been the first known troubadour, Guillaume IX of Aquitaine, and she was a patron of the arts, especially the love song, bringing the most famous of the troubadours Bernard de Ventadour to her court in Poitiers. Another patron of literature was Robert, Earl of Gloucester, the illegitimate son of Henry I. Soldier and politician, spending his time between England and Normandy, and the chief supporter of his half-sister Matilda during the years of anarchy, it's hard to see how he found much time for reading as William of Malmesbury says he did in the dedication of his history. 'You yet snatch some hours to yourself, for the purpose of reading or hearing others read ... whilst you love books, you manifest how deeply you have drunk of the stream of philosophy.'

William of Malmesbury wrote his *History of the Kings of England*, which included the three Normans, at the request, he says, of the wife of Henry I, Queen Matilda. She died before it was finished and he was tempted not to go on, but he had gone too far to give up. When it was finished, a copy was sent to her daughter Matilda, known as the Empress to distinguish her from her mother and because she had been married to the Emperor of Germany. Through her mother she was a descendant of Edmund Ironside, and the kings of Scotland. She was also patron of William's abbey of Malmesbury, which had been without an abbot since her mother's death. An abbey without a powerful head, usually related to the noble family that had founded it, lost status. In praising the Empress's ancestors on her mother's side William hoped to regain the family's patronage.

According to William, God had turned his face away from the English because of Harold's broken oath to Duke William, and they were never more 'to breathe freedom'. The very fact that England is an island makes it easy to control, he says, because there is no escape. Only its internal conflicts are a cause for concern. William was clearly expressing a deliberate Norman policy to keep the English subjugated and isolated. But at what might be seen as the lowest time for the native English he nevertheless chose to praise their kings, whom he calls 'ours', and their living representative and descendant, Matilda.

Matilda's brother, Robert of Gloucester, was also interested in history. Patron not only of William of Malmesbury, but also of another contemporary historian, Henry of Huntingdon, his most influential protégé was Geoffrey of Monmouth whose *History of the Kings of Britain*, written in the 1130s, sparked off the whole romance literature of Arthur. Using Gildas and Nennius and, he claims, a book in the British language given to him by one Archdeacon Walter of Oxford, a provost of St George's, at Oseney, Geoffrey tells the story of the British up to the time of Cadwallo, whom he claims as the last true king of the island of Britain. Significantly the author is full of praise for those Britons who emigrated to France to become Bretons, suggesting that Geoffrey himself was of Breton descent.

Fifteen or so years later the Jersey writer Wace, probably also of Breton extraction, produced a French version of Geoffrey's history, dedicated to Eleanor of Aquitaine. Not to be left out, a Worcestershire priest, Layamon, had written an English version, by the latest in 1250 according to some authorities, though the language and form suggest a date much sooner after Wace. Indeed, it's hard to see why an English version should have had to wait nearly a hundred years, especially since there had been an even earlier French *Estorie des Englais* written for the wife of an Anglo-Norman knight, Constance Fitzgilbert of Lincolnshire, which was also an extended reworking of Geoffrey of Monmouth.

Layamon's epic of over six thousand lines was called *Brut*, like its two French forerunners, because of the tradition that it was the mythical Roman leader, Brutus, who had founded Britain, and is crucial to the re-emergence of English as a national language. Yet hardly anyone, except for academics and students of English, even knows of its existence or its author's name. Layamon, sometimes modernized to Lawman, in his preface calls himself a priest, son of Leovenath, living in Areley Kings in Worcestershire, not far from the Severn and the Welsh marches. He was therefore close to Geoffrey of Monmouth's origins, and those of the later William Langland of Malvern, the author of *Piers Plowman*, which carries on in style and tone from Layamon.

Layamon's English *Brut* is a deliberate act of cultural guerrilla warfare, a kind of 'why should the devil, in this case the Norman French, have all the best tunes?'. He is taking back the history of Britain for the English and '*Engelene londe*'. He makes this clear in a passage towards the end of his account of the founding of London and the different changes in its name. Originally called Trinovant, after the tribe of the Celtic Trinobantes, it was renamed Kaer Lud by King 'Lud', then Londinium after a foreign invasion, then again Lundene by the Saxons, 'a name that lasted long in this land', and finally 'Londres' by the Normans. They came, writes Layamon, 'with their evil ways . . . they have destroyed (or massacred) all this people'. The whole country has suffered because of the foreigners who are driven away again. The original passage in Layamon's sourcebook by the Frenchman Wace has nothing about the Normans' 'evil ways' nor the destruction of the English people and neither does it say that the 'foreigners' are finally driven away.

Brut has another significant statement after the death of Arthur, or rather after his being taken away to the Isle of Avalon to be healed of his wound, a passage in which the English version is as romantically effective as Mallory or Tennyson. Layamon reports the legend that Arthur will return to save the British but repeats it again to say that 'an Arthur will yet come to help *the people of England*' (or 'the English' – my italics). There was indeed an Arthur in Brittany, a grandson of Henry II and therefore a descendant of the kings of Wessex and England, named as Richard I's heir, who died in 1203, which may give a clue to the actual date of Layamon's epic.

Wace says that he writes to please the rich; Geoffrey of Monmouth chose patrons from the ruling house; Gaimar, author of the other French version, wrote for a rich Norman. Layamon has no patron except a possible 'good knight' whose chaplain he might have been. Who were his audience? Obviously they preferred to read English rather than Latin or French. They may have been Englishwomen, educated enough to read or to be read a very long poem in a complex alliterative style that harked back to the full Anglo-Saxon classical epics like *Beowulf* or *The Battle of Maldon*. The *Brut* is much less warrior-centred than its linguistic forerunners and women have a far more equal role in it. The sheer size and complexity of it presupposes a sophisticated native audience.

Not far from where Layamon lived three English sisters, presumably from the remnants of the native gentry, had retired to live as hermits. For them someone, almost certainly a priest, produced a prose handbook on how to conduct their practical and spiritual lives at about the same time as Layamon's epic. It was copied extensively and translated into both French and Latin. Also in the late twelfth or early thirteenth century there appeared a long poem in English, but using French rhyme and metre, which is a dialogue between two female birds, *The Owl and the Nightingale*, preserved in the same manuscript in the British Library as Layamon's poem. Putting those three instances together it looks as if Englishwomen were being provided with a literature that incidentally fostered the preservation of the language itself at a time when it might have been in most danger of disappearing since it had been relegated to the English underclass. Had it done so, French would now be the major world language, spoken in all the former British colonies, on analogy with the complete supersession by Latin Romance languages of the native Celtic and Germanic tongues of, for example, France and Spain. It would have been indeed a true lingua franca. It would now also be the language of the Internet and international flight. English would have dwindled to a minority language like Welsh or died out completely.

Much of what was written in all three languages current at this crucial period has been lost. What has survived is due to chance, like the survival of English itself. Gradually, by the middle of the fourteenth century, English emerged again as the dominant language, understood by everyone:

> Both learnt and lewd, old and young
> All understand in English tongue.

In John of Trevisa's *Dialogue Between a Lord and a Clerk*, the lord puts the case for translating Ranulf of Chester's Latin *Chronicles* into English in terms that Alfred the Great would have applauded, that they may be made accessible to 'as many as possible'.

The language itself had changed, of course, as it does all the time. Usually the changes are minor; these were radical. Old English had been a highly inflected, grammatically rigid language, standardized in its written form by the scribes of Alfred's Wessex. Beginning in the Scandinavian north of the Danelaw, where Danish and Norwegian had died out by the end of William the Conqueror's reign, Middle English took on many words from the languages it had superseded in these areas, as well as others from the conquering Normans. At the same time the sentence structure became simpler. Instead of cases and declensions being used as in German, Latin and Anglo-Saxon, prepositions and word order began to dictate the meaning. By the last entries in the *Anglo-Saxon Chronicle*, dealing with the conflict between Stephen and Matilda in the 1140s, the process is well under way. The modern sentence structure of subject, verb, object has already largely replaced the earlier Germanic construction of leaving the verb to the end of the sentence, as in King Alfred's prose. The language became a simplified yet rich and flexible instrument, fit for a Shakespeare or a computer game. Only our spelling remains idiosyncratic and archaic, though at least by the end of Chaucer's life we had got rid of þ, ð, æ and ʒ, replacing the first two with 'th', the next with 'a', and the last with 'gh' and 'y'. The invention of printing further accelerated the process of simplification and standardization.

In the end even the Norman royal family and the barons adopted English, perhaps because of a stubborn refusal by the bulk of the English to learn a 'foreign' language. Henry IV is said to have been the first king since the conquest for whom it was his mother tongue. Nothing, of course, unifies a country so much as a foreign enemy, a unity reinforced by confinement within an island boundary. When King John Lackland, Robin Hood's adversary, mislaid most of the Plantagenets' northern French possessions by the end of his reign, earning his nickname in the process, even his Norman barons had to begin to think of themselves as English gentlemen.

5

Revolting Peasants

PART OF OUR English myth is that when the rest, that is, Europe, were labouring under feudalism and despotism, we reinvented democracy with Parliament and Magna Carta. While admitting that the Greeks thought of it first, we credit ourselves with its modern, that is, mediaeval, introduction. Henry II's long reign brought us our 'common law' system and the beginnings of a civil service. He kept the barons in order by having his own mercenaries, paid for by the barons in cash instead of military service, and a militia of freemen with standardized weapons. The only event to blot his reign was the wrangle with Archbishop Thomas Becket over who had the power to sentence priests who had been judged guilty of serious crimes, Church or state. The 'turbulent priest' Thomas was finally martyred in Canterbury Cathedral. Henry was made to do penance by the pope but the Church courts were confirmed in their right to impose the lightest of sentences on convicted felons who could read and write, and were therefore able to claim benefit of clergy, that is to be judged by the ecclesiastical courts as if they were priests. Becket became St Thomas and his shrine at Canterbury attracted pilgrims from all over Christendom, including Chaucer's pilgrims of *The Canterbury Tales*.

Much of Henry's time was spent defending his French territones. We became so used to an absentee king that when his son, Richard Lionheart, also spent most of his reign fighting or being imprisoned abroad, either in France or on crusade, the country continued more or less to run itself until the intervention of his brother John. John is a clownish figure who reputedly lost his baggage in the Wash and died of a surfeit of lampreys, a relative of the eel. He was also a greedy extortionist, and murderer of his nephew, who may be the Arthur destined, Layamon had hoped, to return to save the British people. John was also a military incompetent. By 1215, after plunging the country into civil war, he was detested by Church, barons and people alike. At Runnymede near Windsor he was forced by the barons to agree to a limitation to the royal power. The charter contained a famous clause which the English believe enshrines our rights. 'No freeman shall be arrested or imprisoned or dispossessed or outlawed or banished or in any way molested, nor will we go upon him nor send upon him, except by the lawful judgement of his peers and the law of the land.'

These words have mistakenly given rise to the belief that an Englishman is somehow born free, and that 'it's a free country'. The words in fact enshrined a principle that only freemen have rights, not the ninety per cent of the country still composed of unfree villeins and serfs. It's true that the numbers of freemen increased through the King's rapacity, which led him to sell charters to towns granting them the right to hold fairs, govern themselves and confer the status of freedom on successful merchants, shop-keepers and tradesmen. The extension of the rank of freeman and freeholder was largely a product of urban expansion. As the population grew and the country became more settled, the need increased for consumer goods and luxuries, clothes, food and wine, furniture, the arts of literature and music to fill the castles of the nobility, and the homes of the gentry and merchants.

The expanding Church also needed goods, services and especi-ally manpower. Two universities were founded, as well as the Inns of Court for the lawyers between the Westminster court and the commercial city. London had its first annually elected Lord Mayor in 1215 by courtesy of King John. The rural poor, tied to the land and its owners, tended the sheep on whose wool this new prosperity was based, while themselves continuing in a life of virtual slavery and seasonal poverty, brilliantly described by William Langland in his *Piers Plowman*, three-quarters of the way through the fourteenth century.

Our other contribution, as we see it, to democracy was the institution of Parliament, which also came about as an attempt to control a despotic king, John's son Henry III. He had outraged the barons and the Church by filling both lay and clerical posts with foreigners. In 1265 Simon de Montfort, leader of the reforming party, had two burgesses, leading members from the town councils and two knights of every shire summoned to Parliament, the first time that the commons, that is the communities, urban and rural, had been represented. It didn't of course mean the common people, any more than Magna Carta had applied to them. The expansion of the king's council, which was what this talking shop for parlaying was, had been gradually growing as a way to more efficient government, by consent of both parties, the king and the nation, meaning first the barons, lay and clerical, then the gentry, then the merchants. At first there was only one House presided over by the monarch or his chancellor sitting on a woolsack, symbol of contemporary trade and wealth. Gradually the representatives of the communities began to meet together in the chapter house of Westminster Abbey to consider their collective response to questions raised by their superiors and in the many royal petitions from both sides, ruler and ruled, including the always thorny question of taxation.

After the loss of most of the Plantagenets' French possessions by King John, his successors were forced to reinvent themselves as English kings ruling an English state, rather than Norman barons with an English fiefdom whose main interests were in France.

Such a state had to be English because there were still the untamed Welsh, Irish and Scots who might ally themselves with France if they weren't brought under English control. The son of Henry III, Edward I, who as Prince Edward had defeated the barons under Simon de Montfort a few months after the first Parliament, set about restoring the power of the monarchy and reducing the threat from the Celtic fringe. First he put down a Welsh rebellion by Llewelyn ap Griffith, who had supported Simon de Montfort, blockading his army by land and sea until he forced their surrender. Then after he had suppressed a second rebellion, he built a series of castles at Conway, Harlech, Beaumaris and Carnarvon where his eldest son was born. The title Prince of Wales, which the child was given, was intended to put paid to any further ideas of Welsh independence.

In 1296 Edward found an excuse in a dispute over the succession to the Scottish throne to invade Scotland. The Scots were defeated and Edward symbolically carried off the Stone of Scone on which their kings had been crowned. The Scots fought back under William Wallace but he too was defeated and executed. They found a new and more successful leader in Robert Bruce. Edward died at Carlisle in 1307 on his way to a fourth invasion of Scotland, having earned himself the title of Hammer of the Scots.

He was succeeded by his twenty-three-year-old son, Edward II, whose tragic story would make good drama in the hands of the Elizabethan playwright Christopher Marlowe, but was bad governance. His youth and his passion for a young Gascon, Piers Gaveston, gave the barons a chance to make a comeback. Gaveston was murdered and government taken from the king. The Scots invaded under Robert Bruce, now King Robert, and defeated the barons' army at Bannockburn. With this national humiliation supporters returned to Edward. King and Parliament joined against the barons and defeated them at Boroughbridge. But Edward didn't live long to enjoy his new freedom and the support of his people. He had found a new favourite to replace Gaveston, the young

Hugh le Despenser. This relationship alienated his French queen, Isabella, who conspired to dethrone him in 1326 in favour of their son. The king fled to the west but was captured in Neath. Edward was imprisoned in Berkeley Castle and brutally murdered by his gaolers.

His son, a boy of fifteen, succeeded him as Edward III and not surprisingly for the first four years of his reign was in his mother's power. At twenty, however, he retired his mother to 'honourable confinement'. Through her he had a claim to the throne of France, which he was determined to pursue. Edward made a settlement with the Scots to prevent them invading as soon as his back was turned, and embarked on what was to be known as the Hundred Years War in 1337. The new king would complete the process of reinventing the myth of England and the English begun by his grandfather, Edward I, in the wars with France. This time when 'Our king went forth to Normandy', it was England that would 'shout and cry "Deo gratias"'. Edward was no longer a Norman baron trying to regain long lost possessions, though the claim, through his mother, to the throne of France on which this new invasion was based was equally specious. This time he sallied out as an English king invading another sovereign state with the unrealistic intention for the time of annexing it to its island neighbour.

The Englishmen who followed the king were as keen on the war as he was. A rich country like France with towns, religious houses and castles to plunder was much more enticing than fighting over the barren mountains of Wales and Scotland. Then there were the wealthy prisoners to be taken for ransom, and the licence to loot and rape expected to be given to foreign troops. At first the army had been made up of volunteers and conscripts picked from among the freemen of every shire, but gradually, as the war went on and on, they were superseded by companies of professional soldiers, in the pay of knights or nobles who hired them out to the king at cheap rates, on the understanding that they would supplement their pay by plunder as their noble captains did. With such good deals Parliament was happy to go on voting taxes for the king to carry on the war.

The process of reinventing the myth had been helped by our isolation from the Continent, in spite of the fact that the Welsh and the Scots still counted a large part of the island as theirs. Already that part of the myth identifying England with the whole island was under way.

Armed with the longbow, the English were at first very successful, winning the battles of Crécy, Poitiers and eventually, under Henry V, Agincourt. It was Edward I who had first recognized the power the Welsh archers could get from the longbow on his campaigns in Wales, and had made it the symbolic English artillery weapon, both for an English rebel like Robin Hood and for the 'bowmen of England' whose arrows bored through the French knights at the battle of Crécy. Along with the spitfire, the longbow has become the mythical weapon of England. Men were required by royal decree to practise constantly at the butts behind the village churchyard. Handball, even football, hockey, cockfighting and coursing were prohibited in case they interfered with these serious martial arts. This proficiency meant that the king could leave behind a trained militia while he was away in France.

Between Crécy and the Black Prince's victory at Poitiers, Europe, and particularly England, was swept by a plague in 1348, the Black Death, in which nearly half the population died. The immediate result was a shortage of peasant labour, both to farm their own lands to pay the rent and to till the lord's fields. Those with some degree of choice, freemen and better-off villeins, both raised the price of their labour and refused to work on the lord's domain lands, part of their obligatory rent as tenants. The response of king and Parliament, under pressure from the ruling classes, was to fix wages and prices by a Statute of Labourers but increasingly the lords of the manor found it hard to enforce since there simply weren't enough labourers left alive to do the work.

In theory and usually in practice, those who were unfree were still tied to the land. The manor courts imposed a series of local taxes for everything from marriage to the transfer of fields or animals between tenants, for using the mill to grind corn, as well as rents in cash and kind, all of which, in addition to the plunder of foreign wars, provided the lord's income. Tenants weren't free to leave, though some did run away to the anonymity of the growing towns.

The French war accelerated the end of French as a spoken language for the law courts and the nobility. At the same time Latin came under attack as the sole language of religion. John Wycliffe, the Oxford scholar and teacher, began to teach that the Bible should be translated into English for everyone to read, as indeed it had been in part in King Alfred's time. Socio-religious theory underpinned the status quo. Sermons preached that society was divinely divided into three orders: those who fought and protected it: the knights; those who prayed: the clergy; and those who laboured. Foremost among the labourers was the symbolic figure of the ploughman, Piers or Peterkin, the hero of William Langland's poem.

The ploughman was both the salt of the earth who maintained the rest of society with his labour, and a ritual figure of great sexual power whose ploughshare fertilized mother earth. The ceremonies of plough Monday, when the first furrow was turned, involved explicit sexual imagery, sometimes even coupling in the fields. The jolly ploughboy keeps his eroticism until the collapse of agriculture in the last quarter of the nineteenth century, but his political symbolism passed with the later industrial revolution to such princes of the working class as train drivers and miners.

Piers represents an alternative form of the English myth first embodied in the Peasants' Revolt of 1381. His natural partner is the outlaw, Robin Hood, whose exploits were already circulating in verse when Langland referred to them in *Piers Plowman*, which was being written and rewritten throughout this period of unrest.

Piers becomes a symbol for the rebels whose demand wasn't just for the repeal of the laws fixing wages but for freedom itself; no less than the abolition of villeinage and serfdom. The demand was encapsulated in the couplet, rewritten by John Ball, the itinerant priest who preached this new concept, from a poem by the mystic Richard Rolle of Hampole:

> *When Adam delved and Eve span*
> *Who was then the gentleman?*

When God made our first parents, the argument goes, there were no class divisions, no gentle and common, no bond and free, only the free and equal labourers in the garden. The class system, including the subjugation of women (though this would take much longer to be realized) is therefore the invention of fallen, sinful mankind, not God or nature. This revolutionary concept would be opposed by the Church with:

> *The rich man in his castle,*
> *The poor man at his gate,*
> *God made them high and lowly*
> *And ordered their estate.*

Put into John Ball's simple form the couplet lies behind all English socialist thinking until the advent of New Labour. Its pragmatism is the embodiment of the peculiarly English version of conservative socialism. Only now that it's become so hard for us to identify the heirs of *Piers Plowman*, have the words lost much of their resonance. This loss constitutes a real problem for British socialism since the aspiration of New Labour's modernizers is to be freed of the old associations which seemed to have died as a useful political image with the defeat of the miners' strike of 1986. The concept of 'honest toil' and 'the dignity of labour', which in part of the English myth goes back at least to the fourteenth century and *Piers Plowman*, has always been associated with earning one's bread by the sweat of one's brow, but with the rundown of manufacturing industry this becomes increasingly hard to sustain. We are all middle class now, except, of course, the upper class, the managerial and financial executives, and the underclass whose aspirations are bounded by sink estates and schools, with the rather less romantic drug barons as the modern version of the outlaw and highwayman.

The strand of myth woven from Robin Hood who robbed the rich to give to the poor, and defied official authority in the person of the Sheriff of Nottingham, intertwined with Piers himself, underlay the events which erupted in 1381, first in East Anglia, after an attempt to collect a poll tax to support the French war, then going badly for the English after the earlier successes. John Ball, the theoretician of the rebellion, which included the abolition of serfdom among its chief demands, was himself from Essex where the rebellion began. There's some evidence that the physical leader, Wat Tyler, was also from East Anglia. The rebels marched to London where John Ball preached a rousing sermon at Blackheath on our common Biblical ancestors, Adam and Eve. The boy king, Richard II, was encouraged by his advisers to ride out to Mile End where he promised the rebels pardon and emancipation. At a second meeting the next day at Smithfield, after most of the Essex men, relying on the king's word, had gone home with the promise of charters of manumission, their release from servitude, Tyler again presented the rebels' demands to the king, which included, as well as freedom, 'all men to be of one condition', the redistribution of monastic wealth and the abolition of the use of outlawry as a punishment.

Richard agreed to everything and Tyler called for beer, either to quench his thirst or to celebrate the rebel victory. Hearing a king's man accuse him of being the 'greatest thief and robber in Kent', he ordered one of his followers to kill the speaker, said by some chroniclers to be the keeper of Rochester Castle, Sir John

Newtontone, who repeated his accusation that Tyler was a thief. Exasperated, Tyler drew his own dagger, a treasonable act in the presence of the king, at which the Mayor of London, Walworth, struck him with his sword, wounding him. This assault was followed up by Ralph Standish, another of the king's men, who attacked him again. Tyler tried to flee but fell from his horse half dead. His followers carried him into St Bartholomew's Hospital where Walworth eventually found him and had him brought out and beheaded.

John Ball too was hunted down and hanged, drawn and quartered. Others who had taken part were savagely punished and the promises given by the king were all revoked. Nevertheless the process of emancipation continued, partly because labour remained in great demand, partly because the rebels had taken care to burn the manor court records that could alone prove the 'unfree' status, which had governed every aspect of their lives, from the right to leave the estate they were bound to, to the right to marry or sell a cow without both the lord's consent and payment of a fee.

All the contemporary chroniclers of the uprising were hostile, which was only to be expected of king's men and clergy. The rebels' demands for the redistribution of monastic wealth reflect the increased worldliness and riches of the monks, expressed also at the same period in *Piers Plowman* and Chaucer's *Prologue* to the *Canterbury Tales*, as well as in many other ballads and narratives. It's a monk who betrays Robin Hood in the earliest poem we have of him, *The Geste of Robin Hood*, and a nun-princess who tries to bleed him to death. The religious were often barons in their own right, and among the most repressive and backward-looking landlords, with their ability to appeal to the teaching of the Church in support of the status quo.

The hostile portrait from the chroniclers is still part of our ambiguous reaction to this strand of our English myth of freedom, manifest in the reporting of the eighties poll tax riot, and of direct action in general, which has included everything from the Civil

War through Chartism, the suffragettes, animal rights protests and Swampy, the environmental tunneller. John Ball and his fellows sleep like Arthur and Sir Francis Drake in the national subconscious, to be invoked whenever the situation seems to demand it.

Journalists or perhaps their editors appear to be shocked by such goings-on, and contemptuous of the often scruffy appearance of anti-bypass protesters, and the women of the Greenham Common peace camp in their makeshift shelters or 'benders'. They of course, like the suffragettes, attracted male hostility, which is also not a new phenomenon. One of the accusations against the followers of John Wycliffe in his proto-Protestantism, the heavily persecuted Lollards, was that they encouraged women to become scholars and to discuss theology. The same hostility from a male hierarchy has characterized the attempt to deny women priesthood and power in the Christian Church, a power which, to some extent at least, they had been able to exercise as heads of monasteries, like Hilda of Whitby, before the conquest.

Where had these ideas of the free Englishman, equality and the redistribution of wealth come from in the late fourteenth century? They appear to be home grown. The French peasants who had attempted a similar rising, the Jacquerie of over twenty years before, were in a far tighter feudal society and their demands were more pragmatic, in the face of famine and with English soldiers plundering the countryside. Yet they were ruthlessly suppressed and their demands weren't met until the French Revolution.

The English leaders of the Peasants' Revolt, like John Ball, were educated but poor, secular clergy or lesser gentry like Robin Hood's good knight, Sir Richard of the Lee, or Chaucer's and William Langland's. The knightly class was seen as having a clear function in society: to be the protector of poor as well as rich from robbers and armed gangs, and the land itself from foreign invaders. The poor knight embodied what we might now call traditional values of simplicity and integrity. His successor would eventually be the country squire. The idea of freedom embedded in Magna Carta must have seeped down through country pulpits, although Ball, like John Wesley later, often preached in church-yards and at market crosses. Ball's career lasted over twenty years, during which he was excommunicated and imprisoned. Wycliffe himself, who was attached to Oxford until expelled for denying the doctrine of transubstantiation, undoubtedly passed his views on to other members of the university as well as his Lollard fol-lowers. His insistence on English, the mother tongue, itself embodied ideas of equality as distinct from the closed hierarchical world of the Latin Vulgate. The bishops seized and burnt the English Bibles produced by his followers. It would be another one hundred and fifty years until the advent of Luther, before a full English Bible was printed – abroad.

Ball's central doctrine – 'We are come from one father and one mother, Adam and Eve' – with its implied demand for equality, is essentially political, even though the rebels' specific grievances against the game laws, rent in kind and labour services, as well as criminalization by outlawry, are social and economic. It was this political message that the authorities feared, realizing that it under-pinned the demands for economic change. It demanded no less than the restructuring of society and is akin to the movements for the abolition of slavery, reform of the franchise and votes for women. 'How can the gentry show that they are greater lords than we? Yet they make us labour for their pleasure.'

This deep taproot in the English, and particularly the Old Labour working-class unconscious, poses a problem for New Labour, which now tries to avoid the emotional tone traditionally vested in this heroic myth of protest inimical to equally traditional middle-class values of reticence and conformity. The loss of this symbolic, passionate dimension makes New Labour appear bland, uncaring and shifty. Labour's modernizers can point with justification, and some exasperation, to all that has been, or is being, brought about from the received Labour Party agenda: reform of the House of Lords, devolution for Scotland and Wales, extra funding for health and education, a minimum wage, higher employment. Without the sense of community and crusade these reforms appear to have no substance because their appeal is to reason not to myth. The achievements confer no sense of identity. The very real danger is that this emotional vacuum will be filled by another powerful strand of the myth, reinforced at the same time as the Peasants' Revolt by the French war, the English nationalism of 'God for Harry, England and St George', and reinvented by Shakespeare in Tudor times when the new threat was from Spain.

It was Edward III who incorporated St George into the English myth, and his red cross on a white ground is England's flag, although according to a recent poll few people, apart from English football supporters, recognize it, and her contribution to the Union Jack. Hagiographers are divided about whether George was a Cappadocian or a Roman soldier. His reputation as dragon slayer and rescuer of maidens from a fate worse than death made him a suitable emblem of that chivalry Edward III called upon to dress up his militarism with the institution of the Knights of the Garter. According to popular legend, the Countess of Salisbury dropped her garter during a court ball. Shock and horror greeted this faux pas but the king, sensing an opportunity that could be turned to his own ends, picked it up with the immortal words: *Honi soit qui mal y pense*. This became the motto of the newly instituted Order of the Garter, which still meets appropriately in St George's Chapel at Windsor Castle. With all the deftness of a modern spin doctor, the king had invented a symbol for his nation state, in opposition to other nation states, a flag to rally behind, but he had also brought the barons under royal control with his ability to confer what would become the most coveted honour in the land. The deliberate echo of King Arthur's Knights of the Round Table of popular romance would nowadays be an ad-man's dream.

Traditionally this strand of historical nationalism in the myth belongs to the Tory Party, which is in process of raising it against a 'Cool Britannia' that offers no heroes and little warmth. The working class finds itself without a distinct culture or image, fragmented into competing family units. The result is at best political apathy, at worst the tribalism of 'stuff the foreigner', and in particular our fellow Europeans with whom we now compete on the football field and for the best players. But our own identity is at risk, if we could only see it, not from the French, Germans, Italians and so on who are sure who they are, but from within, in the collapse of our old class structure, and without, from corporate globalization and the dominance of an American, English-speaking, empire.

Edward III reigned for fifty years. He and his sons, the Black Prince and John of Gaunt, carried on the war against France, laying waste and plundering. A French war correspondent of the time, Froissart, wrote that the English would never love or honour their king, 'unless he was victorious and a lover of arms and war against their neighbours and especially against such as are greater and richer than themselves. Their land was more filled with riches and all manner of goods when they were at war. They took great delight and solace in battles and slaughter and were covetous and envious of other men's wealth.' Yet he was forced to admire their military prowess.

Gradually the French fought back, replacing their chain mail, which was so vulnerable to the English archers, with plate armour. In the last years of Edward III's reign the French found a brilliant tactician, du Guesclin, who introduced guerrilla tactics, avoiding pitched battles, pouncing on isolated units and destroying the enemy's castle walls with his new use of cannon. By the time Edward died the French had won back most of their lands.

Edward was succeeded by his grandson, the boy king Richard II, who had to confront the revolting peasants just four years into his reign. Once again, bad governance made good drama for Elizabethan playwrights and Shakespeare's poetic account of his downfall is what is most remembered about him. In 1399 he was deposed by a packed Parliament and replaced as king by his cousin Henry Bolingbroke, a further example of the power of the English people over their monarchs, as Queen Elizabeth I fully understood when she banned Shakespeare's play from being performed during the Essex rebellion. For the first time since the Norman conquest over three hundred years before, a would-be English king laid claim to 'this reyme of Ingland and the Corone' in an English that although now heavily laced with French was nevertheless understandable by all his subjects. He reigned for only fourteen years, always at the mercy of the barons who now controlled the king through the Parliament that could depose him.

He was succeeded by his son Henry V. Because of Shakespeare and Laurence Olivier, Henry V has come down in history as a sympathetic soldier king who licked the French at Agincourt with the help of sturdy English yeomen and married a French princess. In reality he prolonged the agony of two countries by renewing the English claim to France. In 1415, with a lesson learnt from the French, he battered down the walls of Harfleur with guns able to hurl two hundred-pound missiles at a throw. When Henry V died, after his better-known success at Agincourt and only two years after being acknowledged heir to the French throne by the Treaty of Troyes, his son, Henry VI, a minor and mad, was technically king of both countries. This gave the French their opportunity to try to regain their land.

Under the inspiration and leadership of Joan of Arc, whose story needs no retelling and whose treatment certainly adds nothing honourable to the myth of England, the French began the task of getting rid of the English, completed in 1453 with a final battle in Gascony, leaving only Calais to be engraved on our hearts. Joan, of course, was rewarded by betrayal, tried for witchcraft and burnt at the stake. At home the Hundred Years War had encouraged anarchy, litigation and lawlessness as the lords built up their private armies to go in search of plunder in France. When France was lost the mercenary bands came back to fight the Wars of the Roses.

At the same time the aristocracy brought back cultural loot that produced the exquisite artistic flowering of the late Middle Ages: the delicate tracery of English perpendicular architecture, the lyrics of Lydgate, Dunbar and Henryson, the music of John Dunstable, mathematician and astronomer as well as composer, said by his continental successors to have invented polyphony. The two writers who best embody the ambiguities of the period are Sir Thomas Malory and Charles of Orleans. Malory wrote his great retelling of Arthurian romance, *Le Morte Darthur*, in prison, probably for crimes of violence, rape and theft that epitomize the lawlessness of the times, while his book deals in chivalry, passion and religious quest. Charles of Orleans was taken prisoner at Agincourt, aged only twenty-one, and held captive in England for twenty-five years, after which he returned to his castle in France to be briefly the patron of the brilliant vagabond poet François Villon. Charles eked out his captivity by writing love lyrics in both English and French, that carry on the courtly tradition of the troubadours and trouvères.

The Wars of the Roses now means an annual cricket contest between two neighbouring and rival counties, Yorkshire and Lancashire, inheritors of the white rose and the red. On and off, as one side or the other gained the upper hand, this civil war ravaged the country for thirty years, beginning at St Albans with the capture of the mad King Henry VI by his cousin the Duke of York. Henry represented the red rose of Lancaster through his descent from John of Gaunt, duke of that country; the Yorkists were represented by the white rose. There's something, of course, very romantic about a battle of roses and very English, too. The reality was very different.

The Lancastrians fought back, capturing and then murdering the Duke of York at Wakefield, only to be beaten in 1461 at Towton, after the Earl of Warwick, known to history as the kingmaker, had brought about the coronation of the new Duke of York as Edward IV. A House of Commons packed with Yorkist supporters thanked Edward for getting rid of the Lancastrian usurpers and the deranged Henry VI was thrown into the Tower of London.

Many of the nobles on both sides had perished in the conflict, murdered, executed or killed in battle, for neither side showed any of the chivalry they loved to read about when they were in the ascendant. Parliament too had been weakened and the new king, Edward IV, enriched by all the estates which had devolved to the crown on the deaths of their owners, had no need to call on it for revenue from taxes. He enjoyed himself, spending freely and marrying an attractive widow. None of this suited Warwick, who now changed sides to Lancaster, Queen Margaret and her son Prince Edward, and the sad king still in the Tower.

Warwick was killed in battle at Barnet and Queen Margaret's army was beaten a month later at Tewkesbury. Her son, Prince Edward, was captured and killed, and his sad, mad father finally put to death. The only Lancastrian claimant to the throne left was a son of the great-grandaughter of John of Gaunt, Margaret Beaufort who had married a Welsh Knight, Edward Tudor. Wisely he had fled to France.

Edward IV had two younger brothers, Clarence and Gloucester, who were at each other's throats in pursuit of Warwick's estates and the crown itself. Clarence was accused of treason, sent to the Tower and murdered. According to one tradition he was drowned in a barrel of sweet malmsey. When Edward died soon after, his son, also Edward, succeeded him. A boy of twelve, he was declared illegitimate by his uncle Gloucester, who was himself crowned king as Richard III. The boy king and his younger brother disappeared into the Tower, and into history and legend. Shakespeare, who was anxious to justify the legitimacy of the Tudor monarchy, accepted the story that the two young princes were murdered by order of their wicked uncle Richard, known as Crookback, but

the truth is still unknown and there are those who believe passion-
ately that Richard III was a deeply maligned monarch, such a hold
do the myths of England and her history have on the English
imagination.

Meanwhile Henry Tudor had been growing up and biding his
time. Edward IV had been very popular with the London citizens
and their wives, the first burgher king, but Richard was another
matter. It was widely believed that he had brought about the deaths
of the young princes, if not done the deed himself. Reports must
have reached Henry that now, while the country was disaffected
and before the new king could get a grip on the throne, would
be a good moment to make his bid.

With a small band of French mercenaries and English dissidents
he landed on the south-west coast of Wales at Milford Haven in
1485. His countrymen flocked to him, for the Tudors, the Welsh
form of Theodore, claimed descent from the British princes and
Henry's banner was the red dragon of Wales. Much of the fighting
in the Wars of the Roses had involved the lords of Welsh marches,
still relatively unsubdued, often in cahoots with the northern lords
of even more lawless regions, like the Percies of Northumberland.

Myth must have villains as well as heroes to be worthy opponents
that enhance the glory of the hero, and Richard Crookback has
been cast as one of the blackest. Even so Shakespeare, the Tudor
apologist, has to show his courage at the battle of Bosworth to
make him a worthy opponent for Henry Tudor, with the famous
but curiously ambiguous cry: 'A horse, a horse, my kingdom for
a horse.' Does he mean that he would give his kingdom for a
horse or that his kingdom is lost for lack of a horse? Henry Tudor,
Earl of Richmond, kills him and is crowned king but he fails to
pass into the myth as an attractive figure, perhaps because of his
very Welshness. Cautious and parsimonious, he shuffles through
history in a long gown and flat cap that appear moth-eaten. The
psychologist could put up an easy and convincing defence of Henry

VII, based on a childhood spent in exile with the constant threat of the assassin's dagger.

Wisely he married a Yorkist princess, combining the white and the red in the Tudor rose, and, in spite of two false claimants to the throne, Lambert Simnel and Perkin Warbeck, whom he treated with surprising leniency for the time, his reign was a consolidation of the peace he had won at Bosworth, that lasted twenty-four years. His great sadness was the death of his eldest son, the handsome and accomplished Prince Arthur, in whose shadow his brother Henry would receive the crown in 1509, having been already dynastically married off to his brother's widow, Catherine of Aragon, in a bid to appease the great power of Spain.

Though Henry VII is such a dim figure he does fit in with an aspect of our myth that we have found serviceable and even comforting from time to time. This is the pipe and slippers image we can have of ourselves. In the words of Paddy Roberts:

> *Oh the Englishman is noted for his sang-froid . . .*
> *And he loves his pipe and slippers*
> *And the missus and the nippers*
> *And he's happy simply growing old . . .*

Smug, making do, careful with money, sedate, not flashy and volatile like our Latin neighbours, it's a useful image for times of consolidation and retrenchment.

The reign of Henry VII in the wake of the Wars of the Roses, when the country was left in an impoverished condition, is similar in tone to that of the Depression between the two world wars of the twentieth century; the other period when this aspect of the myth flourished in a damp way, redolent of galoshes, while we huddled over the wireless with our cups of cocoa.

6

Blame It on the Bard

FROM HIS FATHER, the new king Henry VIII inherited with the crown a full treasury and an England at peace that he was able, through his own Welshness, to unite with Wales in the first act of union, taming the wild men of the marches. His father's version of our myth held no attraction for an ambitious young man, thirsting to be a gilded Renaissance prince, with a glittering court and a nation state to equal any in Europe. But while his father had been reuniting a fractured England, France and Spain had built themselves into superpowers, controlling the seas, the new territories and trade routes, and Holland and Portugal were only just behind them in the exploitation of these rich sources of exotic goods and raw materials. We were marginalized on our offshore island.

Henry VIII's reign coincided with one of those multiple changes that with hindsight can be seen as the end of an era. The discovery of worlds new to Christian Europeans by Spanish and Portuguese sailors, the invention of the printing press, the rediscovery of pre-Christian classical culture, brought about the movements known to history as the Renaissance and the Reformation, and threw the long accepted view of the universe into question. Was there any place for little England at the high table of this brave new world?

William Caxton set up his printing press in Westminster in 1476 and had produced nearly a hundred books by the time he died in 1491. William Tyndale translated the New Testament into English, anticipating Luther's German version by a few years. John Colet preached against corruption in the Church, and Thomas More produced his vision of Utopia. The eighteen-year old king, handsome, lithe, athletic, a poet and musician, welcomed the new learning and arts, importing painters from Germany, Jewish musicians from Italy and the great scholar Erasmus from Holland to grace his Renaissance court. England might not be able to compete with the superpowers of France and Spain in military might, even though Henry invaded France and gained a victory of sorts at the Battle of Spurs, but in developing a culture, funded by the cloth traders and his father's frugality, she might hold her own.

After his uninspiring French expedition, which must have taught him in the face of French cannon that the age of chivalry had died with his brother Arthur, Henry set about building a navy to rival those of the Continent, acknowledging that we were an island and must defend and supply ourselves by sea. Ships were redesigned to be longer and more stable, capable of regularly crossing the Atlantic, and to be efficient gun platforms with cannon firing through their new gunports, such as the *Great Harry* and the *Mary Tudor*. Without his naval innovations England might well have become in his daughter Elizabeth's time, like the Low Countries, a province of Spain. Yet Henry isn't remembered for these or his other achievements. Instead, by a manifestation of that very English, prurient interest in the sex lives of our royals, it's Henry's marriages that have passed into the myth. While pretending, as 'the cold English', not to be interested in sex (a part of the myth largely eroded since the swinging sixties), we have always been fascinated by gossip and scandal, especially about our upper classes. We are at the same time enthralled and disgusted.

Divorced, beheaded, died. Divorced, beheaded, survived.

As the son of a king whose claim to the throne rested on a shaky line of descent and victory in battle, Henry was obsessed with establishing a dynasty that couldn't be questioned. When his marriage to his brother's widow resulted in only a surviving daughter by the time his wife was forty-two and he was thirty-seven, he was ripe to replace her with Nan Bullen, her lady-in-waiting, young, attractive and vivacious, who could reasonably be expected to provide a male heir. At first Henry took the usual route to royal divorce: he asked for an annulment, on the grounds that he should never have married his sister-in-law, a relationship within the bounds of consanguinity and therefore forbidden. Unfortunately for Henry the pope, Clement VII, was, after the recent sack of Rome, in the power of the Emperor Charles V who was Catherine's nephew and protector and also King of Spain.

The man charged with negotiating the divorce was Thomas Wolsey, Cardinal, Chancellor and Archbishop of York, an ambitious and wealthy priest who had enlarged his London home, built himself a palace on the Thames at Hampton Court and endowed at Oxford his Cardinal College, now Christ Church. His failure to move the pope brought him down, and he only escaped execution by a timely death. Henry took over the London house since his palace at Westminster had just burnt down, re-naming it Whitehall, and requisitioned the magnificent palace of Hampton Court. He made Thomas Cromwell, Wolsey's secretary, his chief minister.

There were already those questioning why an English king should have to ask the bishop of Rome for a divorce. Weren't there bishops enough in England of sufficient authority to do this simple job? Among them was Cranmer, Archbishop of Canterbury, who had preached that the English Church could go it alone in such a matter. There was also Parliament, which could make kings and could therefore unmake queens. Henry called a Parliament that was to sit for seven years and sever England from Rome.

The Act of Supremacy by which it did this in 1534 made the king head of the Church of England with power to order all things within the Church and to abolish the monasteries. It says a lot for how strong nationalism had grown, and how far the new thinking of the humanists had penetrated, with its support for the Bible in English, primacy of the individual conscience and disgust with clerical luxury, that there was only one Catholic uprising, known as the Pilgrimage of Grace, in Yorkshire. England became protestant with a small 'p', without either a civil war such as the rise of the Huguenots had precipitated in France, or the bloodbaths of Germany and Holland.

Anticlericalism had been a popular source of satire and outrage in England for centuries, manifest in the work of Chaucer and Langland, and in the Robin Hood and other ballads. When Henry suppressed the monasteries, either taking their wealth into his own hands or rewarding his supporters among the nobility and gentry with the sale of monastic lands, there was little protest. The duty of providing for the sick and the poor now fell on the lay parish rather than the monastery. Ironically, two of the most prestigious martyrs to the change were Fisher, Bishop of Rochester, and Sir Thomas More, both of whom had encouraged the new learning that had helped to bring about the reformation of the Church with the Acts of Succession and of Supremacy, which they were unable to accept and for which they lost their heads.

Queen Nan Bullen, as Anne Boleyn was debunkingly called, soon followed them after the birth of a mere daughter, succeeded by that of a dead son and allegations that she had been unfaithful with a galaxy of lovers, including her own brother, and the poet Sir Thomas Wyatt, who confessed to the king and saved his neck. Henry, who had pursued her for seven years before his divorce, had fallen out of love soon after marriage. Almost certainly she was set up by Thomas Cromwell, who knew that the King was now in love with Jane Seymour and had convinced himself that

Anne wouldn't provide a male heir. Besides, if she was unfaithful any male child might not be his son and the country could be plunged into civil war again. Technically if Anne had been unfaithful she had committed treason by running the risk of putting a bastard on the throne and disinheriting the real heir. The myth, which must have its heroes and villains to act itself out on the stage of our collective and individual imaginations, has tended to approve of Anne and see her as a victim while being titillated by her supposed sexual exploits.

The new young queen was a scholar and a Protestant, and the reformation towards a pure form of protestantism continued even after her death giving birth to a living, though only just, boy child, a year after marriage. Her painful and protracted labour became the subject of a ballad, an indication of Henry's continuing popularity in spite of his religious changes.

King Henry went mourning, and so did his men,
And so did the dear baby, for Queen Jane did die then.
And how deep was the mourning, how black were the bands,
How yellow, yellow were the flamboys they carried in their hands.
There was fiddling and dancing on the day the babe was born
But poor Queen Jane belov'd lay cold as a stone.

The Bible in English was to be displayed in every parish church and Parliament enacted the six articles of religion which reaffirmed transubstantiation. The health of the king's son, however, gave him cause for concern. He married again, sight unseen, a German princess, Anne of Cleves, so ugly the marriage was speedily annulled and the new bride allowed to be 'a sister' to the king. Next he tried a Catholic girl, Catherine Howard, niece to the powerful Duke of Norfolk who, if she had supplied the king with a male Catholic heir who outlived his sickly Protestant brother, might have helped reverse the trend towards Protestantism, but she lasted only just over a year before going the way of Nan Bullen and on the same grounds.

The following year he took on the widow Catherine Parr, a careful Protestant. Now Henry tried to broker a marriage between the young Prince Edward and the infant Mary, Queen of Scots, his own grandniece. When the Scots refused to be united with England, Henry tried to force them and found himself at war with the French who came to their support. The expense led him to complete the annexation of the monasteries and to debase the coinage, but his navy succeeded in defeating a French seaborne invasion. When he died, although the treasury was empty, he was admired by the English people for making them a nation state again that could stand up against the pope, France and ultimately Spain.

Under the young King Edward and his two protectors, the Dukes of Somerset and Northumberland, the Reformation gathered pace, flowering in Archbishop Cranmer's English prayer book and his friend Hugh Latimer's sermons, preached at Paul's Cross to the public and in the king's garden to the court. It gave the moral underpinning to the revised Church that now became part of the myth of England, Protestant, Anglican, C of E, the prop of the Establishment, of empire and the middle classes over the next four hundred years. The pace of that change during Edward's six-year reign nearly undid the whole Reformation.

The destruction of images including the stained glass in churches, the imposition of the prayer book, however beautiful its language, by the Act of Uniformity caused two rebellions in 1549 and the fall of Protector Somerset. The rapacity of his successor, Northumberland, alienated still more of the people. As the king, still not sixteen, lay dying, Northumberland persuaded him to set aside his sisters, Mary and Elizabeth, in favour of Lady Jane Grey, a great-granddaughter of Henry VII, whom he was careful to marry to one of his own sons. Lady Jane became 'the nine-days queen', before Mary was swept to power by popular demand, even in Protestant London. The English, naturally conservative, had had enough of reform and in any case had a strong sense of what was 'fair play', an enduring element in our myth. Mary was old Harry's daughter and in the popular view the rightful heir.

Had Mary been content to build on her initial popularity and slowly reverse the more extreme changes of Edward's reign, she would almost certainly have succeeded in returning the country to Catholicism. Unfortunately for her wishes, she and her politics ran up against the national myth. Half Spanish herself, she didn't realize that the strongest element in the English psyche wasn't religion but identity, separateness. Her mistake was to marry Philip II of Spain, and try to make England subject to Spain and the pope again. When she met with resistance she revived the statute for burning heretics and lit her own funeral pyre.

She began with a clutch of bishops who refused to revert: Hooper, Ridley and Latimer, and then, after an initial recantation on his part, Cranmer himself, bravely holding the offending hand that had signed the recantation in the fire so that it should be consumed first. In five years three hundred men and women of all ages were burnt, mostly at Smithfield in London. Foxe's *Book of Martyrs* detailed their sufferings and became a best-seller after Mary's death. Her final mistake was to drag England into the Spanish war with France, losing Calais, the conduit for the English wool trade, which she cried would be found engraved on her heart after her death.

When Mary died, having become the Bloody Mary of legend, those who had welcomed her so few years before lit bonfires in the streets in celebration of her Protestant sister. Elizabeth was twenty-five. Like her grandfather Henry VII she had been taught prudence by a childhood of terror and poverty. Like her father she was intelligent, educated and tough. Philip of Spain had supported her claim to the throne as Mary was dying since the alternative was Mary, Queen of Scots, who was married to the Dauphin of France, the son of his arch rival. Elizabeth held out the hope to Philip that she might marry him or someone of his choice when in reality she had seen only too clearly, both in her father and her sister, what disasters marriage could bring. When even the Commons and her Privy Council urged her, early in her reign, to take a husband to secure the succession, she answered, drawing off her ring, that she marvelled they had forgotten that she had already on her coronation joined herself in marriage to a husband, namely the kingdom of England. 'And do not upbraid me with miserable lack of children: for every one of you, and as many as are Englishmen, are as Children and Kinsmen to me.' This didn't, of course, stop her flirting outrageously with her own courtiers as well as with foreign ambassadors and princes.

It was up to Elizabeth to reinvent the myth of England as a distinct and sovereign state for her people and her age, that age that has come down to us as the legendary Elizabethan Age. To do this Elizabeth shamelessly, and ambisexually, used the rhetoric of England to suit her needs. She could be queen or king, mother or spouse while yet a virgin: a shape-shifting icon that was still always recognizable as 'her majesty'. She identified herself as 'mere English' on her accession, in contrast to her sister who had spoken to herself in Spanish, and therefore probably thought in it too, and who had been happy to see England an appendage of Spain, forbidden by her husband Philip to take any part in exploration of, or trade with, the Americas. In claiming England as her 'husband', Elizabeth puts herself in the position of wife, or even, like a nun, as the bride of Christ, a point underlined by the closing words of the epitaph that she wished engraved on her tomb: 'Here lieth Elizabeth, which reigned a Virgin, and died a Virgin.'

In the famous speech to the troops at Tilbury, on the eve of the defeat of the Armada, she claimed 'the heart and stomach of a King, and of a King of England too'. Henry V could have done no more and her words were received with thunderous cheers. The Spanish were the enemies 'of my God, of my Kingdom, and of my people'. The speech was printed and sold by booksellers but also by itinerant hawkers like Autolycus in *As You Like It*. A copy may well have come Shakespeare's way, to be echoed in *Henry V* a few years later.

Elizabeth's god was the Protestant god, her kingdom was England and Wales subsumed into it. Scotland was dangerously independent, though there had been a move in her father's time for a union and in 1559 John Knox, leader of the Scottish Protestant nobility known as the Congregation, renewed the proposal. The new kingdom was to be known as Great Britain. To accept, Elizabeth realized, would have meant instant war with France. It was, however, an understandable temptation when Mary, Queen of Scots, under the influence of her French father-in-law and uncles, had signed herself 'Queen of England' and quartered the English arms with those of Scotland and France. Instead of marriage Elizabeth chose independence. She was helped in her identification of herself with England and England with itself by her courtier poets and the playwrights.

Scholars still disagree about when Shakespeare arrived in London and the exact dates of his first plays. A list by Francis Meres in 1598 includes the early comedies – *Two Gentlemen of Verona*, *Comedy of Errors*, *The Taming of the Shrew*, *Love's Labours Lost* and the disputed *Love's Labours Won*, *The Merchant of Venice* and *A Midsummer Nights' Dream*, the histories of *Richard II*, *Richard III*, *Henry IV* and *King John*; and the tragedies of *Romeo and Juliet* and *Titus Andronicus*: thirteen plays with the two parts of *Henry IV* and excluding the mysterious *Love's Labour's Won*. There are three plays missing from Meres's list, the three parts of *Henry VI*, accepted as the earliest of the histories. This would make sixteen plays which at the rate of two or three plays a year, plus collaborations and his own career as a performer, would take his arrival back to the middle or late eighties.

The early comedies lean heavily on the theatricals of John Lyly whose works were written for boy actors to be performed at court or the Inns of Court. The earliest, *Campaspe*, was published in 1584. Lyly was best known for his prose romance, *Euphues, The Anatomie of Wit*, written in a high-flown style echoed in the *Two*

Gentlemen of Verona, which sounds as if it was intended for a similar audience and setting. With *Henry VI* Shakespeare makes a quantum leap both in his art and into unknown territory.

There had been a popular dramatic version of *Henry V* before the Spanish Armada arrived in 1588, but Shakespeare's *Henry VI* is the first serious attributable history play, or rather historical dramatic sequence, to survive. If the early comedies were written for quasi-private performance, *Henry VI* was intended for the public stage. The year before the Armada the expanded *Chronicles* by Raphael Holinshed, edited by John Hooker, were published and became the source for several dramatists. First published in 1577, as a new history and description of England, their reappearance at this date in an extended version itself reflects a growing nationalism under pressure from Catholic France and Spain. The queen took a lively interest in this first complete account of the history of England, ordering the excision of politically offensive passages. No doubt the Lord Chamberlain did the same on her behalf with *Henry VI*.

The three parts dealing with the life of the unhappy king, whose madness Shakespeare wisely glosses over, lead up to *Richard III*, which ends with Elizabeth's grandfather killing the tyrant, as he is depicted, and assuming the crown. It's fashionable to suppose that Shakespeare wrote simply to order of the company, with bums on seats foremost in his mind. This is to misunderstand the nature of the act of creation and to impose a cynical postmodern interpretation on a complex process.

Henry VI was certainly popular. Shakespeare implies as much at the end of *Henry V* where he refers to his own plays:

> *Henry the Sixth, in infant bands crown'd king*
> *Of France and England did this king succeed;*
> *Whose state so many had the managing*
> *That they lost France and made his England bleed;*
> *Which oft on stage hath shown . . .*

It hit the mood of the times when England's nationhood was menaced by France and Spain, and in the euphoria that followed the defeat of the Armada. The historical sequence was conceived as a whole, since each part, although it stands alone as an evening's or rather an afternoon's entertainment, leads us, with its unresolving resolution, to want the next.

This first sequence was to be followed by another which began with *Richard II*, included the two parts of *Henry IV*, and climaxed in *Henry V*. Though Falstaff was the great popular draw, all the plays were rightly understood as political commentaries, and by the queen herself, to whom the clown pays homage in the epilogue to *Henry IV*: '. . . and so kneel down before you; but, indeed, to pray for the queen,' he says before breaking into a jig.

Elizabeth so far identified with the sequence that the scene that portrays the deposition of the lawful king in *Richard II* was never printed in her lifetime. Foolishly, when Essex tried to lead a rebellion to dethrone Elizabeth, the conspirators persuaded the players to put on *Richard II* for an increased fee although the company in their subsequent defence alleged that they had tried to talk Essex's supporters out of the performance. The queen even asked the old antiquarian William Lambarde whether there were any portraits of Richard so that she could see whether she resembled him. The old man said there were none except those that everyone knew. 'This tragedy', she told him, 'was played forty times in open streets and houses. . . . I am Richard II, know ye not that.'

In his historical political plays Shakespeare ran the risk of being misinterpreted and giving offence, for the authorities were understandably very touchy. But it was the rhetoric and mood engendered by Elizabeth herself as the Protestant icon of England that first set him on this course. It can be no accident, given the freedoms he takes with the received history of his time, particularly by foreshortening events, that the villain of the first plays is a Catholic cardinal, Beaufort of Winchester, although Shakespeare himself, like his contemporary John Donne, poet, priest of the

Church of England and eventually dean of St Paul's, had almost certainly been brought up a Catholic. It inaugurates Shakespeare's own public identification with England, and his elaboration of the myth into its fullest and most lyrical expression before Kipling.

The Shakespeare of the histories is our English Shakespeare; the comedies and tragedies belong to the world even where, as with *King Lear* and *Cymbeline*, they deal with the myths of Britain. The best-known and most defining contribution to the English myth is John of Gaunt's speech from that *Richard II* Elizabeth so feared.

> This royal throne of Kings, this scepter'd isle
> This earth of majesty, this seat of Mars,
> This other Eden, demi-paradise,
> This fortress built by nature for herself
> Against infection and the hand of war,
> This happy breed of men, this little world,
> This precious stone set in the silver sea,
> Which serves it in the office of a wall,
> Or as a moat defensive to a house,
> Against the envy of less happier lands;
> This blessed plot, this earth, this realm, this England,
> This nurse, this teeming womb of royal kings,
> Fear'd by their breed and famous by their birth,
> Renowned for their deeds, as far from home,
> For Christian service and true chivalry,
> As is the sepulchre . . .
> This land of such dear souls, this dear, dear land
> Dear for her reputation through the world . . .

Set to music or as a verse-speaking examination piece, the speech is usually stopped short of Gaunt's main point that England has become 'like to a tenement or pelting farm . . . bound in with shame, / With inky blots and rotten parchment bonds: / That England that was wont to conquer others, / Hath made a shameful conquest of itself'. The images of the first part act on us like the singing of 'Rule Britannia' on the last night of the Proms. They serve as a drug feeding an addiction to nationalism, showing us how we want to see ourselves and our country. Yet they are false or at the best inaccurate. Britain is the island, not England, and even so it hadn't been proof 'against infection and the hand of war' as the Black Death, the frequent epidemics of Tudor times and the Roman, Saxon and Norman conquests had shown. Gaunt presumably refers back to Richard Coeur de Lion and Henry V as the kings 'renowned for Christian service and true chivalry', 'feared by their breed and famous by their birth'. Elizabeth had claimed the heart and stomach of a king 'and of a King of England too'. In Gaunt's speech England is a 'teeming womb'. The very visceral imagery of Shakespeare echoes Elizabeth and reinforces her claim to be almost, physically, the mother of her people. The whole speech sounds like a piece of conscious, post-Armada propaganda. It's ready-made to be reinvoked at need to galvanize us into action with its tear-jerking sentimentality of 'this dear, dear land', so at odds with another part of the myth, traditional English or British phlegm, that reinforces, for the foreigner, the image of coldness, of the 'stiff upper lip'. It's hard to tell where the author himself stands; whether with old Gaunt or with Richard's comment on the old man's rebuke later in the scene: 'A lunatic, lean-witted fool', reducing him to a babbling Polonius.

Shakespeare himself points out in *Cymbeline* that Britain is the 'isle', and he can be critical of the English in Falstaff's complaint that it's a 'trick of our English nation if they have a good thing to make it too common'. *King John* returns to patriotic rhetoric at the end with the death of a weak king and the accession of a nine-year-old prince who, in historical terms, had a long and largely unsatisfactory reign that gave Shakespeare nothing to work on. *King John* stands alone. It shows England invaded by the French, together with English rebels, defended by the bastard Faulconbridge, and rescued by the oily Cardinal Pandulph and the loss of the French supply boats. The final message is delivered by the bastard who remains true to King John as the rightful ruler whatever his faults. The moral was one that would appeal to the queen.

> *This England never did, nor never shall,*
> *Lie at the proud foot of a conqueror,*
> *But when it first did help to wound itself.*
> *Now these her princes are come home again,*
> *Come the three corners of the world in arms,*
> *And we shall shock them. Nought shall make us rue,*
> *If England to itself do rest but true.*

If this is anything other than the dramatist's final flourish with drums and trumpets, it's a warning to those who would encourage factionalism. Much as Shakespeare admired his patron Henry Wriothesley, Earl of Southampton, he would have been unlikely to support his friend Essex in his ambition and the rebellion of 1601. But the rhetoric is another echo of Armada and the Spanish war, an exhortation to pull together against the foreigner, repeating Gaunt's false claim that England is inviolable unless betrayed from within.

Shakespeare's patriotic rhetoric, whether he intended all of it to be unreflectingly nationalistic (as much of his audience would surely have taken it to be) or not, is lodged in the national unconscious and can be called on by a Churchill to 'stiffen the sinews, summon up the blood' at will or need. Even those who hadn't been educationally reared on Shakespeare, that ninety per cent of the population who left senior school at fourteen, could be moved by the rhythms, based on the bard's blank-verse line, into which English speech naturally falls. In the rhetoric of Churchill, 'Men shall say of them, "This was their finest hour,"' or 'Never in the field of human conflict was so much owed by so many to so few', it's the pull of the strong rhythm as well as the imagery that quickens the collective English heartbeat. His cadences echo those of *Henry V* which, as a film starring Laurence Olivier, became a self-congratulatory piece of propaganda of the end of the Second World War to an exhausted nation, which believed it had won the war and yet was about to lose both its empire and centre stage in world affairs. At its best, when the cause is right, the rhetoric can produce the superhuman efforts of the early war years of 1940–3, the island race standing alone against the world, protected by the sea and the weight of history.

The downside is arrogance bred of this isolationist image, arguably obsolete in an age of global communications, multinational conglomerates, space travel and the Channel tunnel. It works against our membership of Europe and the common currency. We would prefer to go it alone, even against all economic reason, while our old enemies combine to protect peace in Europe and build a counterweight to America's economic dominance. We secretly admire the simplification of motive and of our lives that are the appendages of war and, once we have settled down to it, we are rather good at it. It appeals to a liking for order and discipline, to our pragmatism that prefers to deal in practice rather than theory.

Our attitude to Shakespeare himself is similarly ambiguous. With our preference for the pragmatic and distrust of intellectuals, we would have preferred our national monument to be a soldier rather than an artist, even in the most pragmatic and democratic of the arts, literature. Shakespeare's plays demand an intellectual effort from us because of their language and complexity.

Our fear of being thought intellectually 'show off', and of Hamlet's disease of 'thinking too precisely on the event' – and look where that got him – makes us reluctant to commit ourselves to them. Better to mow the lawn than risk being thought pretentious. If it weren't for the homage of the rest of the world and the financial support that brings through the tourist industry, the plays would probably by now be unperformed. It took an American, Sam Wanamaker junior, to reinvent the Globe Theatre which, against all the scepticism expressed during its construction, has turned out a success. The sheer size of Shakespeare is unEnglish in its showiness, its universality, for a people which prides itself on reticence and lack of ostentation.

Yet we look back to the Elizabethan Age with nostalgia, as in a sense our finest hour, apart from that designated by Churchill, as a time when we defeated a major power, Spain, and our privateers like Sir Francis Drake held the world's shipping to ransom. The age seems itself to be a jewel set in the silver sea, when we weren't ashamed to indulge, as we are inclined to see it, in all the arts, in the music of Tallis, Byrd, Dowland and many more, in building and adorning the great houses, in the exquisite miniatures of Hilliard and Oliver, in jewellery and dandy clothes, even in developing commerce and industry, and in the exploration of new worlds both actual and scientific before the dead hand of gentility tried to strangle initiative. We look at it with admiration not unmixed with surprise, rather as we do at Henry VIII's great suit of armour in the Tower of London. Were we really such giants, full of confidence and a sense of ourselves?

Given the choice of time travel it's the period most of us would choose to revisit. We knew who we were, even though, then as now, we were an island state apart from the greater continental powers. We couldn't know that we were poised to overtake France and Spain in the power race with our industrial revolution. Hindsight gives us the dangerous sense that what we did once we can do again and the myth of 'this scepter'd isle' encourages us, in a completely changed world, still to go it alone.

7

Masquerade

THE AGE OF the Stuarts is like one of their own glittering masques played out through most of the seventeenth century and encapsulated in Dryden's epitaph on his age, spoken just before his death in 1700:

> *All, all of a piece throughout,*
> *Thy chase had a beast in view;*
> *Thy wars brought nothing about,*
> *Thy lovers were all untrue.*

Elizabeth, revered as herself, the mother of her people and old Harry's daughter, had left the myth of England and how we see ourselves in good shape. We could be proud of us as a nation and of our achievements. The danger from the superpowers, France and Spain, had receded as they succumbed to their own problems, leaving us space to carve out our own trading territories. The difficulty with Elizabeth's projection of herself as the myth's chief icon was that her death left a vacuum where her carefully constructed image had filled centre stage. As she approached her death she was persuaded by Robert Cecil, son of her lifelong adviser

Lord Burghley, to name as her successor James VI of Scotland, son of Mary, Queen of Scots and Henry Stewart, Lord Darnley, her second husband, murdered by her third, James Hepburn, Earl of Bothwell. Indeed, Mary's marital career might have been designed to show up the wisdom of Elizabeth's virginity, until it came to the question of the succession.

Mary and Elizabeth were cousins, the only remaining descendants of Henry VII. Unfortunately, James had imbibed from his mother, and her upbringing at the French court, the doctrine, as Alexander Pope would later describe it, of 'the right divine of Kings to govern wrong'. He was the first king to unite all four countries under the English crown, although Scotland and Ireland were still separate entities, with their own Parliaments and forms of religion. James disliked the extreme puritanism in which he had been raised and set about imposing conformity to the Church of England and its prayer book in his new realm, leaving the Scots to their own form of worship but increasing the number of bishops who might counterbalance the democratic Assemblies.

James's policy was directed towards peace. He ended the long-running war with Spain, even proposing the marriage of his son Charles to the Spanish infanta, against the will of Parliament and people who foresaw in it a repetition of the disastrous events of Mary Tudor's reign. Charles's actual marriage, to the equally Catholic Henrietta Maria of France, was also disapproved of for the same reasons but nevertheless went ahead. The fear of a return to Catholicism seemed confirmed by Guy Fawkes's gunpowder plot to blow up Parliament early in James's reign, a non-event which claimed a powerful place in the myth of embattled Protestant England with its annual ritual burnings akin to the Orange marches in Northern Ireland.

Shakespeare's career had ten more years to run after the accession of James in 1603. Fortunately for him, James and his queen, Anna of Denmark, were determined to cut a dash before other nations' ambassadors with the brilliance of their court, which meant frequent plays, masques, music and dancing. Anna took on Inigo Jones who, as well as designing her masques, built the sugar cube of the Queen's House at Greenwich for her. Shakespeare and his troupe at the Globe became the King's Servants by letters patent, with the right to act in public anywhere in the kingdom, as well as for the royal pleasure whenever required to do so.

The new reign and culture coincided with Shakespeare's artistic maturity and must have excited his imagination. Anna's homeland had itself undergone a modernizing renaissance under her father and brother. Shakespeare's fellow actors had visited the court of Denmark and acted at the town of Helsingør in 1585–6. They may have contributed to his reworking of an earlier version of *Hamlet*, which established him as the foremost dramatist and poet of his time in the last years of Elizabeth's life. It was followed by the anxious and weary *Troilus and Cressida*, echoing the cynical and uncertain mood as the great queen's candle guttered to its end.

> *The mortal moon hath her eclipse endured*
> *And the sad augurs mock their own presage;*
> *Incertainties now crown themselves assured,*
> *And peace proclaims olives of endless age.*

James brought peace and stability for the actors. He was rewarded with *Measure for Measure*, *Macbeth*, *King Lear* and *Cymbeline*. The days of the English nationalism of the Henry plays were over. Now it was the matter of Britain, out of respect for a Scottish king. It freed Shakespeare's imagination to rise increasingly to the universality and status he enjoys abroad. His Englishness now resides in the alleys of London and the enamelled countryside that provide the backdrop to the actions of British kings and Roman emperors.

By ending the war with Spain James had absolved himself from having to call another Parliament to ask it to vote him money.

He believed in any case that he should be able to raise taxes himself, not by the agreement of a parliament that resembled the church assemblies of Scotland, where lay and cleric sat together to debate affairs of religion. He failed to understand the elective element there had always been in the English monarchy, which isn't hereditary in the strictest sense but depends on the will of the people. He probably mistook the shouts of acclamation at his coronation as cries of joy, when they were actually the people giving their acceptance without which no English monarch can govern.

Parliament had grown in experience and power during the long wars of Elizabeth's reign, and it was largely the Queen's ability to manipulate Parliament that had kept her successful and popular for so long. By now knights of the shire and burgesses from the towns were dedicating themselves to being members of Parliament as a counter to the monarch, a development which would eventually evolve into the constitution as it exists today, where the monarch's function is symbolic.

We like the ambiguity of this duality. It gives us an emblematic head to carry out the ceremonial that's so much a metaphor for the tradition and stability that underpins the state. We can at once criticize the royals and begrudge them their money while needing them to embody England. Elizabeth was the last English monarch to have both symbolic and actual power. The Stuarts' attempts not only to prolong her role but to push it towards autocracy were bound to end in tears before bedtime.

Under Elizabeth, yeomen and freemen could vote in elections, and the expanding economy produced many more of them. As the population grew and with it the towns, so did the number of free craftsmen and service providers, as they would now be called. Because of the long war, Elizabeth herself had no money for foreign exploration. It was left to mariners and merchants to open up new markets when not plundering the merchant ships of other nations. James followed her practice of not funding national expeditions to set up new colonies but didn't stand in the way of private entrepreneurs, although his failure to maintain the Tudor navy gave English merchants little protection from Spanish, Portuguese, French and eventually Dutch attack.

As the towns grew, they needed more food to support them and the countryside flourished in response, with the heyday of the yeoman farmer in his manor house, able to think of sending a son to university on as little as twenty acres. It has become fashionable to say that enclosure of common lands, the absorption of small farms by the bigger landowners who could afford to transport surplus produce to London and bring back London muck to fertilize their enlarged fields, began the industrialization of the agribusiness and was therefore a good thing. But in terms of the English myth, for the greater part of the population in towns and villages, this was the period of the development of the individual. A trawl through manor records will show how many, men at least, could read and write, while electoral returns and subsidy rolls document the growing numbers of freeholders, and their levels of goods and property. This relative economic growth, with its increased emphasis on the individual as consumer and free agent, contributed as much as anything else to the climate which ended in civil war, the execution of Charles I and the Commonwealth.

The Stuart period also produced the beginning of empire. Although the English could get no entry to Spanish South America they began to set up colonies in the Caribbean and North America, while the East India Company gained its real first foothold in Asia when it defeated the Portuguese off the coast of north-west India and set up a trading post at Surat in Gujarat. The family that runs the corner shop may have a four-hundred-year-old history of trade with England. Driven out of the Spice Islands by the Dutch just before the death of James, the East India Company nevertheless extended their contacts in mainland India with trading stations in Bengal and the building of, typically, Fort St George at Madras. Raleigh who was executed in 1618 to appease the Spanish after an imprisonment in the Tower of thirteen years on a trumped-up charge of treason, had settled a plantation in Virginia in 1587, named for Elizabeth, which was refounded in 1607. It became the destination for a wave of economic migrants before the Puritans in the *Mayflower*, missing their way in 1620, set up a new colony in the north at Massachusetts. It was just in time to receive the thousands who would flee from the attempt, at the beginning of the reign of Charles I, to impose conformity to a more ritualistic version of Anglicanism. James I's own settlement of thousands of Scottish Protestants in the north of Ireland, to contain the Irish Catholics who might let the Spanish or French in by the back door, sowed the ground with dragon's teeth that are still springing up as armed men nearly four centuries later.

The antipathy to the Catholic Continent, and the study of the Bible in English, together with the writings of foreign Protestants and their persecution by Catholic monarchs, turned England from a half-hearted reformed Church into a noticably Protestant one, with a puritan wing, strong among the urban middle class. It set the Stuart monarchy, quasi-Catholic (especially the foreign wives, mothers of future kings, Queen Anna, Henrietta Maria and finally Catherine of Braganza), apart from the people and the Parliament whose power increased every time the king was forced to ask for money. James I, more pragmatic than his son Charles I and grandson James II, managed, like his other grandson Charles II, to find a kind of accommodation with his people and die in his bed.

Unfortunately his son Charles forgot the elective element in the English monarchy, and that in the end English kings rule by the will of the people and can be deposed. Puritanism rejected the show, as it was perceived, of the Stuart monarchs. Towards the end of Shakespeare's life the burgesses of Stratford renewed the ban on the acting of plays in corporation property on the grounds that they encouraged immorality, while happily taking the playwright's immoral earnings when he bought a share in the civic titles. Private conscience replaced public conformity. Shakespeare's daughter Susanna was summoned for not taking the Anglican sacrament of Easter 1606, under a new and detested law against those 'popishly affected' which would also catch Puritans in its net. We increasingly saw ourselves as a Protestant people, widening the distance between us and the mainly Catholic Continent. Bourgeois Protestantism became a major strand in our identity, and for a time myth and monarch began to drift apart.

James I's weakness for handsome men led to the rise of Charles Villiers, Duke of Buckingham, brilliant, volatile and ambitious, whose unsuccessful attempts at diplomacy and military expeditions involved England in a war with Spain and France. James's daughter Elizabeth, known as the Winter Queen, was married to a German prince who, as a leader of the Protestant cause, lost his kingdom in the Thirty Years War that had just begun. James tried to raise money to help him but failed, and Elizabeth with her two sons, Prince Rupert and Prince Maurice, was forced into exile. They would be in place to fight for the Stuart cause in the coming Civil War.

When James died in 1625 Buckingham's influence was just as strong on the new king, Charles. Attempts were made to help the French Huguenots, and other continental Protestants, but without an adequate army and navy they ended in disaster. Charles tried to raise taxes without Parliament, taking other aspects of the law into his own hands by imprisoning those who refused to pay, and bypassing the traditional system of common law administered by justices of the peace and judges with his own court of Star Chamber. Driven by lack of money to call a new Parliament in 1628, he was forced to accept the Petition of Right, which tried to curb the king's arbitrary behaviour by upholding the established English system of common law against the king's use of his own courts, a right that harked back to Magna Carta. Buckingham was assassinated by a disaffected Puritan. The grieving Charles imprisoned three members of Parliament who refused to support him.

Without money he had to withdraw from the war, and for

eleven years governed without Parliament by retrenching, selling baronetcies and reviving old taxes like Tonnage and Poundage and Ship Money, to try to restore the navy. Charles's last great mistake was to attempt to force religious conformity to the high church prayerbook of Archbishop Laud in more puritan Scotland. Scottish mercenaries returned from abroad to defend the Protestant covenant, and an army camped on the borders with England.

Buckingham's successor in the king's favour was Thomas Wentworth, elevated to be Earl of Strafford, who now came back from governing Ireland to help Charles in this emergency. He advised the summoning of a Parliament, first the Short which lasted only a few weeks and then the Long which would outlive the king. Laud and Strafford were impeached and Strafford executed for encouraging the king in his despotism. The rule of common law and the powers of Parliament were restored. Meanwhile the Irish Catholics had risen in revolt. Who was to control the forces needed to defeat them and the Scots? King or Parliament? Charles tried to resolve the matter by arresting the five most vociferous members of the House who only escaped by fleeing in a boat from Westminster to the safety of the city of London. Charles himself fled to the North. The Civil War had begun.

These events pose a problem for the myth, resolved by a typical piece of English ambiguity, or hypocrisy, depending on your viewpoint. The concept of English freedom and the growth of democracy demands that we support the puritan Roundheads but glamour envelops the Cavaliers. Rather like the Homeric account of the war between Greeks and Trojans, we have to be on both sides at once, or, at some periods, successively. My generation was reared on the schoolroom picture by W. F. Yeames, *When Did You Last See Your Father*, painted in 1878 at the height of empire and Victoria's popularity. It shows the son of a Cavalier family, in satin and ruffles, standing on a stool in front of the captain of the Roundheads, surrounded by stern troopers while his sisters huddle together at the side. The implication is that the blond curly-haired boy is being bullied into betraying the whereabouts of his father. In Captain Marryat's nineteenth-century literary version, *Children of the New Forest*, the Cavalier children escape to a romantic life in the woods, aided by the honest forester. This was followed rather later by the novels of Margaret Irwin, which focused on the equally romantic charms of their Royalist heroes, Charles II and his sister Minette; Rupert of the Rhine and Montrose, the Proud Servant, ensured that my generation was Royalist. The glamour of the Stuarts, the romantic mess of their lives, their sexual freedom and encouragement of music, art, poetry and theatre, set against a wartime and grey post-war upbringing, cast a spell that was finally acted out in the explosion of the sixties when even the flowing hairstyles were Cavalier in contrast to the short-back-and-sides Roundheads of the forties and fifties.

Marryat's novel had been published in 1847 and was still being read a hundred years later. Recently revived on television, none of its monarchical fervour was dimmed for the late twentieth century. Yeames's painting continued the Victorian preference for the myth, which glorified monarchy and the established order against the movements for reform. The new risk of civil war, seen still by the English Establishment in the lurid light of the French Revolution and recently given new life in France with the Third Republic, coincided with a period of Disraelian Conservative government when Victoria was declared Empress of India, persuaded to put aside her grief at the death of her husband, Albert, the Prince Consort, and restore the popularity of the monarchy.

Yeames's Roundheads, helmeted, in dusty, snuff-coloured clothes, the antithesis of charm and lightness, the epitome of brutal repression, are an easy symbol for the totalitarian state, bogeymen to frighten the politically naïve. Cromwell himself is still both admired and feared, as he was by his contemporaries like Samuel Pepys. His psychological error was to be driven to agreeing to the execution of Charles, making the king a martyr, and causing centuries of revulsion at an act seen as out of character with the

English exaltation of fair play and dislike of extremes; a revulsion that has continued to set back the republican and reformist cause for centuries whenever it seemed to be making progress. We had our revolution, the argument goes, before anyone else and look what happened. It was much better, and truer to our nature, to proceed with caution, even if in the process thousands were driven to the edge of poverty and despair by the lack of political, economic and social reform which led in the nineteenth century to the execution or transportation of thousands for minor crimes of theft.

Cromwell, 'our chief of men', was himself offered the crown. He had restored the credibility of England as a military and naval force. The Scots and Irish were defeated, as were the Dutch at sea. The colonies of Virginia and Barbados, who had withdrawn their allegiance, were retaken and Jamaica added from Spain. There was religious toleration for the different strands of Protestantism that had proliferated with the intense religio-political debates that consumed the country and were given more permanent form in thousands of pamphlets and broad sheets. Although theatres were closed, music and literature flourished and the first English opera, *The Siege of Rhodes*, with music principally by the Cavalier Henry Lawes, was produced with a woman on stage.

Education, especially for girls, spread through more levels of society than ever before as the urban, mercantile and professional class expanded. Women were drawn more into the management of businesses and, as widows, into ownership of property, and therefore to a voice in politics if not a vote. Though religious music, apart from psalms and hymns, was forbidden, the secular flourished with the Lawes brothers, Matthew Locke, John Jenkins and the elder Henry Purcell, among the composers and performers. At the wedding of Cromwell's daughters the dancing went on all night.

Cromwell's death left a vacuum, which warring factions threatened to fill with chaos. The country wanted no more of it but a return to the order of monarchy, suitably restrained, of course.

Charles II was restored, determined not to make his father's mistakes of absolutism or go on his travels again. Only those who had had a direct hand in Charles I's execution were themselves executed while those who had helped the young prince escape after the battle of Marston Moor, by dressing him in women's clothes and hiding him among the leaves of an English oak, were rewarded. Theatres reopened. Song, dance, poetry and sex beguiled the court. London and trade expanded but so did religious conflict. The terms Tory and Whig were invented, from the Irish for a plunderer and the Scottish for a horse thief respectively. The image of the Merry Monarch was added to the stockpile of myth along with a revived Britannia, his mistress, the Duchess of Portsmouth.

The forerunner of Bernard Shaw's Eliza Doolittle, Nell Gwyn, 'the Protestant whore' as Nell called out to the London mob when they threatened to overturn her carriage, embodied the new freedoms for women, though it's now politically correct to see her and her acting colleagues as simply sexually exploited. But Mistress Nelly's persona of 'pretty and witty' should in truth be seen as a feminist icon for its courage, independence, common sense and sheer talent. Few women stand out in history as she does. To reduce her to merely victim, as some feminist historians have tended to do, is to connive at the prurience that emphasizes her time as an orange-seller, before her theatrical abilities took playgoers like Pepys by storm, and before she was forced to give up her public career in favour of Charles II's royal bed.

Charles was half French through his mother, Henrietta Maria, who returned to England with her son and kept her own court and Catholic chapel at Somerset House. Having spent his years of exile partly at the French court, Charles treated England as his Versailles, a playground for his amusement where he could saunter in St James's Park feeding his beloved ducks, or plan what he hoped would be his real Versailles, far from the politically tumultuous city, at Winchester. He had to disguise until his deathbed the acknowledgement of his return to his mother's religion, already preceded by his brother James II. What neither of them could accept was that Protestantism was now deeply embedded in the English character, as we perceived ourselves, while we became the 'nation of shopkeepers', as we would be seen by others. A return to Catholicism would have meant abandoning our evolving English myth in a regression to autocracy and feudalism which, in the case of France, would only be dissolved by a bloody revolution. We believed we had already suffered a civil war and our own revolution and we weren't prepared to put the clock back.

The new Englishman was embodied in the diarist and chronicler of the early part of Charles II's reign, Samuel Pepys. Part of the lasting appeal of Pepys is that in his diaries he displays a portrait of an Englishman we can still recognize: his guilty and fumbling sexuality, combined with a genuine love for his wife that kept him single after her death, his financial and social opportunism, pragmatic attention to detail and genuine interest in naval administration, his consumerist delight in comfort and physical possessions, his lack of intellectual pretension, his ability to express shock-horror while being titillated by his sexual experiences; his genuine passion for England coupled with alarm at what he sees as its moral and economic backsliding and neglect of its own best interests. He is a prototype of the kind of Englishman celebrated in Pont cartoons or again, in Paddy Roberts's mocking, but in the end self-congratulatory, song, 'The Englishman with His Usual Bloody Cold'.

> He thinks the way the French behave is absolutely nuts.
> He'd like to try it really but he hasn't got the guts.
> He's scared to death the neighbours might be told.
> The Englishman with his usual bloody cold.

Pepys's very use of code writing for his pathetic confessions to his secret diary is somehow itself a very English stratagem, that makes us such good code makers and breakers, masters of the spy genre in fiction which is, at the same time, capable of sending itself up as Graham Greene does in *Our Man in Havana*.

Three years after Charles II's death civil war broke out briefly again in defence of pragmatic Protestantism. James II and his family fled to France. The Glorious Revolution set William and Mary jointly on the throne. They inherited the true glory of English music in Henry Purcell, and the first woman professional writer in Aphra Behn. High Tory and fervent supporter of Charles and James II, defender of the right of women to love, to choose their own partners and to write for the public stage, she refused to conform to the new bourgeois mode and contrived to die a few days after William's and Mary's coronation. Both she and Purcell were to fall out of favour, almost out of the national consciousness, as attention focused increasingly on trade and business. Puritanism took hold, with its counterpart, an increasing rationalism that in its emphasis on reason and common sense could leave little room for the imagination.

Rationalism under various guises had been a thread in our culture at least since Francis Bacon's *The Advancement of Learning* of 1605. From there the baton passed to philosophers Thomas Hobbes and John Locke, and then to those of the Scottish Enlightenment: David Hume who brought the French advocate of the noble savage, Jean Jacques Rousseau, to England in 1766, and Adam Smith who is recorded as first responsible for the expression 'a nation of shopkeepers' in his *Wealth of Nations* of 1776, later and more famously applied to the English during his exile by Napoleon in 1822. The rationalist line was further extended into the utilitarianism of Jeremy Bentham and John Stuart Mill in the nineteenth century, and represents the Englishman's preferred stance as theologically Deist, with a vague idea of there being 'something' up or out there, yet philosophically pragmatic and secular, unlike America's more categorically religious position, which still contains strong elements of its origins in both Puritanism, which was rejected by British rationalists as the 'enthusiasm' of Quakers and Shakers, and in Irish Catholicism.

Those who couldn't live with the Anglican broad Church left to find religious freedom in the growing British possessions, which were still a ragbag of trading posts, plantations and colonies, mainly in North America and the Caribbean, and often still at the mercy of native peoples and competing European imperialist interests. In deference to the Scottish Stuarts, England had become for a time Dryden's and Purcell's Britain, the 'fairest isle, all isles excelling, seat of pleasure and of loves'. The song, 'Britons strike home', from Purcell's musical version of the Boadicea story, *Bonduca*, is the forerunner of 'Rule Britannia'. The Union of England and Scotland under Queen Anne, the last of the Stuarts, in 1707 absorbed Scotland and her Parliament into England, which could now be seen by an outsider as a single political entity, while never of course diminishing Scotland's own sense of identity.

When George succeeded Anne, Britain once again retired into the background in favour of England and English. Power was concentrated at Westminster in the hands of the English upper classes, some of whom might indeed own large tracts of land in Scotland and Ireland, and have unEnglish titles. The years of Anne's reign saw a renewal of the war with France under John Churchill, Duke of Marlborough. The intermarriage of royal houses had brought the real danger that Louis XIV's grandson would rule Spain, the Netherlands and the Spanish colonies in the Americas. Louis also recognized James Stuart, the Old Pretender, son of James II, as rightful king of England rather than his half-brother-in-law William, the sitting tenant, or his successor Anne. Looked at logically, James III's claim as the legitimate male heir was indisputable and several among the High Tory party wanted to restore him, especially after the death of Anne in 1714, but there was little support in the country for another Catholic Stuart brought up in France, and the attempted rebellion in his favour in Scotland in 1715 was quickly and brutally suppressed.

A king who could speak no English was necessarily dependent on his ministers, who had given him the crown, to run the government. George handed over the chairmanship of his council to the leader of the ruling party, the Whigs, and so created the first prime minister and Cabinet. The end of the war with France in the year before Anne's death had left England in a position of strength. France was contained; our sea rivals the Dutch were given to the Austrians who had little interest in sea power. England had meanwhile added Gibraltar, Minorca, Nova Scotia and Newfoundland to her colonies. The road was open for an explosion of finance and trade, for what Dr Johnson, epitomizing the ethos of the time, described as 'few ways in which a man can be more innocently occupied . . . getting money'.

The essential mechanism for this development, the Bank of England, had been set up by William III in 1694, to fund the war with France and finance the National Debt. mainly from the wealthy Whig merchants of the City of London. Together with the London Stock Exchange, the merchant banks like Hoare's and the first insurance companies, all products of the seventeenth and early eighteenth centuries, the old lady of Threadneedle Street began the rise of London as a great commercial centre, still only rivalled by America's Wall Street and, for over two hundred years, unopposed. It has fostered the myth of the gentility of money, of finance and stocks and shares, rather than trade, the creation and distribution of goods, which was left to the lower and middle-middle classes to soil their hands with when the industrial revolution arrived.

At first, trade meant importing foreign desirables: wine from France and Spain, then spices and silk from old civilizations like China and India, and raw materials like wood, exotic fruits and vegetables, sugar and furs from the New World, Russia and the Baltic, to be processed by English craftsmen: cabinet makers, tailors, cooks. The landed gentry might take a share in such enterprises but mainly they lived off their rents, acquiring more land by enclosure and buying out their smaller neighbours who became first their tenants and eventually their labourers.

There's still part of the myth that clings to this historical division. 'The City' is an acceptable milieu for the sons and daughters of the upper classes. Money breeds money without dirty manufacture. But inherent in our preference for a financial rather than a manufacturing career is the short termism of the English economy. Since money has to generate money, shareholders come first and must be constantly appeased and rewarded. Manufacture is a long-term business that therefore in our economy suffers from chronic underfunding. We are very good at invention and discovery but unwilling to tie up our money in the lengthy expense of development. We're secretly glad that the dirty industries of coal and steel and their products have gone away, with their undesirable concomitants of working-class solidarity and culture. Now we can all be individuals, responsive only to our immediate family and friends, refusing to involve ourselves in our communities or even to vote. Our passions, as evidenced in magazines and television programmes, are for our homes and gardens, and for the repository of our remaining nationalism and regionalism: sport.

8

Empire Day

AS TRADE WITH the colonies and the rest of the world grew, London sucked more and more people into herself, becoming 'the great wen', as William Cobbett, the roving journalist of the early nineteenth century, called her, a blot on the landscape, or abnormal growth. By 1800 the city had grown to just under a million and was 'the grandest city in the West'. It had sprouted like a frontier town, without planning since Charles II's and Sir Christopher Wren's aborted attempt at urban design after the great fire, and without any coherent local government. It still relied on the parishes to administer some kind of poor law and welfare system, a situation to be repeated with local councils in the late twentieth century when Mrs Thatcher abolished the GLC. As the city grew it divided into three classes: those who had money and power, the craftsmen and retailers who supplied their needs and a heaving mass, the 'mobile', who picked up a living as best they could. Beyond the fashionable West End were whole areas like Ratcliff Highway in Wapping, where the sailors, who brought the goods and prosperity to the city, came ashore to spend their pay. It was a whirl of 'dissolute sailors, blackmailing watermen, rowdy fishermen, stock fish hawkers, quarrelsome chairmen, audacious highwaymen, sneak thieves and professional cheats . . . footpads, deserters, prisoners of war on parole, bravos, bullies and river vultures'. And, of course, harlots to service the male gallants of every class. The nineteenth-century myth would present us as a quiet, respectable people but the reality of eighteenth-century London life was very different. The world of the pinstriped city gent with his bowler hat and rolled umbrella is a late manifestation of the myth, itself superseded by the shirt-sleeved yuppy.

A German visitor, Georg Christoph Lichtenberg, who had longed to visit London and finally made it in the 1770s, wrote, with fascination, of the street women that they were available 'got up in any way you like, dressed, bound up, hitched up, tightlaced, loose, painted, done up or raw, scented, in silk or wool, with or without sugar, in short, what a man cannot obtain here, if he have money, upon my word let him not look for it anywhere in this world of ours'.

Already versions of the pub and the more temperate coffee bar were the places for everyday social life, in a city where lodgings were the general rule and even if clean, were cramped spaces mainly for sleeping. Fast-food takeaways and cheap eating houses provided the solid food, until the gin craze of the 1730s and 1740s when an average of two pints a week was drunk for every man, woman and child in London. Hogarth showed its devastating effects in *Gin Lane*, while the novelist and magistrate, Henry Fielding, wrote that 'gin is the principal sustenance (if it may be called so) of more than a hundred thousand people in the metropolis . . . the intoxicating draught itself disqualifies them from any honest means to acquire it, at the same time that it removes sense of fear and shame and emboldens them to commit every wicked and desperate enterprise'. The author of *Tom Jones* was no dreary puritan but he believed that 'should the drinking of this poison be continued at its present height during the next twenty years, there will be by that time few of the common people left to enjoy it'.

Now we would think in terms of the evils of drugs rather than gin but addiction itself is nothing new.

The underclass was an object of fascination for the respectable and the men of fashion, 'the flash blades', for whom it was a kind of sport to finish off a night's rambling and drinking in a backstreet gin shop, after a visit to a gambling den and a smart club in St James's, a ride in Hyde Park and a cockfight.

The laissez-faire, free-trade philosophy that provided the climate for these developments was encouraged by the corrupt politics of rigged elections that gave the governing classes a free hand to expand trade and make money. But the libertarian view extended downwards too to all classes who believed themselves to be free-born Englishmen, even if they were merely free to starve. The only limit to freedom was money or the lack of it. The Lord Mayor's Day crowd, according to a Swiss visitor in the 1730s, 'is particularly insolent and rowdy turning into lawless freedom for the great liberty it enjoys. At these times it is almost dangerous for an honest man, and more particularly a foreigner, if at all well dressed, to walk in the streets, for he runs a great risk of being insulted by the vulgar populace, which is the most cursed brood in existence. He is sure of not only being jeered at and being bespattered with mud, but as likely as not dead dogs and cats will be thrown at him, for the mob makes a provision before of these playthings . . .' Our tendency to xenophobia has a history as long as that of addiction, and can be very quickly reanimated by the unscrupulous whether politician or press.

These reports didn't stop foreigners flocking to see this phenomenon, a city without an effective royal court, since the German-speaking early-Hanoverian Georges made little attempt to keep a court, unlike their princely continental cousins and counterparts, but still a capital city which was the financial and trading centre of the world, noisy with its teeming people who seemed to be always running after their business and pleasure, to the music of street fiddlers, organ grinders, the bells and cries of hundreds of vendors, or to the clubs of the fashionable male world where a 'thousand meadows and cornfields are staked at every throw and as many villages lost as in the earthquakes that overwhelmed Herculaneum and Pompeii'. One observer reported that even in the worst of winter the pie shops and bakers were forced to keep their windows fully open so that the scurrying passers-by could seize their food on the run, and toss the appropriate coin through the window without stopping.

Some, like Boswell and Johnson, found the metropolis exhilarating, others were glad to retreat to the contrasting elegance of their country houses where they could be painted at ease by Gainsborough and Reynolds or with their dogs and horses by Stubbs. Often in these pictures both men and women are attended by black servants brought back from the colonies. The patrons look out from a classical background of drapes and stylized landscape while the servant, or a dog, gazes up at them, both suggesting fidelity to the power icon. Less swagger than the Van Dyck portraits that preceded them, these are cool, composed, elegant without ostentation. The world they embody is ordered, civil in contrast to the disorder of the city underworld.

The best of all worlds was Bath, free of the embarrassments of trade and business. There the commerce was the discreet pursuit of property through the marriage stakes, disguised as sophisticated pleasure and even, in the case of Jane Austen's novels, as love.

Austen's sailor brothers represent the other side of the coin. It's hard now to recapture, in the age of the aeroplane, telephone, Channel tunnel and Internet, the isolation of England, surrounded by seas over which all her trade had to be conveyed and her wars fought. The navy, the senior service, was our lifeline for the two hundred and fifty years in which we built and lost an empire. Yet this very isolation drove us to break out. Islands can be claustrophobic.

As well as fighting the French, we desperately admired their cultural achievements. Civilization began at Calais, with the boorishness of a Squire Booby and the English peasantry left behind. The Continent was there to be both culturally and actually pillaged for adornments to the new country houses, the new musical theatres and concert rooms, and to teach the latest dances. It led to a neglect amounting to suppression of English talent, especially music, in favour of Italian, French and German. Foreign books filled the library shelves, imported statuary turned the long gallery into an avenue of classical figures.

Beyond Europe lay more and more lands to be colonized and eventually annexed. A low point in English fortunes came in the middle of the eighteenth century just before the beginning of the Seven Years War between England and France, when the French had routed the English in Pennsylvania and the Ohio Valley, and attempted to take over the Carnatic coast in India.

The end of the Mogul Empire in India had left many small independent states whose rulers were wooed in turn by both the English and French East India Companies. In June 1756 an event took place that has passed into English mythology with an expression for anything that's dark and suffocating like the punishment cells of an army barracks or even an unlit cellar. The Nawab of Bengal imprisoned a hundred and forty-six English traders, including a woman, in the cellar of the East India Company's Fort William, which he had captured. Less than twenty by fifteen feet square, the Black Hole of Calcutta suffocated all but twenty-two men and the woman. Passing into legend, it became the spur to Robert Clive's conquest of Bengal with his victory at Plassey the following year.

Meanwhile, on the Continent William Pitt the Elder, now prime minister, made common cause with Frederick the Great of Prussia against the Austrian Empire, which was trying to swallow Frederick's little kingdom. Pitt's strategy was to keep the French and Austrians from dividing Europe between them, and then turning their undivided attention to the invasion of England. Minorca was lost and Byng, the admiral held responsible, shot '*pour encourager les autres*' as Voltaire put it in *Candide*, suggesting that it was something the English did from time to time.

'I will conquer Canada [then largely a French possession] in Germany,' Pitt said, as his justification for supporting Frederick the Great. Unable because of the war against Prussia and England to get reinforcements from France, Montcalm, the gallant French commander, was finally defeated by General James Wolfe's daring stratagem of scaling the Heights of Abraham to take Quebec, both commanders being killed within minutes of each other. The peace settlement in 1763 gave Canada to the English, who also seized French colonies in West Africa and the West Indies. Seven years later Captain Cook raised the Union Jack at Botany Bay, adding Australia to the colonies.

The idea of empire gained strength from the middle of the century, when George Berkeley, the Irish-born philosopher and Anglican Bishop of Cloyne who had visited America in 1728, published his poem 'On the Prospect of Planting Arts and Learning in America', written before his trip in 1752. It contained a line which was to be often quoted:

Westward the course of empire takes its way . . .

Ironically this concept of a British Empire was given its fullest expression just as the first part of it was about to be lost. Both Edmund Burke and Adam Smith refer to it: Burke in his *On Conciliation with America* published on the eve of the War of Independence, advising accommodation and tolerance; Smith in the *Wealth of Nations* published on the very day of the Declaration of Independence.

Burke writes of the need to give the American colonists freedom, 'that sole bond which originally made and must still preserve the unity of the empire . . . a great empire and little minds go ill together'. Smith, advocating their inclusion in the Parliament at Westminster, says: 'If any of the provinces of the British Empire cannot be made to contribute towards the support of the whole empire, it is surely time that Great Britain should free herself from the expense of defending those provinces in time of war, and of supporting any part of their civil or military establishments in time of peace, and endeavour to accommodate her future views and designs to the real mediocrity of her circumstances.'

George III had succeeded his father in 1760 as the first 'Briton' on the throne since Queen Anne, determined to restore the powers of the crown as they had been at the Glorious Revolution of 1688, before, as he saw it, his German antecedents George I and II had fallen into the hands of Parliament, the Whig merchants and their prime ministers. Unfortunately the king suffered from the genetic disorder porphyria, which turned his urine intermittently blue, heralding severe attacks of madness, although perhaps from the national viewpoint these periods of incapacity saved us from an effective despotism.

The attempt to impose taxes on the American colonists, which Adam Smith was justifying even as independence was declared, climaxed in the Boston Tea Party of 1773. The colonists had demanded 'No taxation without representation', which Smith supported, but rather than allow them to elect representatives to Parliament as members on an equal footing with the British, the king and his first minister, the obsequious Lord North, first imposed taxes from Westminster and a legal stamp duty, which they were then forced by riots in Boston to repeal, except for the tea tax. Rejecting even this, the colonists poured the East India Company's tea into Boston harbour. The Boston Tea Party, as it has come to be known, belongs to the myth of America not England but it's interesting to speculate how different world history might have been if we had been prepared to grant the colonists seats in the English House of Commons.

The dispute went much deeper than taxation. The Americans, as they now saw themselves, wanted self-government and freedom from the motherland's apron strings. The temper and tone of the two states were quite different: the new Americans thrusting and energetic with their Protestant work ethic; the English appearing almost somnolent, prepared to live off colonial enterprise and taxation while fighting the old enemy France, who saw in the imperial conflict a chance to get her own back.

The war lasted six years, with the whole of the Continent supporting the Americans and the Irish seizing the opportunity to advance a little home rule for themselves. Only Canada, now the home of thousands of Scotsmen, many of them highlanders who had settled there after their bitter defeat at Culloden put an end to Bonnie Prince Charlie's aspirations to restore the Stuart monarchy, stood firmly by England. Peace was made in 1782 with the former thirteen colonies transforming themselves into the United States of America under a president, their successful commander-in-chief George Washington.

Significantly, Edmund Gibbon had published the first volume of *The Decline and Fall of the Roman Empire* just a few months before the American Declaration of Independence. At the end of Book IV he wrote: 'The decline of Rome was the natural and inevitable effect of immoderate greatness. Prosperity ripened the principle of decay; the causes of destruction multiplied with the extent of conquest; and as soon as time or accident had removed the artificial supports, the stupendous fabric yielded to the pressure of its own weight; and instead of inquiring why the Roman empire was destroyed, we should rather be surprised that it had subsisted so long.' The moral was clear: all empires carried within them the seeds of their own destruction. Britain's first empire had fallen almost before it had begun. The obvious implication, however, ran contrary to our self-interest and we at once began again on a new empire. This time we would concentrate on places where we had the supposed advantages of being Christian and civilized, unlike the natives with their assorted non-white skins and 'bizarre' religions.

Yet in one respect we were morally in the van of the American colonists seeking their independence. At the same time as we were fighting to hold on to our colonies and extending our empire yet further, agitation was growing to abolish the slave trade on which many of them had been built. It would take a civil war in America to abolish slavery, twenty-five years after it was abolished in Britain, and a world war a century later before an end was put to its vile offspring, segregation.

Cynically it could be argued that by abolishing the trade in slaves, which came about in 1807, we were merely trying to damage the provision of cheap labour to our new, fast-growing commercial rivals. However, abolition must also in their eyes have damaged the Dons of Barbados and the British colonies of the Caribbean, which is perhaps partly why it took another twenty-six years to abolish slavery itself. Meanwhile other ways had to be found to provide labour for the remaining colonies, especially the newly discovered Australasia, where the natives were either too few or too hostile to be pressed into service and there weren't old, skilled civilizations like India and China to exploit.

Gibbon regarded Cook's voyages of discovery, 'undertaken by the command of his present Majesty' (George III) as 'inspired by the pure and generous love of science and mankind' and praised the king for introducing into the islands of the South Seas 'the vegetables and animals most useful to human life'. Gibbon died in 1799, ten years after Australia had been put to use as a penal colony to replace America, which was now closed to us. Cook himself was murdered by enraged Hawaiians when he was forced to return to the islands to repair his ship.

The population of England was growing. By the end of George II's reign it had doubled to over fourteen million. At the same time the new technologies of the industrial revolution were changing the lives of millions.

I am a handweaver to me trade.
I fell in love with a factory maid.
A factory maid although she be,
Blessed be the man that enjoys she.

Women were the first to be industrialized, along with their children. The cottage spinning wheel was overtaken by Arkwright's spinning jenny driven by water power and patented in 1769.

Where are the girls? I'll tell you then
The girls have gone to weave by steam
And if you would find them you must rise at dawn
And trudge to the mill in the early morn.

James Watt's invention of the steam engine began a new stage of taking people out of their homes into the huge shed-like factories of the Midlands. The slave trade was abolished to be replaced by the import of cotton picked by slaves, which came in as they had gone out through the western ports of Bristol and Liverpool, to be processed by the Lancashire and Scottish lasses and their children. The men continued to weave at home, thousands of them abandoning other employment, including in some cases their own smallholdings, to process the masses of spun cotton and wool coming off the women's machines. Canals were opened up in the 1760s to transport coal, which was also carried on land in horse-drawn trucks running on wooden rails. Coal was to be the black gold that, with water, would power the new steam engines to turn everything from threshing machines to trains and ships. Roads were surfaced with a crushed stone process invented by a Scottish engineer, John McAdam. Indeed, the Scots were everywhere devising and implementing the new technologies. Gradually even the handlooms began to be brought together by 'the masters', the manufacturers, under one roof. 'A factory', said a witness to the Committee on the Woollen Trade of 1806, 'is where they

130

employ perhaps two hundred hands in the same building.' Increasingly these would include some of the élite of the industry, the croppers, who dressed the cloth in the finishing process.

Grouping people together within the same four walls encouraged solidarity, the feared combination against authority that became the subject of harsh laws after the outbreak of the French Revolution in 1789. The cause of Wordsworth's 'bliss was it in that dawn to be alive' and the politician, Charles James Fox's, initial 'delight' turned to repugnance and fear as the just revolution was succeeded by the terror of the tumbrils to the guillotine three years later, and the execution of the French royal family. Whether the English Parliament conveniently forgot that it had done much the same thing, or whether it remembered only too well, the extreme reaction at home included the suspension of habeas corpus, a new law of treason, a ban on public meetings, suppression of cheap newspapers by a stamp duty and the anti-union legislation of 1799, the Combination Acts, forbidding people to combine together for improvements either in wages or working conditions. Laissez-faire had become laissez mourir.

The solidarity might be general, to a class, trade or workforce, or personal. It could be felt and expressed by either men or women. The mill girls felt it towards their own forewoman, the 'doffing mistress'.

> *Oh do you know her or do you not*
> *This new doffing mistress we have got?*
> *Elsie Thompson it is her name,*
> *And she helps her doffers on every frame.*
>
> *Sometimes the boss he looks in the door.*
> *'Tie your ends up doffers,' he will roar.*
> *Tie our ends up we surely do;*
> *For Elsie Thompson but not for you.*

The wars at the end of the century and the beginning of the next brought food shortages, unemployment or greatly depressed wages for thousands, while the landowners who had managed to increase their acreage, and the manufacturers, especially those supplying the army and navy with equipment, uniforms and provisions, flourished. There was no minimum wage to cushion either urban or rural labourers, many of whom were 'on the parish', which gave relief according to the price of corn and the number of children, and helped to keep wages low.

William Cobbett, the radical reformer and chronicler of his times, who saw the effects of all this at first hand, travelling the length and breadth of England on his *Rural Rides*, published from 1821, wrote: 'These things are the price of efforts to crush freedom in France, lest the example of France should produce a reform in England. These things are the price of that undertaking.' Cobbett had begun as an anti-radical, producing his pro-Tory *Political Register* from 1802, but observation changed his opinion and two years' imprisonment for an article against flogging in the army only accelerated the reversal, which he expressed in prose that Hazlitt called 'plain, broad, downright English'. It's largely this that makes him part of English mythology, as a vigorous, no-nonsense pragmatist even when his politics are unfashionable.

The agricultural labourers themselves saw the situation with a dash of humorous cynicism:

No wonder that butter's a shilling a pound
See those rich farmers' daughters how they ride up and down
When you ask them the reason they say, 'bon alas'.
There is a French war and the cows have no grass.
Honesty's all out of fashion. These are the rigs of the time,
Time my boys. These are the rigs of the time.

The figures of John Ball and *Piers Plowman*, now renamed General Ned Ludd or Captain Swing, preside over the recurring outbreaks of machine breaking and rick burning that were only ended by a change of government and monarch, and the reforms of the 1830s. The symbols of the Peterloo Massacre, the Tolpuddle Martyrs and Botany Bay itself, the graveyard of those men and women who took direct action and were transported rather than hanged during the worst phase of bitter suppression, have all passed into this strand of our iconography. Significantly, E. P. Thompson's great study is called: *The Making of the English Working Class*; not of the 'British' working class, for it was among English labourers, both rural and urban, that the movement that was to become our very English version of socialism began.

The English forces abroad fighting the French did badly on land at first, especially when Napoleon, the little corporal of genius, took over. It was left to the navy under Nelson to win a series of sea battles, holding the empire together and staving off the threatened invasion from France. Nelson was England's new darling, a role he reinforced with his famous pre-Trafalgar signal 'England expects . . .' France was at war with England not Britain. Scotland or Ireland might join forces with the enemy and repudiate the infant union. Still the French had eventually to be defeated on land by Wellington before the peace could be finally won.

As usual long wars, and especially the threat of invasion, made little Englanders of even the most impoverished. By the end of it more colonies had been added, almost by accident, to the empire: Ceylon, Cape Colony, more of India and the East and West Indies. It had become the global empire on which the sun never set, which stained vast tracts of the map of the world red and would arouse such envy in others as to be in the end more trouble than it was worth, especially when Hitler tried to emulate it by acquiring a German empire in the east.

Psychologically it was of great use to governments of whatever political colour. Not only did it provide a way of siphoning off criminals, it also provided lands to which the energetic poor could be encouraged to emigrate. Those left behind were either the least adventurous and most docile, or those most attached to their homes and families and less likely to risk losing them, or their rights to parish support in hard times. However oppressed they might be they could still see themselves as freeborn Englishmen, a class above the other members of the empire who were at best rude colonials if white and Christian and, if not, coloured heathens.

There was a moment after the end of the French war when the country hovered again on the edge of rebellion. A law was passed against the import of cheap foreign corn. America, with its vast prairies for cereal, was already taking over as the granary of the world. This law tried to kill two birds with one stone: denying the Americans an English market and keeping up rents at home by making corn dear. A cartoon showing the end of the Manchester demonstration against the corn laws and the high price of bread, and for parliamentary reform in 1819, which has passed into history as the massacre at Peterloo, has the mounted hussars and yeomanry striking down and trampling men and women, and is captioned: 'Britons strike home', a satire on Purcell's still popular song from *Bonduca*, that musical version of Boadicea.

Eleven people were killed; at least six hundred claimed serious injury, of whom over a hundred were women and girls. The government and the Prince Regent congratulated the magistrates for calling out the troops but there was also an upsurge of popular sympathy for the demonstrators. When one of their leaders, Henry Hunt, went to London between his arrest and trial, three hundred thousand people lined the streets to see him.

What frightened the government most was the orderliness and organization of such numbers of the 'lower orders', with their stewards, divisions and banners. 'The peaceable demeanour of so many thousand unemployed men is not natural,' General Byng said of an earlier strike procession of spinners in Manchester. Thousands of disbanded soldiers, who had learnt discipline fighting Napoleon, had returned to unemployment or low wages in their villages. They knew how battles were planned and armies assembled, and the value of identification with comrades, a cause and a regiment, which is still the basis for the organization and training of the British army.

The banners and bands, the orderly organized procession of protest, endured until the last decades of the twentieth century. The miners' return of the eighties behind their historic red banner, beaten but unbowed, still had power to raise the lump in the throat of pride and tears, after nearly two centuries. The immediate result of Peterloo was a repression that failed because it had the effect of allying the shopkeepers and skilled artisans and middle-class radicals to the labourers and operatives. The Reform Bill of 1832, which gave the vote to the 'ten pound householders' and tenant farmers, added to the previous year's redrawing of constituencies and abolition of the old 'rotten boroughs', succeeded at first simply in splitting off their old allies from the labourers but was still the beginning of the progress, however slow, to one man or woman, one vote. A nation of middle-class shopkeepers had been enfranchised.

The concept of a property qualification as an entitlement to vote, instead of birth, though the two still often went hand in hand, made empowerment theoretically within the reach of everyone. All that was needed was the Protestant work ethic: be good and work hard. The journeyman could become a master; the apprentice aspire to his own shop. Self-help would give you the vote and keep you out of the workhouse. The ethos of the 'respectable working class' became imbued with middle-class values that could keep its poor members from falling over the edge into the chaos of the underclass. The chapels sanctified it with a touch of Methodism.

Respectability was coupled with our innate conservatism and dislike of change: the 'if it ain't broke don't fix it' of English tradition, further yoked to the concept of the Englishman's home as his castle. 'Keep yourself to yourself and don't owe anything to anyone' were the self-limiting virtues. Even these were often impossible to live up to. In lodgings, tenements and subdivided terraced houses, which continued to house the working classes, seventy-five per cent of the population until after the Second

World War, privacy was often impossible, while unemployment and periodic economic depression left thousands owing rent, with goods 'on tick' at the corner shop or in hock to the pawnbroker.

What could provoke serious unrest when added to extreme poverty was the perception of 'unfairness' which, like our civil law system, was a matter of case rather than constitution. A song written at about this time, 'The Poor Cotton Weaver', composed by a weaver, Joseph Lees, and a spinner, Joseph Coupe, both from Oldham, sets this out in the last verse. Also known as 'John o'Grinfilt's Ramble', and immensely popular, it was published in Manchester in a broadside, the cheap single sheet that most people could afford, and parodied many times.

> I'm a poor cotton weaver as many a one knows.
> I've nowt to eat in the house, and I've wore out me clothes.
> Me clogs are both broken and stockings I've none,
> You'd hardly give tuppence for all I've got on. . . .
>
> Our parish church parson kept telling us long,
> We'd see better times if we'd but hold our tongue,
> I've holden me tongue till I've near lost me breath
> An' I think in me heart he means to starve us to death . . .
>
> We held on six weeks thinkin' each day were the last.
> We harried and shifted till now we're quite fast.
> We lived upon nettles while nettles was good,
> And Waterloo porridge the best that we could.
>
> Now old Bill o'Dans sent bailiffs one day
> For shop score he's owed that I couldn't pay.
> But he's just too late for old Billy o'Bent
> Had sent round his cart and ta'en goods for rent.
> > They left nowt but a stool that'd seats for two
> > And on it sat Margit an'me

Our Margit declares if she'd clothes to put on
She'd go up to London to see the great man,
An' if things didn't alter when there she had been,
She says she'd begin an' fight, blood up to the een.
She's not against king, but she likes a fair thing
An' she says she can tell when she's hurt.

Political reforms didn't abolish economic problems of poverty and unemployment. The new Parliament still saw trades unions as hotbeds of sedition and improper demands, and struggled to suppress them. Six Dorset farm workers who became known as the Tolpuddle Martyrs, were prosecuted for 'administering illegal oaths' in connection with the Agricultural Labourers,' Friendly Society and transported two years after the passing of the Reform Bill, even though they were pardoned two years later, after fierce protests. By the 1830s some four thousand people a year were being convicted of assorted crimes and sent to Australia. Many of those transported either chose, or were forced through lack of funds to buy a passage home, to stay in Australia. Some sent for their families, others began new ones with female transportees when they were released. It became a new region of white settlement, with the aboriginal people marginalized in the outback, and black or Asian immigrants discouraged from settling there until after the middle of the twentieth century.

Labourers were particularly eager to emigrate if they were promised land and even, for a time, a bounty, but the administration of the empire was in the hands of the colonial service, staffed by the professional civil servants of the middle and upper classes. In India and Africa particularly, the younger sons of the gentry could find government employment with all the perks of handsome houses and devoted servants, whereas their position on the family ladder at home in England would have meant at best a country parsonage or military service, itself increasingly, if not at sea, on land in the same colonies.

Merchants and planters themselves settled in the colonies to be the allies of the British administration and of ruling petty princes, kept divided from each other by flattery and a share in the spoils from the export of spices, silks and beautiful artefacts crafted by skilled but cheap labour. When the Anglo gentry retired 'home', where their children were sent to learn to be English at public boarding schools, they built town mansions like those in Richmond or Blackheath, or acquired country houses to begin new dynasties.

Not all the benefit was to the colonists. Countries which had developed highly sophisticated but non-industrial civilizations were brought into contact with all the technological developments of the West, which would make India, for example, after the trauma of independence and partition, ready to become a world player in science and technology.

We are still dogged by the myth of our empire and its aftermath. Centuries of regarding ourselves, however impoverished economically and culturally, as at least 'better than the heathen' adds to our feelings of superiority over all foreigners which, when it is seen to be manifestly untrue as in European league tables for education, child poverty or sports, turns to aggression and arrogance born of shame and frustration.

9

Rural Idyll

BY ONE OF those ambiguities or ironies for which we are famous, just as England's 'green and pleasant land' was subsiding under the weight of the new 'dark satanic mills', a wave of interest in rural life began with the publication of *Poems on Several Subjects* by Stephen Duck, 'lately a poor thresher in a barn in the County of Wilts, at the wages of four shillings and sixpence per week'. Written by the time he was twenty-five, Duck's poems were read aloud to Queen Caroline in the drawing room at Windsor Castle, by Mrs Clayton, lady of the bedchamber. In 1736 the queen made him a yeoman of the guard, and gave him a house at Richmond and a pension of £30 a year. The collection ran into many editions. Duck's work was the only treatment of rural life that his successor, George Crabbe, thought had any authenticity, so much so that parts of his own *The Village*, of 1783, are close enough to be almost plagiarism.

Duck's success led eventually to his taking holy orders, but four years later he drowned himself. He begins a line that reaches apotheosis in John Clare, whose *Poems Descriptive of Rural Life and Scenery* started his own publishing career in 1820. Along the rural way Thomas Gray published his *Elegy Written In A Country*

Churchyard in 1751, Oliver Goldsmith produced *The Deserted Village* in 1770, and Robert Bloomfield brought out *The Farmer's Boy* in 1800, which sold 26,000 copies in the first three years and was translated into Italian and French. Mary Collier, laundress and fieldhand, a contemporary of Stephen Duck, and Anne Yearsley, the Bristol Milkwoman, whose poems appeared in 1785, added the working woman's viewpoint.

Gray, Crabbe and Goldsmith represent the gentlemen, and the others the players, in this village green tradition, but all were concerned to repudiate the concept of the rural idyll as expressed in conventional pastoral poetry and its images of a Golden Age: of pretty china shepherds and shepherdesses, with their flower-entwined crooks and curly lambs, who were really sixteenth- and seventeenth-century aristocrats like Sir Philip Sidney in the disguises of Arcadia. Goldsmith comes closest to it, succumbing to both the pastoral myth and the very English weakness for nostalgia in his reinvocation of times past when village life was still flourishing before wholesale emigration to cities or colonies, and before enclosure and the industrialization of agriculture, a continuing process that Clare would still be depicting angrily fifty years after Goldsmith.

Stephen Duck seems to have taught himself to read and write before being sent to school, where he learnt so fast that the schoolmaster complained to his mother who immediately took him away: 'lest he might become too fine a gentleman for the family that produced him.' Undeterred, he took his favourite poet Milton out to the fields and barns where he worked, along with *The Spectator* and Bailey's English dictionary. At home he laboured over his poetry, scanning the lines out loud on his fingers until his wife ran out of their cottage telling the neighbourhood that 'her husband dealt with the devil and was going mad'.

'The Thresher's Labour' takes him through the farming year, beginning with the winter's work in whichever barn the master directs them to:

'Come, strip, and try, let's see what you can do.'
Divested of our clothes, with flail in hand,
At a just distance front to front we stand;
And first the threshhall's gently swung to prove
Whether with just exactness it will move:
That once secure, more quick we whirl them round,
From the strong planks our crab-tree staves rebound,
And echoing barns return the rattling sound.
Now in the air our knotty weapons fly;
And now with equal force descend on high . . .
In briny streams our sweat descends apace,
Drops from our locks and trickles down our face . . .
When sooty peas we thresh, you scarce can know
Our native colour, as from work we go;
The sweat, the dust, and suffocating smoke,
Make us so much like Ethiopians look:
We scare our wives when evening brings us home;
And frightened infants think the bugbear's come.

After the winter threshing comes late-spring haymaking, at first a pleasure out in the open air.

But when the scorching sun is mounted high,
And no kind barns with friendly shades are nigh,
Our weary scythes entangle in the grass
And streams of sweat run trickling down a-pace.

At night they stagger home exhausted to dumpling and boiled bacon supper. The next morning the girls arrive in the fields 'arm'd with rake and prong' to spread out and turn the grass, until they break for dinner and are forced by a shower to shelter under the hedge, scenes like those painted by Stubbs in his haymaking pictures.

The year ends with harvest.

Before us we perplexing thistles find
And corn blown adverse with the ruffling wind.
Behind our backs the female gleaners wait,
Who sometimes stoop, and sometimes hold a chat . . .
Confusion soon o'er all the field appears
And stunning clamours fill the workmen's ears;
The bells and clashing whips, alternate sound
And rattling waggons thunder o'er the ground.

The last load is taken home with a loud cheer and the master, the farmer, treats them to the harvest supper where they down 'the jugs of humming beer . . . so fast / We think no toil's to come, nor mind the past'. In the morning it's back to the barns to begin the winter threshing:

Thus as the year's revolving course goes round,
No respite from our labour can be found.

The vividness of these scenes sprang from Stephen Duck's own experience. Separated from his roots, in comparative comfort, he lost his touch and his verses became conventional pastorals in eighteenth-century diction. His early poems are the first examples of the authentic voice of the English agricultural labourer to be heard in our literature, but their very realism is unsuited to myth. The sweat, the aching muscles, the monotony, the dumplings and boiled bacon, which anticipate by nearly three centuries the modern interest in personal testimony as an historical source, leave us with an image that after the initial interest tends to undermine that part of the myth in its rural aspect that we really want: a refined melancholy soothed by nature.

Gray's elegy picks up the story with the gentleman meditating on the humble dead, the rude forefathers, who are Duck's village successors, in some of the best-known lines in English poetry.

> *Full many a flower is born to blush unseen,*
> *And waste its sweetness on the desert air . . .*

Gray exhorted his readers not to despise those who, even if they died unknown, at least had done little harm to anyone:

> *their crimes confined;*
> *Forbad to wade through slaughter to a throne*
> *And shut the gates of mercy on mankind. . . .*

> *Far from the madding crowd's ignoble strife,*
> *Their sober wishes never learned to stray;*
> *Along the cool sequestered vale of life*
> *They kept the noiseless tenor of their way.*

He begins an idealizing strand in the green wellies myth of England that results in the present flight from city to country as a place of innocence to bring up children, even when the children themselves are sent away to the enclosed sophistication of boarding school for most of the year.

Goldsmith reinforced the bleaker, more realistic view of what rural life was becoming twenty years later:

> *Sweet smiling village, loveliest of the lawn,*
> *Thy sports are fled, and all thy charms withdrawn;*
> *Amidst thy bowers the tyrant's hand is seen,*
> *And desolation shadows all the green:*
> *One only master grasps the whole domain,*
> *And half a tillage stings thy smiling plain.*

The brook is choked with weed, the cottages in ruins, the paths overgrown. The man of wealth and price

Takes up a space that many poor supplied;
Space for his lake, his park's extended bounds,
Space for his horses, equipage and hounds;
The robe that wraps his limbs in silken sloth
Has robb'd the neighbouring fields of half their growth . . .

George Crabbe's *Village* isn't deserted. It still has a pub, a church and a full workhouse for the dying, the mad, orphans and single mothers. The poor are vicious and coarse, only differing from the rich in that they can't disguise their vices. There's nothing idyllic about the rustic life he describes. Even nature herself and the landscape share in the poverty and corruption:

Hardy and high, above the slender sheaf
The slimy mallow waves her silky leaf;
O'er the young shoot the charlock throws a shade,
And clasping tares cling round the sickly blade.

The Farmer's Boy of fifteen years later paints a much rosier picture of Giles the orphan's life, of grinding labour but with some joy too. Its author, Robert Bloomfield, who went from his Suffolk village to become a shoemaker in London, was remembering his own childhood and this may account for the charm of the poem as it follows the boy through the seasons. Giles isn't coarsened by his hard life, and Bloomfield writes with great compassion and real understanding of the animals who are his daily companions. The poem must have been a relief to the middle classes still rocked by fears of an English revolution.

The Farmer's Boy was written as an antidote to the cult of the sublime, affected in the second half of the eighteenth century, particularly by those who had been on the Grand Tour and been moved by spectacular Alpine scenery of

> *The roaring cataract, the snow topped hill,*
> *Inspiring awe, till breath itself stands still.*

In spite of his success Bloomfield died in poverty. Like Clare, who admired his work, he was first taken up and then dropped by the literary world. Indeed, none of the player-peasant poets were able to enjoy their success. Stephen Duck committed suicide, Bloomfield's poverty was exacerbated by a crippled son, Clare declined into madness.

Clare is the angriest and the finest of the rural literary line of descent but the poem of his that fits best into this tradition, 'The Parish', was never published in his lifetime. Too dangerously satirical and bleak, it outCrabbes Crabbe whom, together with Goldsmith, Clare was reading as he wrote 'The Parish' in a conscious effort to go one better. 'I mean to have a good race with him and have conceit enough to have little fears in breaking his wind . . . – what's he know of the distresses of the poor musing over a snug coal fire in his parsonage box . . .'

His own description of the workhouse owes much either to Crabbe or to their common experience and perception, a Hogarthian bedlam close to hell itself.

> *Shoved as a nuisance from pride's scornful sight . . .*
> *A makeshift shed for misery . . .*
> *. . . 'Twas not contriv'd for want to live but die.*

In his prefatory note Clare says that the poem was 'begun and finished under the pressure of heavy distress with embittered feelings under a state of anxiety and oppression almost amounting to slavery – when the prosperity of one class was founded on the adversity and distress of the other – the haughty demand by the master to his labourer was work for the little I choose to allow you and go to the parish for the rest – or starve'.

The first part of the note stems from Clare's personal circumstances but the second clearly refers to the Speenhamland system of poor relief which kept wages low by topping them up from the poor rate. It was only abolished by the New Poor Law of 1834. In the last part of the note Clare acknowledges the improvements of 'better times and better prospects . . . that have opened a peaceful establishment of more sociable feeling and kindness', presumably following the reforms.

All the poets except Duck and Bloomfield refer to enclosure, and the ostentation of the rich, as making the situation of the poor more unacceptable. Economics may be used to justify the reverse side of the complaint, but against that must be weighed not only the distress but the very English refusal to accept it that brought the country to the brink of revolution before the other very English manifestation of innate conservatism was prepared to give way a little and compromise. Among other reforms, some recognition of the loss of common grazing was made by the allotments acts of the early part of the nineteenth century and onwards.

While the cottage gardens fell into decay and the big estates were rationalized by takeover and enclosure, Launcelot 'Capability' Brown, William Kent and Humphrey Repton were being called in to integrate the newly acquired landscape. Each country house, even those of the nouveau-riche factory owners and merchants, had to have its park, its lake and terrace, the backdrop of Austen's novels and the subject themselves of largely undistinguished verses.

Gardening wasn't a new pastime in England. The Romans had internal walled courtyards with fountains, statues and roses. Eleanor of Aquitaine and *Le Roman de la Rose* had popularized the bower among the aristocracy, with its intimate, hedge-walled little rooms for the flirtations of courtly love. The Tudor garden had been formal with edged paths, beds laid out in squares of colour and the green sculpture of topiary. New colonies brought new plants. Religious immigrants from the Continent brought new gardening styles, including market gardening. The Restoration produced an explosion of interest encouraged by Charles II himself. The garden became a cultural action zone for which the diarist John Evelyn's advice was frequently required, to ensure the owner's taste was in line with fashion.

The pursuit of the sublime, which sent the rich abroad, was translated at home into the romantic neo-classicism of the landscapers, in particular Brown:

> But you great artist, like the source of light,
> Gild every scene with beauty and delight;
> At Blenheim, Croome and Daversham we trace
> Salvator's wildness, Claude's enlivening grace,
> Cascades and lakes as fine as Rysdale drew,
> While Nature's varied in each charming view . . .
> Born to grace Nature, and her works complete
> With all that's beautiful, sublime and great!
> For him each muse enwreathes the laurel crown
> And consecrates to fame immortal Brown.

So Joseph Wharton in 1767. But not everyone was overwhelmed by the new style. The Swan of Lichfield, Anna Seward, by 1790 in *The Lake: Or, Modern Improvement in Landscape* expresses a view that would be immediately accepted by today's environmentalists.

> Fall'n are the woods, and lawn adoring oaks!
> Fled every varied charm boon Nature gave,
> No green field blossoms, and no hedgerows wave!
> On the dim waters nods the useless sail . . .

At the demand of fashion, 'the gaudy despot . . . foe of beauty and the bane of sense' his lordship, the owner, cuts down the woods and floods the valley. The contagion spreads from the great to the little. The farmers' wives and daughters of the folksong 'The Rigs of the Time', now call their farm or farmhouse The Lodge, The Cottage or The Place and the cottage garden, walled in, has a shrubbery and exotic espaliered fruit trees 'Of which the lady scarcely knows the name'.

Town gardens had always been cultivated for as long as we have records, and the growing middle class in their urban villas aped the landscaping of the gentry rather than the mere utilitarian cottage gardens of the rural poor, which were there to fill the table with cabbages and the medicine chest with herbs. The first gardening magazine appeared in 1826 under the editorship of John Claudius Loudon who had already published his *Encylopaedia of Gardening* four years before. By 1838 he had produced, with his wife Diane, *The Suburban Gardener and Villa Companion*, a comprehensive gardening book of the sort that flood the bookshops at Christmas, full of advice on the design and care of small gardens. It needed only Joseph Paxton, the designer of the Crystal Palace and recreator of Chatsworth, to complete our downfall with his *Gardener's Chronicle* of 1841, followed by G. W. Johnson's *Cottage Garden*, seven years later, that included his own invention for recycling filtered household sewage, which doubled the size of his asparagus. His magazine also charts the progress of the potato blight that was to bring famine to England as well as Ireland in the 'hungry forties'.

Gardening clubs and societies sprang up all over the country, their annual competitions usually taking place at the local pub, with prizes then as now for the biggest and brightest in every class. The growth in education with the founding of more church schools must have encouraged more of the 'lower orders' to read these gardening books and magazines, and follow their advice. Unlike other nations who were building apartment blocks in their cities, our dwellings were still typically discrete family units, each with its own yard, if not garden. The pace of educational reform was still slow, encouraging the development of a practical rather than an intellectual cast of thought, which might have produced dangerously radical ideas akin to those across the Channel. The result is that our chief cultural activities are still practical: either gardening, with its indoor extension DIY, or sport.

A Frenchman who had been living as a student in England pinpointed the difference between us and our neighbours in an article in the Eurostar magazine in 1999. Aurelic Lambillon writes: 'The French enjoy cultural activities whereas the English have three main passions – DIY, gardening and football – which form the basis of their leisure activities. Hours of backbreaking work go into keeping the famous English garden looking its best. Mowing the lawn, pruning the roses and clipping the hedge are all part and parcel of this popular hobby. Imitate nature to the point of resembling her . . . The English make their gardens into botanical parks, delicate works that they observe with a tender but critical eye . . .' It could be argued that Lambillon's comments merely embody well-known elements of the myths the French tell about themselves and the English, but that is their point. So strong is myth in its hold on the popular imagination that even when it's clearly no longer true or has been overtaken by historical events, it continues to colour the way we are perceived or perceive ourselves, and therefore the reactions between 'us' and 'them'.

Gardening, our national hobby, panders to our preference for the pragmatic, often to the exclusion of the other arts. Television and radio have now joined literature in its service. The garden allows us to be alone, and removes the need for messy human contact, rather like our relations with our pets. We can be quietly competitive, critical of what's over the neighbour's hedge. But because gardening is a medium that aspires to no commercial gain, competition is kept to a minimum. It fulfils our preference for the gentleman over the players since we are all amateurs, apart from the telly pop stars of horticulture and the true specialists.

Our gardens involve us in no embarrassing intellectual or artistic decisions. With nature, even our version of stylized nature, we can't go wrong. Our plots are little stages on which we are the only players, making three-dimensional installation art as the stage designer does with a maquette and the final set.

Gardening is both democratic and class-bound at the same time. Anyone can do it, even in a window box. Plants can be grown from cheap packets of seed, compost made from kitchen waste, tools resharpened. Yet we can visit the gardens of the living or dead rich, like Vita Sackville-West's Sissinghurst or Stourhead, by courtesy of the present owners, which may well be the National Trust. These visits reinforce our residual class structure by showing us what we can aspire to but never attain except by joining the truly rich who are able to employ an army of gardeners. The network of country house gardens with their plant and home-made produce shops enables us to bring away a little bit of them, a touch of class that caters to our passion for gardens, our snobbery ('Wasn't that the duke in that old straw gardening hat?') and nostalgia for country life. The network also exposes the English garden to the foreign visitor so that 'English gardens' spring up all over the world, but particularly in the USA, and helps to perpetuate the myth of the eccentric, charming but old-fashioned English upper classes, fixed on film in Hugh Grant's performance in *Four Weddings and a Funeral*.

Our passion usurps reading, except of garden books, and, since the rise of a national interest in cooking after the Second World War, their near relative the cookery book. We prefer it to the other arts, which raise deep suspicions of pretension and fakery; probably no other nation is as susceptible to the story of the emperor's new clothes. The practical nature of our favoured art reassures us that what we are doing when we garden is real, of the earth earthy and natural. It only needed Gertrude Jekyll, under the influence of William Robinson who introduced the concept of the wild garden, to marry with that her own idea of the cottage garden and make our idealization of the natural complete. This concept, which affected the whole layout and planting of gardens great and small, lasted for over a century and is only now under threat from a new formalism that is postmodern and owing more to interior design. The rural muse has become part of a generalized nostalgia, and the garden that was her last retreat, disguised as garden gnome or piddling putto fountain, just another outdoor room.

Plants permit us, the least touching people in Europe according to a survey, to hold them and smooth their leaves, to show our suppressed tenderness. They don't answer back and provoke scenes as small children do in the public spaces of the supermarket and shopping mall. Their only form of protest is not to flourish and ultimately to die on us, when we have poisoned or neglected them, killed them by the kindness of overwatering, or been too ruthless with pruning or dividing up. Now a three-and-a-half-billion-pound industry with twenty-three million confessed practitioners, gardening is the ideal commercial enterprise with its built-in obsolescence and ever changing seasons and fashions. It creates small green lungs everywhere in our crowded, polluted towns, and patches of relief, if not beauty, against the homogeneity of our hoarding and shopping façades. Our choice is often limited by what the garden centre believes is good for us, and them, in any given month. Yet we somehow manage to evade what could be a crushing horticultural uniformity, mainly by exchange of seeds, cuttings, plants and that exercise of eccentricity which may be the final manifestation of the freeborn Englishman.

10

The Green and Pleasant Land

THE ENGLISH LANDSCAPE has been manufactured over at least three thousand years by the constant interaction of 'the natural world and human activities', as Oliver Rackham puts it in his *History of the Countryside*. Our population density is the highest in Europe. Even our moors and hills have been lived on and cultivated at some point in their history. To find the nearest to that sublime the eighteenth-century travellers went in search of, we have to go to the Celtic fringes of mountains and islands: Scotland, Wales, Cornwall and Ireland. Take a metal detector over a Somerset field and it will turn up a hoard of Roman silver coins, beachcomb the edges of the Thames at low tide and there are huge timbers from the Bronze Age London bridge, fly over the land with your camera and it's ridged, furrowed, potholed from end to end. Our dead are constantly underfoot.

Our northerly latitude is almost on a level with Moscow and Canada's snowbound winters, but a climate warmed by the Gulf Stream and misted by the seas all around us gives our light a natural wistfulness. Hardly a day has the same weather throughout its length. These constant changes remind us of the passage of time itself. In England you can never forget mortality. This is the mood encapsulated in Browning's poem of homesickness, 'Home Thoughts from Abroad', intensified in the nineteenth century for those who were either fighting in foreign wars, administering the empire or merely looking for renewed health in a warmer, drier, less humanly polluted climate than Victorian London with its epidemics of cholera and malaria. The 'white man's scourge', tuberculosis, reached into rural cottages as well as city clums, and into every class.

Browning's nostalgia is for an English spring with its slow coming of 'tiny leaf' and the song of a small bird, the chaffinch. He continues with his catalogue of miniature sights and sounds: a whitethroat, swallows, a thrush, dewdrops and blossoms, all culminating in the final comparison, in favour of the English landscape, between the buttercup 'the little children's dower' and 'this gaudy melon-flower'. It's a parallel to Keats's earlier evocation of an English autumn with its very domestic landscape of stubblefields, a cloud of gnats rising and sinking above 'the river sallows'. Keats observes as carefully as Constable might the gathering of migrating swallows and the first winter song of a garden robin.

Constable himself, writing about the countryside of his childhood on the Essex–Suffolk borders, describes the landscape that was the basis of his art, constantly re-imagined after he had left home and rarely revisited it: 'The beauty of the surrounding scenery, the gentle declivities, the luxuriant meadow flats sprinkled with flocks and herds, and well cultivated uplands, the woods and rivers, the numerous scattered villages and churches, with farms and picturesque cottages, all impart to this particular spot an amenity and elegance hardly anywhere else to be found.'

This is 'England's green and pleasant land' as the collective imagination recreates it, in defiance of the reality of the 'dark satanic mills' that by Constable's and Keats's day already sprawled across the North and Midlands, encroached on London itself and, by the time of the Great Exhibition of 1851, were employing nearly as many people as in agriculture. It's the dream of the lost

Golden Age for which we still strive in song, and which can be easily exploited by a countryside lobby, claiming to speak for an industry that even by 1977 employed a mere 1.6 per cent of the British workforce.

Under the influence of Albert, the Prince Consort, who made himself responsible for cultural affairs, English art began to move away from the seemingly parochial towards the more emblematic. Artists were encouraged to study the German school known as the Nazarenes, in particular Friedrich Overbeck and Peter Cornelius. The genius of Gainsborough, Reynolds, Turner and Constable was forgotten, and it began to be believed that the English were no good at painting or music and that we should look to Germany and later France, either exporting our artists to learn abroad or importing our cultural styles and practitioners from the Continent and America. This set a precedent we are still following in appraising our own contemporary literature. Even the theatre was in pre-Wildean, pre-Shavian doldrums until rescued by this pair of Irishmen.

Urban life largely replaced rural as the setting for realist or genre painting, with the new trains and omnibuses favourite backgrounds for crowd scenes of a social mix that emphasized our togetherness, and spilled over into national sporting events like Derby Day, painted by William Frith in 1858. As usual in English life there are two sides to the coin. The flip side is provided by Ford Madox Brown's *The Last of England*, where unwilling immigrants forced from home by poverty, stare back at the retreating white cliffs. Brown used himself and his wife as models for the picture, an image of his own feeling of rejection by the artistic establishment, though he was at first admired by Rossetti.

Dante Gabriel Rossetti, William Holman Hunt and John Everett Millais formed what was known as the Pre-Raphaelite Brotherhood in 1848, at Millais's family house in Gower Street. Their idea was to go back to the simplicity of the early Renaissance. The result is the iconographic, meticulously painted pictures that can so easily look like Victorian sheraton. The subjects are the Bible, Arthurian or Italian romance, contemporary literature (Tennyson was a great source) and historical events. The best-known examples are Hunt's *Light of the World*, *The Scapegoat* and *The Lady of Shalott*, Rossetti's depiction of the Annunciation (*Ecce Ancilla Domini*) and Millais's *Ophelia*.

Many of them have women as their subject, not the fashionably dressed mothers and wives who had sat for Gainsborough and Reynolds, but often diaphanously semi-nude figures that, in their voluptuous contemplation, actually have more in common with their High Renaissance and Baroque forerunners than with anything Giotto would have recognized. Though these artists were attempting a new style, and a new use of paint, their subjects reinforce the ethos of the period, cloyingly religious or queasily romantic, which now seems quintessentially Victorian. It's a relief to turn to the everyday in William Dyce's *Pegwell Bay* or *Ramsgate Sands*, with people paddling, shrimping in rockpools or picnicking.

The forty years after the defeat of Napoleon at Waterloo were a period of comparative calm and stability. This was shattered in 1854 by England's involvement in the Crimean War against Russia, in an attempt to check her growing power in central and eastern Europe, a legacy still affecting us with the late-twentieth-century conflicts in the Balkans. The Crimean War has contributed one of the great female figures that make up an essential part of the myth of England. The story of the Lady with the Lamp who took her forty nurses to the filthy field hospitals of Balaclava and Scutari, who fought the military medical establishment, whose very shadow was kissed by the wounded as she passed, who began the reorganization of army medical services and, incidentally, the emancipation of women, must be set against the other, black, myth of the incompetence of commanders and the courage of the ordinary soldier and his officers: the Charge of the Light Brigade when six hundred were ordered to ride into the mouths of the enemy cannon. As so often, time of war enhances the English myth.

Stories, and those who enact them, pass into the myth uncritically. Examined too closely, with all the tools of a modern historian at our disposal, they lose their magic. Nightingale becomes an autocrat and hysteric, who took to her bed for twenty years in order to get her own way. Nelson is a weak philanderer, enslaved by a pretentious slut, Emma Hamilton. The myth puts this relationship very differently. He is an heroic sailor carried away by his passion like any Jack Tar in a popular sea shanty. Sailors were the backbone of a country dedicated to trade, as the ploughboys had been of agriculture.

Nelson's courage, which some might see as foolhardiness, is celebrated in the legend of his putting his spyglass to his dead eye, and claiming to 'see no ships' when he had been ordered by the admiralty not to engage the enemy before the Battle of the Nile. Even so restrained a classic historian as G. M. Trevelyan says of Nelson, acknowledging his mythical quality: 'There is more in our relation to him than can be accounted for by his genius and our obligation.' He puts this unique relationship down to Nelson's common touch and tells the story of Nelson on the very eve of Trafalgar, ordering the return of the despatch boat taking letters, presumably including his own, home to England, so that the coxswain of the *Victory*, who had been too busy organizing the mailbags, could include his own letter to his wife. Nelson's justification was that the man might be dead the next day.

Nelson probably attracted more legends than any English hero since King Alfred. His hoisting of the famous message to his crews that England expected them all to do their duty is in the direct line of military exhortation from Henry V to Churchill. His enigmatic last words, 'Kiss me Hardy', or as some believe, 'Kismet, Hardy', take their place along with the last words of the dying Robin Hood to Little John, asking to be buried where the arrow falls that he manages to shoot from the window into the garden below while his friend holds him in his arms.

At home the repeal of the corn laws in 1846 allowed cheap

corn into the country to feed the poor. Imports of corn and flour, which had been a mere 405,000 quarters at the end of the eighteenth century, had risen to over 100,000 million hundred-weight by the end of the nineteenth, nearly trebling in the decade from 1860. There followed the collapse of agriculture in the 1870s, which sent thousands more in flight from the desolate countryside, either overseas or, like my own great-grandparents, to the swelling outskirts of the nearest town or city.

The rural economy changed for ever. Villages were again deserted, fields overgrown with weeds, roads dusty tracks. Only for a few years during the Second World War did the country return to full agricultural production. Otherwise England was a floating dock, the head of the world's seaways that brought home the goods of empire. Increasingly we relied on invisible trade, in particular financial services, banking and insurance, to balance the books. Depressed wages, inadequate housing often tied to the job and the final displacement of the agricultural labourer by the machine have made the landscape even more artificial. As Oliver Rackham says, the most artificial place is the centre of a modern cereal field, sterilized except for the desired crop, by pesticides, herbicides, chemical fertilizers and mutant seed. The aggrandiz-ation of holdings begun by enclosure continues. Village houses and small manors, once occupied by tenant farmers and the village professionals, doctor and vicar, became desirable country houses where the middle classes can reproduce the lifestyle of the gentry in miniature, while commuting to the city.

The countryside is now as much a place for leisure pursuits, holiday cottages, theme parks, marinas, and out-of-town shopping and garden centres as of farms, fields and animals. Our nostalgia for the green and pleasant land is eating it up as we now reverse the flight to the city with a flight from it, its crime and pollution. Yet just like those fleeing from the plague, we carry our infection with us in the shape of our cars, our inflated consumer needs, our thirst for constant entertainment. We are threatened with the need for over a million new homes in the south-east that would turn the whole of southern England into a continuous suburb, because we refuse either to make our cities worth living in or to give up the nostalgic yearning for a largely fictional country life that can only be enjoyed by the few at the expense of the many. In the words of Philip Larkin:

> the whole
> . . . Boiling will be bricked in . . .
> And that will be England gone.

It's also part of our myth that until recently we were a great manufacturing nation. The figures show that our exports of cotton, woollen, iron and steel goods all declined steadily from the middle of the nineteenth century to the outbreak of the Second World War. In a table of the main occupation groups in Britain in 1851, based on the census, domestic service, employing roughly a million and a quarter people, women and men, is second only in size to agriculture, while there are more milliners, seamstresses and dressmakers than workers in the woollen industry, including carpet weaving, more washerwomen than seamen.

The myth of our innate fairness and kindness to the weak founders on the fact that child labour was used everywhere throughout the century. The minimum working age didn't reach twelve until 1901. Thousands of children, particularly in the country, continued to skive off from school often to help their low-paid parents earn more. Education was made compulsory in 1880 for those between five and ten years old. Then children were allowed to work part time in factories if they had reached a certain standard. Frequently their parents, and they themselves, could see little point in schooling that seemed unrelated to the work they would do for the rest of their lives and truancy was common. This perception of the uselessness of education survives today in run-down estates, failing schools and areas of high unemployment, in the seven million people whose skills in reading, writing and numeracy are still minimal. For decades it was both sustained and modified in its worst effects by a feeling of community, largely destroyed by the last quarter of the twentieth century, leaving the poor and underskilled exposed to the harshness of individualistic capitalism, a situation reflected in the enormous disparity in income between even middle-range earners and the bottom.

In the first decades of the twentieth century, malnourishment was still common, both in town and country. Treats were the tail of father's bloater or the top off his egg. Breakfast in my mother's family was a piece of bread soaked in the sugary tea dregs from her mother's cup. Father came first because he sustained the family. If he was ill and unable to work or simply refused to co-operate in the unwritten contract of 'with all my wordly goods I thee endow', and withdrew his support, the family unit could collapse unless the mother was strong enough to take on both parental roles.

Traditionally, as seen by other nations, we aren't fond of children though we may spoil them with presents. 'A good hiding' or a 'clipped ear' are still the opinion-poll-sanctioned responses to bad behaviour. The country children who avoided school not to help their parents but themselves, usually boys, felt they were being manly and independent. Girls were often kept off school to help mother with younger or ill siblings. Life in a cottage with no running water, bucket sanitation or a shared outdoor privy, ten children to clothe and feed was a constant strain. Photographs and early film footage tell the same story of dirty children, in cut-down clothes from parents or older brothers and sisters, clearly underfed. George Clausen's painting of the shepherd girl with her angular, pale, anguished face and broken hand-me-down boots, whose hardness we can feel on her soft girl's feet, contrasts her with her round and curly-fleeced lambs, and with the poised, voluptuous upper-class women of Tissot and Orchardson who may have their problems, but of a different order from the elemental needs of the shepherdess.

Seen from the train windows our landscape still appears almost empty, as indeed it increasingly has been for over a hundred and twenty years. The green fields and trees provide a nostalgic antidote to the city, but one that gives few opportunities to those who wish to work there unless they are in the service industries or prepared to take low wages. The younger generation must go away to find jobs and eventually homes, while villages and towns suffer increasing suburbanization. Because we aren't, as a people, happy to live in flats but hanker for a cottage and a garden, a myth of cleaner air, water and neighbourhoods free from crime, while not being prepared to give up our own comfort, we continue a process, begun under Victoria, of denuding the countryside of workers, a process accentuated by global free trade and ever cheaper imported food. If the countryside is to survive as a working industry, farmers will have to develop niche markets in organic and specialized crops that are more labour-intensive. English orchards may even bloom again.

Nowhere is the English myth stronger than in our periodic attempts to return to Victorian values, which we believe will bring us greater happiness and stability. These 'values' fluctuate with their current promoter. Support for the family is always uppermost and is linked to the myth of rural England. Once upon a time we all lived in a two-parent family in a country cottage. We didn't have much but we were happier. Such is the substance of this part of the myth, which we maintain against all the evidence of nineteenth-century statistics of disease and death rates, parish and poor law records, and personal histories. We need to believe that we were happier, simpler, more innocent, to account for our present feeling of unease and dissatisfaction.

Most of us live longer, are better fed and clothed, relieved by machines of domestic drudgery, endlessly entertained, and yet we feel a sense of loss, part an undefined angst, part a lack of purpose and community. I suspect we experience it more than our continental neighbours. We still find it hard to communicate because of our reticent upbringing and phlegmatic ethos. We are each enclosed in an envelope of privacy, a notional space like a glass bubble separating us from the next person. Partly this derives from the Protestant legacy of the unique individual conscience and its responsibility for its own fate, and partly from centuries of over-crowding in cramped homes, streets, slums, factories where it was necessary to 'keep yourself to yourself' while being prepared to help out others in need. The cup of sugar, borrowed or lent, was more than a simple sweetener.

We need a cause to overcome our separation and force us together. It can be a war, a disaster, or simply a community of experience which may express itself as a regiment, a leek-growing club or the annual Service of Remembrance at the Cenotaph. We have to communicate through practical channels. A dose of alcohol in pub or club traditionally oils the wheels. The Frenchman who noted our passion for DIY and gardening in the Eurostar magazine, also noted an unwillingness to go home after work, expressed as a desire after long hours at the office to 'spend hours standing around drinking litres of beer'.

He also wonders at our passion for sport. 'Football is more of an obsession than a hobby. Everyone, even women, support a team and their weekends are dominated by the matches. I can't ever imagine suggesting to a French friend that we go off to watch Paris – Saint-Germain playing. I was in a pub in the City during England's elimination from the World Cup. It was as though a national disaster had occurred.' The Official Handbook for 1983 records over twenty million attendances during the season from August to May, three hundred and fifty clubs affiliated to the English Football Association and forty thousand to regional or district associations. But this is only the visible tip of the iceberg that stretches down to include schools, youth clubs and workplaces. Go to any London village, city or town, park or recreation ground on Saturday morning or afternoon, and there will be teams playing, all in colourful strip with supporters cheering them on.

Our sports were, and to a great extent still are, village sports, played since the Middle Ages on village greens and transported to the green grass of our urban villages. London, all the rest that isn't the City or Westminster, sees itself as a series of villages, each with its shopping centre, high street or broadway and playing ground. Our favourite games, football and cricket, are still played on grass. Even tennis we have transferred to the lawn from the courtyard while other nations have kept it on an enclosed hard surface. Cricket, our summer game, is also played by thousands and was regulated as early as the eighteenth century by the Marylebone Cricket Club. These village beginnings have left a legacy of amateurism.

Whereas other countries have developed a professional funding structure, which may include sports scholarships at universities, English players were, until the full-blown development of sport on television, expected to do it for the love of the game, to develop a sense of fair play, to 'give it your best', to accept losing gracefully and praise the other team. This attitude, especially where football was involved, was often at odds with the purely professional approach of other countries which don't, however, involve almost the entire population at some level of the sport. On the morning after a World Cup qualifying match between England and Scotland, which England lost although their previous score in the first leg meant they were the ones to qualify, my local London street market had disappointed English fans passing from stall to stall, comparing notes and berating their team. 'We were so pathetic. I wanted Scotland to score another goal,' as one stallholder put it.

Football in particular has become a substitute for empire and world leadership. That's why it carries such weight, and a defeat at world class level is seen as a 'national disaster'. What has raised our game from the amateur level, some would say to its loss, is its all-embracing popularity, which in turn makes it a magnet for television because of its great appeal to advertisers through the huge captive audience. This has finally professionalized the game with big injections of television cash for the premier teams.

Both cricket and football were exported with empire, which helped to regulate the games so that they could be played throughout the world according to home rules. Now the tables are turned and our former colonies consistently thrash us at cricket, while the rest of the world beats us at football, both soccer and rugby. We wring our hands and bemoan our fate to have taught these skills to the foreigners, only to be beaten by them. North America alone stands aloof, asserting its independence with its own brands of sport: baseball and American football. At this time we remain still curiously but essentially amateurs, but amateurs who don't like the national humiliation of losing at our own popular pastime, reluctantly forced to embrace professionalism, which seems to increase violence on and off the pitch. Because of the emotional overload we place on sport, and now on being the best, nothing else matters. We may for the time being lead in art or fashion but these don't command our hearts. They don't evoke that wave of common feeling we experience from a Wembley crowd singing 'Abide with me', or from the white figures on a green ground glimpsed through a train window in fading, summer evening light.

Blake's solution for our nostalgia was to offer us the idea that before industrialization Jesus himself might have walked on England's 'mountains green'. He exhorts us to build Jerusalem, the once and golden city, set in the 'green and pleasant' land, which has now become the preferred solution of environmentalists and such organizations as the Campaign for the Protection of Rural England. But our need may be too strong. We demand a right to roam, equal to that of the Finns with only five million people in the greatest European land mass. A million of us belong to the National Trust but millions more visit the houses and, in particular, the gardens owned by the Trust throughout the year, or buy the magazines that service a way of life remote from most of us except in imagination. 'The Everyday Story of Countryfolk', *The Archers*, is our longest-running soap and its television cousins *EastEnders*,

Coronation Street and *Brookside* recreate its village in an urban setting.

The village soaps give us the feeling of community, fed by the gossip once exchanged over the fence, on the doorstep or at the pub. Their characters and the actors who play them become part of thousands of conversations and news articles. They carry on the tradition of Dickens's own part-work publication of his novels that had great numbers of readers hanging on for the next episode and even stopping him in the street to beg him with tears not to let Little Nell die. Perhaps we need these fictional outlets more than other people because of our emotional reticence. As we need our little garden plots to remind us of that fictional Eden from which our modern knowledge of good and ill threatens to exile us for ever.

11

Cut Glass

BEGINNING AS CHARITY schools endowed for the education of poor boys, the public schools, still a mystery to foreigners because of their private status, had by the end of the eighteenth century established themselves as the breeding ground for the aristocracy and gentry. Even as early as 1766 at Eton, fifty boys referred to as 'Mr' were the sons of noblemen, out of a total of four hundred and eighty-three. The 'great schools' were Eton, Harrow, Westminster, Winchester, Christ's Hospital, Shrewsbury, Charterhouse and Rugby after Thomas Arnold's reforms described in the classic *Tom Brown's Schooldays*, and these are the schools that are still thought of, with the addition of Stonyhurst and Ampleforth for Catholics, by the public mind as 'the public schools', though there are also many smaller ones which are unknown even by name to the man or woman in the street. Similarly, asked to name girls' public schools, the woman on the Clapham bus would offer Roedean, Cheltenham Ladies College, St Paul's and possibly North London Collegiate. These are the names behind the popular image.

For much of the eighteenth and early nineteenth century the boys' schools were thought by many parents to be violent and brutal places of drink, gaming and whoring, and even on occasion rioting, and many boys were taught by private tutors at home. Some, like Tom Brown himself, began at the village school and were sent to a private school at nine, then on to public school. The great reformation of public schools followed the headmastership of Thomas Arnold at Rugby from 1827 to 1842. Tom Brown arrived at the school in the early thirties before Arnold's reforms had begun to bite. His father, Squire Brown, reflecting on why the boy is being sent to school, perfectly expresses the Arnoldian public school ethos. 'Tom isn't being sent to school to make him a good scholar: at any rate not for that mainly. I don't care a straw for Greek particles or the digamma; no more does his mother. If he'll only turn out a brave, helpful, truth-telling Englishman, and a gentleman, and a Christian, that's all I want.'

The place he's being sent to learn to be an English gentleman is, before Arnold's reforms, a place of violent bullying, intimidation and arcane ritual where games are seen as much more important than study in forming character, and masters and boys live in a state of natural enmity, 'like a match at football or a battle'. There's no suggestion that he might be taught to think or to have an interest in any of the arts or even in politics, the ultimate profession of many public schoolboys. He's to be taught courage, and conformity to the established Church and the social mores of his class. The schoolboy rituals of Rugby are a preparation for obedience to the rituals of society itself.

These social norms are already established, as is the dialect, which Tom encounters at once on the lips of East. ' "Bless us yes, I forgot," said East, "you've only just come. You see all my tin's been gone this twelve weeks, it hardly ever lasts beyond the first fortnight; and our allowances were all stopped this morning for broken windows, so I haven't a penny. I've got a tick at Sally's of course; but then I hate running it high, you see, towards the end of the half, cause one has to shell out for it all directly one comes back, and that's a bore." Tom didn't understand much of this talk . . . '

Thomas Hughes, Tom's biographer, makes it clear that the public school dialect includes phrasing and intonation, as well as vocabulary and no doubt pronunciation too, although he makes no attempt to represent this graphically as he does Berkshire and other working-class (his term) speech. This new language has to be learnt or rather absorbed by a kind of osmosis. In the terminology of linguistics this is hyperlect, upper-class dialect, known to others at different periods as 'cut glass', 'toff', 'tony' wallah-wallah, nobby, pound-notish, 'Oxford drawl', 'posh' and more recently 'hooray' or 'Sloane'.

A closer examination suggests that its roots lie in seventeenth-century court speech, developed by a court in foreign exile, cut off for twenty years from the mainstream language by politics and the exclusiveness and inclusiveness of the courtier group, and perpetuated after Charles II's restoration by the same factors. Standard English, however, which had been evolving since the fifteenth century very much as a written language of central administration and printed texts, just as Alfred's Wessex had become the standard English of its day, had been further boosted by the radical pamphleteering and sermonizing of the republicans. It was the language of the city and the rising mercantile class, of Cromwell and Milton rather than of the restored court.

The language of the court was transferred to the stage in Restoration comedy, and given a stamp of authority and permanence in the publication of play texts. Aphra Behn's *The Rover* of 1677 makes clear the difference between the speech of the gentry, even though fallen on hard times in exile, racy and self-referential, and that of the country squire Ned Blunt, 'the Essex calf', who keeps his local accent and speech patterns. The hyperlect was to remain closely associated with stage, and ultimately screen, in deference to the middle- and upper-class audience, whose lives the theatre chiefly dealt with, in drawing-room comedy. British films carried on the tradition until the end of the Second World War in their minutely delineated class structure and accents. At its most extreme, the stage version of hyperlect produced a distortion of, for instance, the pronunciation of 'a' as 'e', as in the 'Relex!' of a Binnie Hale or Cicely Courtneidge.

Quite distinct from received pronunciation or BBC English, hyperlect now sounds, in our more egalitarian sonic society, affected and outdated, and has largely been abandoned by the younger generation in favour of a more neutral version, either based on radio and television speak, the over-voice of documentaries, what used to be called 'speaking nicely', or a version of so-called Estuary English. In its heyday the hyperlect was carried to the four corners of the empire by public-school-educated administrators and was the dialect of politicians, the officers of the armed forces, and of the civil service, for roughly a hundred and fifty years. 'What', Lord Rosebery asked at a dinner in 1878 when he and a fellow Etonian, a bishop, were off to India, and an earl was off to govern Canada, 'would Canada have done without Eton? . . . Our Alma Mater goes on turning out the men who govern the Empire almost unconsciously.' Speakers recognized each other at once, and similarly recognized non-hyperlect users, as in Nancy Mitford's 'U and non-U'. The concept of what could or couldn't be said was a reflection of what could or couldn't be done. The omission of intermediate vowels, as in Asc't for Ascot, the conversion of 'room', pronounced by most people as 'rume', to 'rhum', the placing of the accent as in 'controversy' were all de rigueur.

Numerically small, hyperlect speakers not only attended the same schools, they went to the same functions, to each others' dinner parties, weddings, funerals and balls, and either knew each other or knew each others' friends for roughly a hundred years until the last quarter of the twentieth century. Some still do. This exclusive group was the English gentleman in the eyes of the rest of the world, indeed *the* Englishman. The rest were perceived as servants or labourers, speaking unintelligible comic dialects. In *Tom Brown's Schooldays*, a rustic character still uses the alternative form of the verb to be of Alfred's Wessex: I be, thee bis, etc. with its negative form 'baint', retained until after the Second World War in the west of England but now largely replaced by the eastern form, Kentish and London: I am, you are, he – she – it is. Hyperlect itself reaches its most extreme form in the twentieth century during the twenties and thirties in the girls' boarding school stories of Angela Brazil and her colleagues.

In between hyperlect and dialect the nineteenth century saw the expansion of a version of standard English, the language of the growing number of clerks of both sexes, of the service professions and those who'd been in service, women mostly, who would encourage their children to 'talk proper'. It was the language of spreading suburbia with its upward aspirations. The latest form has been dubbed 'Estuary' but it belongs not to the Thames estuary proper, more to the suburbs of the middle reaches, west and south of London, which have gone on expanding in wave after wave since the 1880s building boom. A form of bowdlerized cockney that has lost any connection with the region, it's characeized by a flat intonation, a fondness for cliché and a limited vocabulary. The language of communication rather than expression, it embodies an ethos of conformity. 'Don't show yourself up; keep yourself to yourself.' Its benefits are a calm linguistic politeness that reflects the desire to be genteel, not to excite attention: the embodiment of the concept of 'niceness', which still has a flavour of its original meaning of what is just and accurate, or 'nice'.

This version of standard English is characterized as 'doyle' by its upper-class mockers, from that most typical physical manifestation of its ethos: the lace or paper doily, as in John Betjeman's 'How to get on in Society', which delineates its usage most savagely in his collection of 1954, *A Few Late Chrysanthemums*:

> *Phone for the fish-knives, Norman,*
> *As cook is a little unnerved;*
> *You kiddies have crumpled the serviettes*
> *And I must have things daintily served.*

Are the requisites all in the toilet?
  The frills round the cutlets can wait
Till the girl has replenished the cruets
  And switched on the logs in the grate.

It's ever so close in the lounge, dear,
  But the vestibule's comfy for tea
And Howard's out riding on horseback
  So do come and take some with me.

Now here is a fork for your pastries
  And do use the couch for your feet;
I know what I wanted to ask you –
  Is trifle sufficient for sweet?

Milk and then just as it comes dear?
  I'm afraid the preserve's full of stones;
Beg pardon, I'm soiling the doileys
  With afternoon tea-cakes and scones.

It's questionable whether anyone who wasn't English would understand the underlying premise of these verses and we're probably reaching a time when they will be inaccessible even to the native. Betjeman fans argue that his portraits of bourgeois life are drawn with affection. This poem dates from a period of increasing change although harking back to a much earlier pre-war age of pretension.

Pretentiousness is, seen from the extremes of the social spectrum, the cardinal sin. 'Getting above yourself' was the common phrase to describe it. A peculiarly English phenomenon, it's hard to imagine Americans subscribing to such a concept. The attempt at gentility should logically be praised as a sign of upward mobility. Instead it merely underlines the rigidity of a system that doesn't allow entry to the upper class. Like Zoroastrianism, you have to be born into it.

Betjeman's verses were originally a contribution to a *Time and Tide* competition and, perhaps through haste, once or twice his touch falters. The suggestion that Norman, son or husband, might put his feet up on the 'couch' during tea gives Betjeman the chance to get a laugh out of the doyle use of 'couch' instead of sofa or chaise longue, but offends the social reality that has to underpin the lines for them to work. Similarly the last two lines are very weak but they let him bring in the 'doileys' and 'soiling' instead of 'dirtying' and 'afternoon tea-cakes'. This largely incomprehensible reference reveals that the speaker has risen from a class which had 'tea' as its main meal of the working day at about six. 'High tea' is a nursery meal of the upper classes. 'Tea' filled the gap for them between lunch and dinner, at about four o'clock. The working class had 'dinner' on non-working days at around one p.m.

As opportunities for secondary and tertiary education expanded in the nineteenth century with more university colleges opening, and a growth in the number and catchment of grammar schools, standard English became increasingly identified with the educated and the professional on one side, while on the other it shaded into whatever was the local dialect.

Even so, by 1901 only nine per cent of children aged fourteen were still enrolled in a school and some of those were there because they hadn't reached the standard required to leave. Yet it was better than in 1870 when only two per cent of that age were still in some form of school. Entrance to grammar schools was not only subject to selection but fee-paying until 1945 – so it's hardly surprising that the percentage of children in the fifteen-to-eighteen-year age group still at school had only reached 3.2 by 1921.

The growth of novel reading among the middle-middle and lower-middle classes in the eighteenth and nineteenth centuries helped to fix and stabilize the language in narrative and description. Nevertheless, although the standard-English speaker might have a wider vocabulary and greater linguistic skills than a hyperlect user, until the late twentieth century he or she would be immediately identifiable by accent. After the First World War Siegfried Sassoon once remarked to Stephen Spender of his fellow poet and officer, Wilfred Owen: 'He was embarrassing. He had a grammar school accent.' Spender and Sassoon were public school and Oxbridge. It took the invention of radio and the establishment of the BBC to produce the seeming neutrality of received pronunciation, 'BBC English'.

Clever children from working- or lower-middle-class families had two languages at least: one for dealing with those in power and a more intimate language of home and playground. The only way into the gentry was through sex or the arts. Successful actors could portray, and therefore needed to imitate, the upper classes and, like Noël Coward and Gertrude Lawrence, might gain acceptance. Part of the English myth is that nobs get on best with yobs. Neither feels threatened by the other, as both do by the upwardly mobile middle stratum. They encounter chiefly in the world of sport: racing, hunting, or playing village cricket, or sometimes in bed as in *Lady Chatterley's Lover* or *The Go-Between*.

The relation between middle-middle and either extreme upper or lower is much more uneasy. In the Victorian hierarchy the clerk is the most despised and exploited figure. Dickens's Bob Cratchit is decent, hard-working, a family man full of quiet virtue, terrorized by his employer Scrooge who has the power to reverse the whole family's fortunes. Bob's kind of heroism, self-effacing, uncomplaining, obedient and intelligent, would provide the backbone of the conscript army of two world wars. Yet no one would wish to be a Cratchitt. Such virtues are perceived as boring although they give certain characteristic qualities of kindness, politeness, endurance and tolerance to English mores. They are responsible for the queue rather than the fight for a place on the bus.

The society portrayed by eighteenth- and nineteenth-century novelists is rigidly stratified, a hierarchy of great complexity with yet more layers within the three major divisions of gentry, squirearchy and labourer. These divisions are still both obvious, and yet incomprehensible, to our neighbours. From time to time some politician will proclaim that they are dead, replaced by a meritocracy where anyone can be anything they please, but simple observation shows this to be an oversimplification so great as to be a lie. The shading is more subtle now but circumstances of birth and upbringing still govern the rest of our lives. The exceptions only prove the rule for most people.

There's comfort, of course, to be had from 'knowing your place'. As the world becomes more alien we turn to the warmth of the dialect soaps, still watched by millions, even of those who've never lived in Manchester, Liverpool or East London. We're adept at recreating that hierarchical world in costume drama for film or, especially, television, based on classic novels. Our fascination seems endless. In showing us the extreme form of the class system at its most highly developed, the historical soaps encourage us to feel that we have escaped that world, but our dependence on contemporary dialect versions shows how much we need their sense of tradition and community. And that, according to the latest British Council survey, is how, for all our claims to be modern and cool, the world sees us.

We swing between wanting to draw the curtain of Albert Square or Coronation Street around us while, as the lottery winners and the pop stars prove, aspiring to live in a country house. Our royal family still leads the country life of riding and hunting. Indeed, since the death of Diana, the reversion to traditional modes is more marked and now involves the next generation in the upbringing of the two princes. At the far end of the scale we have some of the most extreme poverty in Europe while our haves and have nots drift further apart. The class struggle in England has not so much been won as faded into a media backdrop against which we play out our imaginative lives. We allow ourselves a myth of all being middle class now that the fastest-growing area of employment is found on the end of a telephone line in the sweatshop of a call centre.

In the matter of language the BBC now accepts a trace of regional dialect in its presenters: like Jeremy Paxman's hard-edged Yorkshire, Huw Edwards's Welsh lilt and even cockney with Janet Street Porter, giving an illusion of the demotic. But the struggle still goes on among educators and linguists about what our children should be taught. Perhaps only in England could the identification of different dialects with the levels of our power structure and access to upward mobility have taken on such a divisive political importance that potentially threatens the development and employability of thousands.

The mirror image of hyperlect, a construct of exclusivity, and as racy and self-referential, is cockney. The term itself to describe 'one born within the city of London' dates at least to 1600. Edwin Pugh, writing of the cockney in 1912, describes the dialect as every day 'enriching the English tongue with new forms of speech, new clichés, new slang, new catch words'. The cockney 'has a notable gift of phrasemaking and nicknaming'. Like the underworld Parisian of François Villon, cockney must have grown out of the need for secrecy, for a code, a thieves' cant which produced rhyming slang. But it was the conflict between city and country life that fostered the delight in constant wordplay and wit. Cockney prided itself in being sharper; in being an 'in' language parallel to the language of the toff, which it encountered on the racecourse, at the boxing ring, outside the theatre, inside the music hall.

Cockney and colonial English fed each other. Australia is the most obvious example because of transportation and immigration, but India too contributed to cockney vocabulary, especially through returning soldiers: buckshee, a brahmah of a woman, tiffin, up the Khyber; and from Turkey: burgoo for porridge. The cockney sentence structure is distinctive too. A question is often phrased as a statement with an auxiliary coda: 'He came, did he?' instead of 'Did he come?'. The chief noun may be at the end of the sentence: 'He came, then, did he, the gasman?' Those who want to hear the authentic voice of the cockney in the first half of the twentieth century can do no better than listen to the songs of Chas and Dave: 'Give me a London Gel', 'Turn that noise down' and 'Gertcha Cowson'. This last is particularly interesting linguistically since the singer-composers claim not to know what the expression means. It translates as: 'Get out of or away from it, you son of a cow', where 'cow' is a euphemism for 'whore'. Nothing that could be turned in cockney was said straight. Unlike the country dialects of southern England, it was a language that, if it knew its place, refused to accept it.

There was, though, a common stratum of working-class idiom that stretched throughout England, even if the accents changed, and the common usage was intermixed with local words and speech patterns. Commenting on poaching at the end of the nineteenth century, the men of Flora Thompson's *Lark Rise* called it 'a mug's game. One month in quod and one out', a remark that would have been perfectly acceptable in a city street, though more likely applied to a pickpocket than a poacher.

In the highly stratified world of *Lark Rise*, where girls still curtsied and boys pulled their forelocks in deference to their betters, religion underpinned the status quo. The Sunday sermon taught

the supreme rightness of the social order as it then existed. God, in his infinite wisdom, had appointed a place for every man, woman, and child on this earth and it was their bounden duty to remain contentedly in their niches. A gentleman might seem to some of his listeners to have a pleasant, easy life, compared to theirs at field labour; but he had his duties and responsibilities, which would be far beyond their capabilities. He had to pay taxes, sit on the Bench of Magistrates, oversee his estate, and keep up his position by entertaining. Could they do these things? No, of course they could not; and he did not suppose a gentleman could cut as straight a furrow or mow or thatch a rick as expertly as they could. So let them be thankful and rejoice in their physical strength and the bounty of the farmer, who found them work on his land and paid them wages with his money.

The expression 'bounden duty' with its overtones of bondage is particularly telling. Thompson continues, 'Less frequently he would preach eternal punishment for sin and touch more lightly upon the bliss reserved for those who worked hard, were contented with their lot and showed proper respect for their superiors. It was not religion he preached but a narrow code of ethics, imposed from above upon the lower orders, which, even in those days, was out of date.'

Thompson singles out Queen Victoria's Jubilee in 1887 as 'the turning point' away from such a hierarchical society. 'People began to speak of "before the Jubilee", much as we in the nineteen twenties spoke of "before the war" either as a golden time or as one of exploded ideas, according to the age of the speaker.' Ten more years of peace led to the Queen's Diamond Jubilee. Two years later the Boer War began to stamp its mark on the new century of bloodshed and violence. The age of innocence was over. It would take another fifty years to complete the changes begun in the last quarter of the nineteenth century. That stratified village world remains part of our folk memory, of the myth of an England which, with hindsight untinted by rose-coloured spectacles, we know we wouldn't have wanted to inhabit but that decorates our greeting cards and calendars with its nostalgic cottage gardens and girls in bonnets and pinafores. East Enders move back to the Essex countryside their great-grandparents came from, only now it's to the suburbia of Harlow New Town and Basildon.

The process of homogenization, begun when Anglo-Saxon and Norman French were forced together, continues. Television has done most to democratize our attitude to the way contemporary English is spoken, and in the beginning of the 2000s, a touch of dialect no longer determines someone's job prospects for the worse, in the media at least. Mid-Atlantic speak is adopted by many, particularly those in public relations departments, as a seemingly neutral medium: 'Hi. This is Sophie's voicemail. I'm away from my desk right now but I'll get back to you as soon as I can . . .' The globalization of English as the language of the Internet, while it introduces new technical terms like website, log on, hit, cybersquatting and so on, diminishes regional and national diversity to mere differences in pronunciation. Even this tends to flatten out. First-generation immigrants of Asian or Afro-Caribbean origin bring their distinctive pronunciations and speech rhythms with them but their children quickly absorb those of the playground and the media. Our language, which for centuries carried the changing versions of the myth embedded in it, has been converted to a global communication currency. Even the sometime richness of our vocabulary for swearing and emphasis has dwindled to variations on the ubiquitous 'Fuck!'

12

Trench Foot

Oh what's the matter wi' you my lass,
An' where's your dashing Jimmy?
The sowdger boys have picked him up
An' sent him far, far from me
Last pay-day he went off to town
An' them red-coated fellows
Enticed him in an' made him drunk
An' he'd better gone to the gallows.

When Jimmy talks about the wars
It's worse than death to hear him,
I must go out an' hide my tears
Because I cannot bear him.
A brigadier or grenadier
He says they're sure to make him,
But aye he jibes an' cracks his jokes
An' bids me not forsake him.

THE ARMY WAS an alternative to farm work for the more adventurous village boys, while their sisters went off into service. There was often a redcoat on leave in *Lark Rise*, visiting his family or the girl he left behind him.

Most of the century it had been service overseas in the empire for Kipling's 'recruitees', the Tommy Atkins of *Barrack Room Ballads*, published in 1892. These were the 'little wars' as Earl Montgomery calls them in his *History of Warfare*, though not of course to the wounded and dead of both sides. The English soldier certainly respected the courage of many of those he was called on to fight as defender of the empire, wearing 'the Widow's Uniform'.

> *We've fought with many men acrost the seas,*
> *An' some of 'em was brave and some was not:*
> *The Paythan, an' the Zulu an' Burmese;*
> *But the Fuzzy was the finest of the lot.*

In 1885 the so-called Fuzzy Wuzzies, under their religious leader the Mahdi, succeeded in besieging Khartoum where General Charles Gordon, a fanatical Christian unable to contemplate evacuating his troops, was murdered with his Bible in his hand; a failure of British arms which lead to the downfall of Gladstone's Liberal government. However, the election that followed was inconclusive. Gladstone meanwhile made an alliance with the Irish leader, Charles Stewart Parnell, to push forward with Home Rule for Ireland, after the model of Canada and Australia.

Ironically, many of the soldiers whom Kipling celebrates were themselves Irish. The same rural poverty that motivated the English ploughboys and colliers had driven them into the army. Taking advantage of the humiliation at Khartoum to whip up imperialist sentiment, the Conservatives, in conjunction with Liberal Unionists who rejected Gladstone's pact with Parnell, won the next election. The grand old man of English politics died two years later at eighty-nine. The Conservatives took on the name they still have of Conservative and Unionist. Their policy of 'killing Home Rule with kindness', by extending local self-government and buying out the English absentee landlords, worked for a while but left a bitter legacy that would erupt continually for the next century.

The empire now reached its greatest extent with the annexation of more parts of Africa, which the European powers were busily carving up between them. Not surprisingly, Britain's share of the available cake and the increased prosperity it brought, though it didn't reach down into the urban and rural poor, attracted the envy of her neighbours France and Germany, in rivalry with each other, building alliances, armies and navies. Though Britain remained in 'splendid isolation', protected by her navy and trying to maintain her favoured position by diplomacy, it should have been obvious that she wouldn't be able to stand apart for ever. Her come-uppance arrived with the second Boer War.

There had been a first in 1880 after the defeat of the Zulus. No longer having to watch their backs for those fierce African warriors, the Boers defeated the British at Majuba and recovered the independence of the Transvaal as the Republic of South Africa. Unfortunately for any peaceful solution, gold and diamond mines were being rapidly developed in the Transvaal, bringing a deluge of immigrants who wanted not only a share of the new wealth but of old land and political power. At the same time the new republic was being squeezed to the north and the west by Cecil Rhodes, in Rhodesia and Bechuanaland. Since the British controlled Egypt it looked possible to extend the African dominions from the Cape of Good Hope to Cairo.

Britain demanded in 1899 that these South African newcomers, mainly British adventurers contrasting starkly with the conservative Boer farmers, should be given the vote. Realizing that this group of new voters could endanger the republic's independence, President Kruger refused and the Boers of both the Transvaal and the Orange Free State declared war. At first it went badly for the British who were outnumbered and outclassed by local militia, crackshot horsemen on home ground, with no problems of supply and the new Mauser rifle. The British were besieged at Ladysmith, Kimberley and Mafeking, and defeated at Colenso and Spion Kop. Not until the beginning of 1900 did reinforcements arrive led by the veteran of the Indian north-west frontier, Field-Marshal Roberts, 'Bobs', and General Kitchener, who relieved the besieged towns and defeated the Boer troops at Diamond Hill and Belfast. Kruger fled but Christian de Wet carried on a guerrilla war for two more years. Kitchener, unable to defeat him by traditional means, began a scorched-earth policy of destroying farms and imprisoning civilians, mainly, of course, women and children, in concentration camps where, according to Montgomery himself, 'inevitably the living conditions were terrible'. The country was divided into garrisoned zones with barbed wire and blockhouses, which were systematically cleansed and subdued.

The settlement, including eventual self-government and material reparation of the damage done to farms, was sensible and the terms kept, but innocence had been lost fighting fellow Protestant Europeans. The concentration camps in which twenty thousand Boers and twelve thousand Africans died, mainly from epidemics of measles and typhoid, outraged many. For the first time rolled celluloid film and the folding camera were available to record a war. The movie camera was first used in wartime to capture the events of the Boer War as they happened by W.K.L. Dixon in 1899. The race between the European powers to expand their empires had inspired the armaments manufacturers to new invention. Technology took a quantum leap with the development of the submarine, telephone, cinema and wireless, the petrol engine and the car, flight and antiseptic surgery. 'By 1900,' Montgomery writes, 'rifles, pistols, carbines and machine-guns had reached the stage of development in which they were to be used during the 1914–18 war,' with the invention of magazine loading and smokeless powder, smaller and therefore lighter and faster bullets with a flatter trajectory for the rifle, automatic pistols, as used by the Boers, and the Maxim gun with the cartidges on a flexible belt, patented in and adopted by the British army as the Vickers machine-gun, weighing only forty pounds and firing six hundred and fifty rounds a minute. 'More than any other weapon it was responsible for trench warfare, and probably no other type of weapon has killed so many soldiers.'

The big guns that were to be such a terrifying feature of the First World War were also refined, with breech loading and a hydraulic recoil carriage. Balloons and airships were built for reconnaissance, to be joined by the first aircraft. Alarmed by the alliance of France and Russia, whose combined fleets were greater than our own, we began a massive shipbuilding programme. The *Dreadnought*, laid down in 1904, incorporated all the latest developments in warships: oil-fired, cased in steel, she carried ten twelve-inch guns. The Germans too were building up their navy and all these fleets vied with each other for bases throughout the world, which increased imperialist competition.

In the last few years leading up to the war the press, and in particular the popular boys' magazines, as Peter Parker makes clear in *The Old Lie*, were full of the premonition of war, including even the threat of aerial invasion of Britain by German balloons, a favourite preoccupation of the press baron, Alfred Harmsworth, later Lord Northcliffe. Imperialism, xenophobia, war as a boy's own adventure made an explosive mixture with the stockpiles of arms and machinery of war. The public school ethos of manliness and *pro patria mori* had carried over into the grammar schools, which in their turn reflected the public school system and mores with houses, prefects, Latin mottoes and school songs. It was the perfect breeding ground for an attitude to the coming war which had no concept of the difference that new technology would make, an attitude that perished for most in the trenches of the Western Front.

It might have been thought that working-class men and women, who formed seventy per cent of the population if shop assistants are counted among them and whose limited education didn't include this specific kind of indoctrination, would have reacted differently to the outbreak of war, but the evidence of enlistment is against this. Everyone knows that the immediate cause of the conflict was the murder in the Balkans, at Sarajevo, of the Austrian heir, Archduke Franz Ferdinand, by a Serbian patriot in June 1914. This gave the Austro-Hungarian leaders the excuse to try to annihilate the Serbs once and for all, since the archduke had been murdered in support of the Bosnian Serbs whose little country had been annexed by the Austrians. An ultimatum was sent to Serbia, which would have meant the end of her existence as an independent state. Russia was Serbia's ally, then as now, while Austria was supported by Germany.

The British tried to broker a European conference that might have avoided war but the Kaiser refused on the grounds that it was a local affair and no one, especially Russia, should intervene. The Russians began to mobilize. The Germans sent an ultimatum of their own to Russia and her ally France. Within five weeks of the murder the German armies were on the move, following a preconceived plan, the Schlieffen, which her generals had been itching to try out, to strike west through Belgium against France and roll up the French army with a dash for the Channel ports, taking in Paris on the way.

Britain had signed the *entente cordiale* with France in 1904 and was pledged to supply sixty thousand men in her support. A British ultimatum was therefore sent to Germany on the 4 August. When it remained unanswered, except by the crushing of any resistance in neutral Belgium, Britain was at war. The British Expeditionary Force of nearly a hundred thousand men was sent to France at once and recruitment began in earnest. The public schools had been in their Officer Training Corps summer camp at the beginning of August. Many of the trainees were excited by the prospect of a real war and rushed to enlist. Lord Kitchener, who had been made Minister of War, was given permission to form a new army of a million men by the end of the year. The public schools of course could provide only a fraction of this. Those with training in the OTC were given commissions and by the end of 1915 there were enough of them to officer some seventy battalions. But the men they were to command had also to be found.

Unlike other European countries Britain didn't have conscription. By late 1915, though, there were nearly two and a half million volunteers but this wasn't enough and conscription was introduced in 1916. At the end of the war in 1918 there were over four million men in uniform, some two million wounded and a million dead. Nevertheless the numbers of early volunteers show that the eagerness to enlist wasn't confined to public schoolboys. G.M. Trevelyan suggests that until the invasion of Belgium and the reports of atrocities committed there by German troops, the 'bayonetted' babies syndrome, England was very lukewarm about being drawn into a war, but he seems to be taking the stance of anti-war politicians like Sir Edward Grey, the Foreign Secretary, or pacifist intellectuals like George Bernard Shaw, as typical of the country as a whole. The evidence from the numbers enlisting, from personal accounts of the feelings of excitement, patriotism and duty the recruits experienced, and the many young men from all classes who lied about their ages in order to join up at once, suggest much more a culture embracing war as an adventure.

Women were not immune to these reactions, even though their opportunities for direct involvement were limited. Rose Macaulay in 'Many Sisters to Many Brothers' expressed their frustration. Envying the man at the front while she is 'knitting a hopeless sock that never gets done', the woman left at home writes:

> Well here's luck my dear,
> And you've got it never fear
> But for me the war is poor fun.

It was women who handed out the white feather of cowardice to young men not in uniform, even when they were merely home on leave, as if the war were a mediaeval tournament and they were ladies who could withhold their favours from cowardly knights. Young men were expected '*pro patria mori*', to die for their country, for the myth of Mother England, which obscured the economic and social shortcomings at home and was meant to drown out the 'monstrous anger of the guns' at the front.

Men and women, apart from coming together for sex, or rather procreation, led largely separate lives. There was women's work and men's work. Her sphere was the home and family; his the workplace. His place of entertainment was the all-male club or the male public bar. Hers was the home, either her own or another woman's. Flora Thompson says that the gender barriers were beginning to come down in the countryside in the early 1900s and that young wives expected more help and companionship from their husbands, but the change was very slow and is still not complete.

Boys and girls were educated apart, not only in public or grammar schools but effectively in senior state schools. They played apart. Girls who tried to run with the boys were fast or tomboyish. Boys who liked the company of girls before they were old enough for courting were sissies. Young men went from single-sex schools or apprenticeships into the comradeship of the regiment and the smaller unit of the platoon. Their daily affection was for the men they fought beside and in particular for a best chum or mate. John Brophy in *The Long Trail* records an incident of a soldier stuck fast in the mud, painted by Captain Alexander Jamieson, with a description of the event. 'It took four nights hard work by the Pioneers to get him free. His comrade stood by him day and night under fire. He fed him by means of a long stick. When eventually saved both went delirious.'

Tell England by Ernest Raymond, who himself survived to write his best-seller after the war, is really the story not as he calls it of 'a lost generation', but of a David and Jonathan passionate friendship. After the death of Edgar Doe from his wounds the narrator, Rupert Ray, says: 'The memories made my breath come fast and jerkily. With madly exalted words I addressed that slight fair-haired figure, which must now for ever be only a memory. "My friend," I said to it; "mine, mine!" In the freshness of my loss, I thought no lover had ever loved as I did. "I loved you – I loved you – I loved you," I repeated. And I even worked myself up into a weary longing to die.'

The later book echoes the love of Tom for East in *Tom Brown's Schooldays*. Homophilia informs both boys' and girls' school stories. They can compass either the love for a chum or the crush on a prefect or teacher. In *Tom Brown* the crush is on the head himself. In *Tell England* it's for the master, Mr Radley, who knowing Rupert Ray has no father takes his sexual education in hand when Ray reaches puberty including, it seems, discussing the evils of masturbation.

Kipling himself was aware of the homoerotic atmosphere of boarding schools and warned his son against 'beastliness'. Kipling had problems with his own misogyny and, typically for his time, was more at ease in the company of men. Men and women of all classes treated each other with amused contempt. Men were 'just like kids'; women were empty-headed gossips. In the working classes the division was particularly strong, in spite of Flora Thompson's perception that customs were changing. Men worked ten hours a day at hard physical labour and, if it could be got, did overtime on Saturday. The weekend was punctuated with visits to the pub. Homes were cramped, ill-lit and poorly heated. The pub was a place of camaraderie with cards, darts, shove ha'penny and dominoes. 'Why burn your own heat and light, when you can burn someone else's' was a common attitude.

Women too worked long hours of hard physical labour, cleaning, scrubbing, washing clothes and linen, lighting the copper, turning the mangle, scrubbing on a board with the newly invented bar of sunlight soap, often in the yard in bitter weather. Shopping and cooking stews, pies, brawn, puddings, cakes and bread had to be done without mechanical help, and for relaxation there was knitting and sewing to clothe the family and provide the soft furnishings. Many women were responsible for painting and decorating the house. Everything had to be ready for the return of father and the children for the main evening meal. Only a slut didn't have the doorstep whitened or the brass polished, and a clean cloth on the table. In return many men passed over an unopened wage packet on Friday night and received back their beer and tobacco money. Others handed over 'the housekeeping' and their wives never knew how much they earned.

Few men interested themselves in the children, unless something went badly wrong. Then the woman would be blamed for spoiling them and the strap brought into play. Affection couldn't be expressed except in practical terms of feeding and clothing. 'Baring emotions to the buff' was satirized as something foreigners and pansy artists went in for. It was a self-protecting attitude, which would serve well in trench warfare. Generations of malnutrition and harsh working conditions had made the working men who enlisted puny and pale, on average five inches shorter than the public schoolboys who commanded them. This obvious difference should have bred disaffection but the young workers, boys themselves, had great understanding of and affection for the young subalterns who had to lead them and suffer with them, keeping their anger and satire for sergeants and the top brass. Kipling's friend and fellow writer Ryder Haggard, who explored every way to find out what had happened to Kipling's son John, missing at Loos after only a few months in the army, heard a story, kept from the grieving parents, which typifies the relationship between men and officers. A guardsman, Michael Bowe, had come across John Kipling, crying with the pain of a mouth wound but made no attempt to help him because he 'was afraid of humiliating' the young officer.

The mouth wound is itself very significant for the tradition of the 'stiff upper lip', kept in place with self-mockery, and making light of danger and discomfort by all ranks. John Kipling in his agony broke the code. He had wanted to join the navy but his sight wasn't good enough. Accounts seem to differ about whether his father had urged him into the army 'to do his bit' for England, or whether he had tried to dissuade him. John had tried to join up twice when he was only seventeen. Kipling went with him to the recruiting office but John's sight was too poor. Kipling finally wrote to Lord Roberts himself and secured him a commission in the Irish Guards. Kipling's own glorification of war and fighting men was swept away by his and his wife's grief at John's death. Perhaps if he had known that his son might have been saved except for what Wilfred Owen called 'the old lie', which encompassed not only the English class structure but a whole way of life, he would have spoken out against the devastation of the war and the peace that followed, and the traditions which had sent so many to their deaths.

By the winter of 1914 the German attack had run out of steam and both sides dug in after the first battle of Ypres. On the first Christmas day of the war soldiers from the opposing armies crossed into no man's land, exchanging cigarettes with each other and even playing football, in a spontaneous fraternization frowned on by both authorities and never to be repeated, though sometimes they would sing across the trenches to each other, as the novelist John Brophy records, like birds singing out their territory.

Singing or whistling on the way back from the line or in some estaminet but never, Brophy says, on their way up and at the front itself unless in competition with their enemy, was a release mechanism for the tensions which for some became unbearable and resulted in them going absent without leave, AWOL, and being captured, tried and shot. But given the nearly five million involved throughout the four years there were very few such cases, or even instances of rebellions more serious than ordinary 'grousing'. Brophy, in *The Soldier's War*, a collection of testimonies published eleven years after the armistice and only four years before Hitler came to power, speaks of

> a reaction against a reaction. Men write letters to the newspaper, and even publish books, to declare that they personally enjoyed the War. They go further, and maintain that most men enjoyed it as the War gave to the civilian turned soldier health, adventure (intermittently), a sense of a tangible and valuable task, profound emotional experiences, and comradeship. But the deaths of millions, the sufferings of the maimed, bereavements and the anguish of uncertainty, the destruction of property, the loosing of greed, hypocrisy, and selfishness, the shattering of nerves – these are too big a price to pay for a few enjoyments otherwise obtainable.

Many of those who came back and didn't write to the newspapers or produce books felt as if they were living an afterlife. 'I should have died there. I did die there with the others,' as one said to me. The rest of their lives, in spite of marriage, children, the experience of the slump and the General Strike, never held the resonance for them that their days in the trenches and at the front line had. Brophy identifies as one of the 'enjoyments' the sense of a 'tangible and valuable task' lacking for most returning soldiers, looking for work in their urban or rural village simply to feed themselves and their families. For the time of their enlistment they had mattered, they had been part of a national enterprise that could be interpreted as having a moral purpose, being on the side of the angels. Out on patrol behind enemy lines, going over the top, were moments of terror and excitement that had no peacetime counterpart. The mud, the lice, bursting gas shells, bombardment have all been woven into our culture as symbols of things that must be endured, that gave us a chance to show what we are traditionally best at: not brilliance but endurance, as Dunkirk and the Blitz would show again twenty years later, and as King Alfred had shown in his long drawn-out struggles with the Danes.

What was new about this war was the degree of articulacy of the combatants from all the armies and, in the case of the English, of all classes and ranks. Millions of letters flowed in both directions across the Channel, many of them still preserved in public archives and among private papers with the censor's mark on them. As Wilfred Owen wrote in his poem 'The Letter', those from the front could say little about the writer's position or even, for fear of alarming mothers or wives at home, about the conditions they endured. They were sent more for the replies they brought back with the illusion of normality, that one day it would all be over and that there was somewhere to come home to.

Forty years of universal if elementary education had now produced a civilian army that could, and did, read and write, though it would be left largely to those officers who survived to produce the literary accounts in prose and verse that have fixed the images of that war for us in our cultural history. The 'war to end wars' is still capable of endless exploration and re-invocation in books and films, even when the very last of those who fought in it are centenarians. Though there were photographers and cameras, and both still and moving picture records, it was a war of the word. The contributors to John Brophy's 1929 anthology became, several of them, household names: Henri Barbusse, Edmund Blunden, Ford Madox Ford, Herbert Read, Francis Brett Young and Arnold Zweig. Of the poets several had died or been killed, leaving a unique verse testimony; Rupert Brooke, Wilfred Owen, Charles Hamilton Sorley, Edward Thomas and Isaac Rosenberg perished while Graves, Sassoon, Binyon and Blunden survived. Ivor Gurney bore out the rest of his post-war life in a mental hospital.

Never before had war been so full of horror, such an assault on all the senses, but also never before had it been subjected to such scrutiny. According to Montgomery's analysis nobody won. 'The 1914–18 war could not be won; it could only be lost in a final failure of endurance by the men of one or the other side. The men on both sides fought with tenacity and courage, but in the end the Germans broke.'

New technology in the shape of the tank, invented by the British and first used in 1916, and most decisively in the battle of Amiens of 8 August 1918, foretold the style of any immediate future war, a lesson Montgomery would put into practice twenty years later. And one that Hitler too learnt. Without the tank trench war might have gone on indefinitely, but the iron juggernauts, although they helped to break the stalemate, added to the sense of alienation, of flesh and blood crushed by the metal monsters that we can now, in theory, give a will of their own until obliterated by a smart missile. *The Shape of Things to Come*, H.G. Wells's doom scenario, owes much to the imagery of the Great War and to the between-the-wars maxim: 'The bomber will always get through.' The film version appeared in 1936, the same year as the reconstruction of *The Charge of the Light Brigade*, that blast against the mismanagement by the brass hats, which Owen and others had inveighed against as the waste of the 'youth of Europe one by one'.

In spite of the victory of Amiens the war went on for another three months while both sides attempted to get the best out of the armistice. In the settlement imposed at Versailles the Austro-Hungarian and the Ottoman Empires were both dissolved and replaced by a collection of nation states. France got Alsace and Lorraine; Poland was given access to the sea. France and Britain acquired new colonies by 'mandate'. Germany was disarmed and made to pay crippling reparations. The League of Nations was set up to end war for ever, largely by the Americans who then decided not to join. Russia, where the Bolsheviks had taken power, was excluded.

The Kaiser went into exile. The Rhineland was declared a demilitarized zone to be occupied by the allies for fifteen years. Yet the German army hadn't been beaten and it was easy for unscrupulous politicians to exploit the bitter emotions the terms of settlement produced.

Returning home to what he had been told would be a land fit for heroes and to homes fit for heroes to live in, the English soldier found that little had changed, except that there were the new rich, racketeers who had made money out of munitions and war supplies. Owen, recovering from neurasthenia at Scarborough and preparing to go back to the front to his death, had written in a letter that he wished 'the Boche' would 'make a clean sweep' of 'all the stinking Leeds and Bradford war-profiteers now reading *John Bull* on Scarborough Sands'. Strikes had broken out in the last years of the war in the munitions and other factories as employers took advantage of wartime to bring in unskilled workers, many of them women, and cut wages while prices rose and conscription took the skilled men. Even the police struck in London and Liverpool. The armistice brought no domestic peace but only increased violence as millions of returning soldiers tried to make the adjustment to civilian life, displacing the women from their temporary independence, while the number of available jobs shrank as armaments were no longer needed and the war machine wound down.

If the officers had suffered the highest percentage of casualties, at least those who had survived, mentally and physically, returned to a world, a social milieu, determined to make up for the lost years. Cut off from the men they'd led and suffered with, they had every inducement to be reabsorbed by the old structures that provided a chance of forgetting, of pleasure and the pick of the girls since so many potential rivals had been killed.

Owen had foreseen that the promised homes for heroes would be long in coming.

> *Head to limp head, the sunk-eyed wounded scanned*
> Yesterday's *Mail; the casualties (typed small)*
> *And (large) Vast Booty From Our Latest Haul.*
> *Also they read of Cheap Homes, not yet planned.*

In the first five years of peace only four hundred thousand houses were built. As a sop, men over twenty-one were all given the vote while the women, who had made the munitions and cared for the wounded, won the suffrage for those of their sisters over thirty, who were ratepayers or the wives of ratepayers. The rate of population growth, which had already declined from its early-nineteenth-century peak, halved from its pre-war figure of forty-nine per cent, even though women were desperate to be married and afraid of being left on the shelf because of the numbers of men killed.

The war had driven the sexes further apart. The male experience had been so different that it couldn't be communicated. To dwell on it was to be a bore or to 'give way'. Millions had left their home villages, and island, for the first time in centuries and had come into contact with foreign men and women, and ways of life. Men had shared not only the terror but the relaxation of drink and casual sex that couldn't be mentioned back at home. At the same time they had been jealous of what their wives and girlfriends might be doing with the dodgers still in England.

Returning officers found the world of the public school with its opportunities for homophilia still intact. The after effects of the trial of Oscar Wilde, which had resulted in his imprisonment and early death at forty-six, lingered on and male homosexual acts were to remain punishable by imprisonment for another thirty years. In spite of this a homoerotic subterranean culture flourished and many of the foremost talents among artists of all kinds were at least bisexual, as the Bloomsbury and other intellectual groupings demonstrate. The steady increase in the number of prosecutions reflects not only greater police activity but the higher profile of homosexuals after a war which had so effectively divided the sexes.

The myth of England always being in the right and the myth of our invincibility, that we would always win through, when we had so often been defeated in battle, had been shown up as an illusion. So too had the mindless exhortation of Henry V:

Once more unto the breach, dear friends, once more,
Or close the wall up with our English dead . . .

The soldiers who went over the top again and again when the whistle blew found themselves playing out an outdated myth that was being blown to bits by the new technology of the big barrage and the scything machine-gun. Too often the breaches made in the line were indeed closed up with English dead for four years without any smell of victory or an end to the war of attrition. Even when the end came, the German army was not defeated. The returning soldiers were disillusioned by all they had suffered for what seemed a paper victory. For a time we would no longer see ourselves as the heirs of Harry of England's bowmen, and this part of the myth would fall into disuse in our longing for peace. It would take the threat of worldwide fascism to revive it.

13

Sugar and Spice

PART OF THE myth of England is the myth of the Englishwoman, seen by both foreigners and natives as, ideally, a blonde with a delicate rose complexion, tall, inclining to the angular, and frigid. In fact, a stereotypical English upper-class gel. It hadn't always been so. An anonymous Italian visitor in 1500 found Englishmen 'somewhat licentious' but he had never noticed anyone, either at court or among the lower orders, to be in love. 'I say this of the men, for I understand it is quite the contrary with the women, who are very violent in their passions.' The Anglo-Italian John Florio, friend of Ben Jonson, reader in Italian to James I's queen, Anna of Denmark, and translator of Montaigne, quoting a common aphorism during Shakespeare's time, had it that 'England is the paradise of women, the purgatory of men and the hell of horses'.

Englishwomen had always had greater freedom until Victorian times, than their continental, Catholic sisters. Though their marriages might be arranged dynastically by their parents in the upper and middle classes, once married the wife became a partner in the enterprise that was the family, as the surviving letters and account books show. If left a widow she frequently took over and ran the family business. Among rural labourers the viability of the family unit depended very much on the wife's abilities as manager, and part provider through her dairy, poultry and herb garden. Englishwomen, even if they weren't queens, spoke their minds, took part in discussions and politics, and began to preach as nonconformists during the Commonwealth. They weren't confined to the house or constantly chaperoned, except by a maid or companion of their choice.

Shakespeare's women, even though some of them were historical characters like Cleopatra and Lady Macbeth and were played by male actors, must have been based on his own observation of contemporary women, including his own family and those he met through his profession, which must have included all classes and all temperaments. Lady Macbeth and the Lear daughters recall the Celtic queens like Boudicca, but Beatrice in *Much Ado About Nothing*, Rosalind in *As You Like It*, both Viola and Olivia in *Twelfth Night* are all women with distinct characters and minds of their own, while Mistress Quickly, Doll Tearsheet and the nurse in *Romeo and Juliet* extend Shakespeare's range through all the social classes, underlining the independence and diversity of the Englishwomen of his time.

By the seventeenth century women were running salons and contributing to artistic and social life. Aphra Behn is the great exemplar with her plea in the 1680s for freedom to write 'for the masculine part, the poet in me' but she was followed by others whose names now fill the gender and women's studies courses, still ghettoized but at least there. Women continued to play a part in regional and rural life but with the advent of Victoria it began to seem as if the mere fact of being ruled by a queen subsumed all that was necessary to cover 'the distaff side'.

The industrial revolution created new employment for women away from their homes in mills and factories. These new 'factory maids' were rather looked down on by the male 'hand' workers who were still self-employed in a cottage industry, until the power looms sucked them in in their turn.

> *I am a hand weaver to me trade.*
> *I fell in love with a factory maid,*
> *And if I could but her favour win,*
> *I'd stand beside her and weave by steam.*

> *My father to me scornful said:*
> *'How could you fancy a factory maid?'*
> *A factory lass although she be,*
> *Blest is the man that enjoys she.*

In the country villages mothers were anxious to get their daughters off their hands and out of the cramped cottage constantly refilled with new babies. Flora Thompson describes the process: 'There was no girl over twelve or thirteen living permanently at home. Some were sent to their first place at eleven . . . As soon as a little girl approached school-leaving age (twelve) her mother would say, "About time you was earnin' your own livin', me gal," or, to a neighbour, "I shan't be sorry when our so-and-so gets her knees under somebody else's table. Five slices for breakfast this morning if you please." From that time onward the child was made to feel herself one too many in the overcrowded home. The first places were called "petty places" and looked upon as stepping stones to better things. It was considered unwise to allow a girl to remain in her petty place more than a year; but a year she must stay whether she liked it or not, for that was the custom. The food in such places was good and abundant, and in a year a girl of thirteen would grow tall and strong enough for the desired "gentleman's service", her wages would buy her a few clothes and she would be learning.'

After a year it was time for a girl 'to better herself' and a place would be found, either by the vicar's daughter or through friends or sisters already in service, as a scullery maid or a 'tweeny'. 'When the place was found, the girl set out alone on what was usually her first train journey, with her yellow tin trunk tied up with thick cord, her bunch of flowers and her brown paper parcel bursting with left overs ... Every month when the girl received her wages, a shilling or more would be sent to "our Mum", and as the wages increased, the mother's portion grew larger.' Once on the first rung of the service ladder, with its promotion as rigidly stratified as the army's, girls usually left only to marry or die.

One of the reasons for the great popularity of the television series *Upstairs, Downstairs* must have been that it dealt with an experience, still lodged in family folk memory, of when mother, auntie or nana was in service, and the stories she could tell about it. Still being sold, and presumably transmitted, abroad, it must give a strange impression of life in England today to anyone without the necessary historical perspective to place it in, like the Italian student who on her first visit to London in the sixties was excited by the thought of seeing 'the poverty of Dickens'.

Once a year the girls were allowed home for a fortnight's holiday. Their mothers would parade them about the village in their best clothes so that everyone could see how well they were doing, and what good places they had. Thompson describes how what they saw in the big houses where they worked affected their own style of living when they came to settle down in married life. The bride bought the furniture out of her savings in service.

> She would try to obtain things as nearly as possible like those in the houses in which she had been employed. Instead of the hard windsor chairs of her childhood's home, she would have small 'parlour chairs' with round backs and seats covered with horsehair or American cloth. The deal centre table would be covered with a brightly coloured woollen cloth. On the chest of drawers which served as a sideboard, her wedding presents from her employers and fellow servants

would be displayed – a best tea service, a shaded lamp, a case of silver teaspoons with the lid propped open, or a pair of owl pepper boxes with green glass eyes . . . Somewhere in the room would be seen a few books and a vase or two of flowers. The two wicker armchairs by the fire would have cushions and antimacassars of the bride's own making. . . . There were fancy touches. . . . Cosy corners were built of old boxes and covered with cretonne; gridirons were covered with pink wool and hung up to serve as letter racks; Japanese fans appeared above picture frames . . . Blue or pink bows figure largely in these new decorative schemes. . . .

Such innovations produced much satire from the older generation. Older men joked about the bride who'd put blue bows on her chamber pot, or flowers on the table at mealtimes which caused her mother-in-law to offer her son a mouthful of sweetpeas. 'But the brides only tossed their heads at such ignorance.' They had begun a tradition that still continues and they would have been perfectly at home in Laura Ashley, or leafing through *Country Living* for their new ideas.

When they moved to the city they took their traditions with them which, in the case of basic foods like the suet pudding in a cloth, eaten in slices as savoury or sweet, with gravy, jam, butter and sugar or golden syrup, and boiled bacon or silverside with pease pudding, persisted until after the Second World War in places like the East End of London.

Before the introduction of radio there was still singing and storytelling. Many of the songs are variations on the 'Lovely Joan' tale of the clever village maid who outwits the squire or lawyer trying to seduce her. Joan runs off with the 'fine young man's gay gold ring and milk white steed', leaving him 'to rage in the meadows green'. There's even a nursery rhyme version, 'Where are you going to my pretty maid?' When in the last two verses the man asks her what her fortune is and she replies 'my face', he says he can't marry her. Her smart answer comes back like a whip: 'Nobody asked you sir,' she said.

The girls in the songs are quick-witted and sometimes sharp-tongued. Lovely Joan, in her version of the intended seduction, at first pretends to agree to give her virginity in return for the ring:

> 'Give me that ring into my hand
> And I will neither stay or stand,
> For that would be more worth to me
> Than fifty maidenheads,' said she.

The girl in 'Blow away the morning dew' compares the young man who has missed his chance to a cock 'that never treads a hen' or to the marigold, both symbols of impotence. The message is that girls should be tough and clever, not just a 'push-over'. Parallel to these songs are the ones of girls deserted by their lovers when 'their aprons are to the chin'. The songs were a lesson to vulnerable girls who might suffer the fate of a Tess of the D'Urbervilles if they allowed themselves to be seduced or forced to have sex before marriage, particularly with a man from another class. Even as late as the 1930s the kindest that could happen if the girl became pregnant and there was no question of a wedding would be for the child to be taken into her family and brought up alongside her siblings as one of them. The worst was that the child would be taken away and the girl confined to an asylum as a moral delinquent, or driven to abandon or murder her baby.

In some ways the regimented life of 'in service' overseen by the upper servants was a method of preserving a girl until she was safely married, and also of getting her out of a tiny cottage where there were growing boys and a sexually active father. Girls in towns who worked in factories and shops, and continued to live at home, had a much more precarious existence but with equally punishing results for those who succumbed and brought disgrace on themselves and their families. Gin and a very hot bath was a favourite folk remedy for inducing a miscarriage and, if all home treatments failed, there was always somebody who knew of a woman who could get rid of an unwanted child.

It wasn't only ideas for furnishing that girls in service could have picked up in the big house, for by the 1890s the movement for women's suffrage had grown enough to be consolidating the different groups into the Foundation of National Union of Women's Suffrage Societies under Millicent Fawcett. The story of that struggle has been the subject of books, films and television, and there's no need to repeat it here in detail, but a few events should be mentioned. The Fawcett Foundation proved too slow and passive for some women, and in 1903 Emmeline Pankhurst and her daughters Christabel and Sylvia formed the Women's Social and Political Union to carry out more militant direct action, which reached its climax in 1910 with arson attacks, mass demonstrations, arrests, prison hunger strikes and their corollary, force feeding through a tube in the nose, which was both painful and disgusting.

The Liberal government, assisted by the largest group of Labour MPs so far elected, continued to hold out against the vote for women. Asquith, then Prime Minister, was again attempting Home Rule for Ireland, and to pass Lloyd George's reform budget which embraced the first Unemployment and Health Insurance Act. Opposed by the House of Lords because it introduced a Land Tax, it was only brought about, *plus ça change*, by curtailing the power of the House of Lords, after the new king, George V, had agreed to create enough new Liberal peers to pass it through. The most favourable interpretation for Asquith's refusal to act on women's suffrage was that the government had enough on its plate, but there was also the old cry about not giving in to terrorism. In 1913 Emily Davidson threw herself in front of the king's horse at the Derby, and the government passed the 'Cat and Mouse'

Act, which allowed hunger-striking women to be released to build up their strength and then rearrested.

How this would all have ended without the intervention of the First World War can't now be judged. Unlike Sinn Fein, the women suspended hostilities for the duration, many serving as nurses and drivers at the front, or making munitions at home. Classic male historians like G. M. Trevelyan continued to refer to the suffragist direct actions as 'outrages', even as late as the forties, and to state categorically that it was only their war work that got women the vote, suggesting that the authorities would have continued recalcitrant if the war hadn't provided them with a face saver. Meanwhile the Irish, carrying on their struggle during wartime with the Easter Uprising in Dublin in 1916, were crushed ferociously. Yet in both cases some measure of acceptance had to be granted once the war was over. In February 1918 a group of women got the vote and the Irish Free State was set up in 1921.

The first woman, Lady Astor, was elected to Parliament in the 1919 election. By 1928 it had become clear that women were even more likely to vote conservatively than men and posed little threat of real change. If anything, enfranchisement emasculated them. The immediate post-war years brought a mini-boom, which soon subsided into slump. Europe, impoverished by the war, had no money to buy our exports which the United States, who had actually profited economically by the war, could in any case produce more cheaply and in greater quantity. Returning soldiers were disgusted by those in England who had grown rich while they suffered and who now, in the words of one commentator, Douglas Goldring, admittedly with a left wing bias but someone who had nevertheless lived through it all, had honours showered upon them. 'KBEs abounded – Cardiff was appropriately nicknamed the "City of Dreadful Knights" – and men whose surnames stank concealed them under titles which recalled the chivalry of Feudal England or the Poetry and romance of Highland glens.'

New money combined with old aristocracy to try to restore pre-war privilege. Even so the shadow of the war hung over the Bright Young Things who were its replacement offspring, encouraging them to exaggerated and highly visible levels of pleasure seeking that produced the image of the flapper, with bobbed hair, short fringed tunic, bound flat chest, single-strap shoes, a cigarette holder in one hand and a champagne glass in the other, charlestoning away the hours while slump followed boom. When so many seen as 'the best' had died, there seemed little point in not making the most of youth and life, which might be equally short. Although the mood was deeply pacifist, 'never again', at the same time a new cynicism questioned the previous values of service and patriotism that had led only to suffering and early death for the individual soldier in the trenches. The traditional concept of what it meant to be English wilted under the febrile reaction to the 'Great War' as it had come to be called.

New inventions, the gramophone, wireless and the development of commercial cinema, provided an antidote to increasingly grim times as the country drifted deeper into depression. Those women who could find husbands retired to their homes, those who had private incomes took up voluntary work among the unemployed and their families. *They Call It Peace* by Irene Rathbone deals with the choices available to upper- and middle-class women, many of whom felt guilty at taking a paid job when there was so much male unemployment, not only among workers in the old industries of mining, shipbuilding and steel but in the professions like teaching and in clerical work. Women in offices were paid less than men and were therefore an attractive proposition to employers in hard times.

The universities began to open their doors to women, mainly with the founding of new single-sex colleges, even though male students would link arms across the road to prevent female students sitting their exams. Some of the sexual barriers had also been breached by the war. Lovers hadn't all been prepared to wait when one of them could be dead in weeks. Although there were attempts to go back to a pre-war morality, women in particular, although still worried by an unwanted pregnancy, demanded more freedom in their private lives.

The twenties, according to the myth which is fixated on the chaste symbol of the English rose, are seen as a time of dangerous and rare female hedonism of which the flapper is the most full-blown image. In reality they were for many women a time of intense political activity on the left, in which women of all classes became deeply involved, often at a local level like the suffragette Hannah Mitchell whose autobiography *The Hard Way Up* ends with her account of her experiences as councillor from 1923 and magistrate from 1926. Looking back in 1946 after another war, she concludes: 'More intensely than ever I believe in women's right to equality, whether married or single, the right to her own individuality, her own soul. A lifetime of drudgery is too high a price to pay for following her natural instincts, a price no man is ever prepared to pay.'

The new freedoms for women weren't exclusively heterosexual. Parallel to the higher profile for male homosexuality was an increased public awareness, and indeed self-awareness, of homosexual women, many of whom had spent the war as drivers of every kind of vehicle, as they were to do in the Second World War. While the authorities worried about them fraternizing with the troops, they should, given the army's persistent homophobia, have been more worried about them sororizing with each other.

D.H. Lawrence's *The Rainbow* of 1915 begins the run of English novels dealing with female homosexuality, followed in 1917 by Clemence Dane's *Regiment of Women*. Although both are unsympathetic to homosexuality in women, their importance lies in their acknowledgement of its existence. From then on the list of writers dealing with the subject, however obliquely, includes Ronald Firbank, Arnold Bennett, Rosamond Lehmann and Virginia Woolf.

A peak was reached in 1928 with Compton Mackenzie's *Extraordinary Women*, Elizabeth Bowen's *The Hostel*, Virginia Woolf's *Orlando* and, notoriously, Radclyffe Hall's *The Well of Loneliness* – where the lovers indeed meet as ambulance drivers during the war.

The Well introduces another stereotype of the Englishwoman, the antithesis of either the flapper or the rose: masculine, tweedy, crop-haired, based on Radclyffe Hall herself, a favourite of cartoonists until the fifties and still around half a century later. She has both a heterosexual and a homosexual manifestation, variously as a member of the women's institute, lady magistrate, or simply bossy wife, or often as one of the women's forces or a cigar-smoking sportswoman, with or without horse, hockey or lacrosse stick. These cartoon versions are perceived as uninterested in sex and so reinforce the stereotype of the frigid Englishwoman more concerned with her hot-water-bottle or her horse.

The flappers, the female half of Evelyn Waugh's Bright Young Things, are silly and pleasure seeking, carried along by events rather than in charge of them. Their extreme femininity, in contrast to their sterner suffragette mothers, is unthreatening after a period of war and gives promise of sex without responsibility, although eventually they too would accept marriage and motherhood. Even the most politically committed who mourned the wasted chances of the twenties had managed to enjoy them. Irene Rathbone's *They Call It Peace* sums up the impression they have left on us:

> The twenties were over . . . Those twenties that in spite of the mist of economic depression, thicker in some countries than in others, had been in a manner gay. Whose very cynicism had vitality, whose unbelief was unqualified, whose flippancy without fear. The twenties that were the extreme of self-consciousness as a decade; that tasted their own flavour and found its bitterness a sort of comfort – appropriate,

'amusing even. The twenties that were aware all the time, that the bottom had fallen out of the world, and had concluded a bottom couldn't fall further.

Meanwhile the Englishwoman carried on. The humourist E.M. Delafield, who had written the introduction to Irene Rathbone's novel of the First World War and its aftermath, *We That Were Young*, typified in her work for *Punch* and in her own trilogy *The Diary of a Provincial Lady* the use of humour to palliate the unpalatable. In a later introduction to a book of cartoons by Pont, published just before the next war, she produced a summary of 'the beliefs of Englishwomen' which are

> *confined to the more domestic problems of life.*
> *That all men are just like children.*
> *That it is better to be dowdy than smart.*
> *That listening to the wireless is meritorious but reading a novel is*
> *a waste of time.*
> *That a Sale is a place where goods can be obtained for less money*
> *than they are really worth.*
> *That children are a blessing to their parents.*

Presumably her comments on the English in general that we have a phenomenal 'power of self-delusion, neither possess, nor wish to possess, any imagination at all' and that 'instead of thoughts, the English have traditions' was equally true of women and men.

Flora Thompson remarked on the lack of physical beauty among her rural neighbours and she would have found the same among the urban poor. Centuries of bad diet, hard physical labour, cramped conditions in cottages, mines and factories, long dark winters, produced the female counterparts to the stunted, thin-chested young soldiers of both world wars. The English beauty, first cousin to the English rose, is either upper class or a rare sport who has usually sprung up on the stage or later the screen. Until the invention of photography she is almost the only Englishwoman to be pictured except in grotesque caricature by a Hogarth or a Rowlandson. Most of us are as the cartoonists show us: short, pale and lumpy, only recently bettered by the addition of African or Asian genes and an improved lifestyle.

For centuries, upper- and, later, middle-class parents have added nurture to nature to give their daughters the best chance in the marriage market. By the seventeenth century girls were already being sent away to school to be 'improved'. The letters of the Verney family, spanning several centuries, have a charming vignette of a Verney father taking his little daughter to see the Westminster Abbey waxworks, before delivering her to the school in Chelsea where Purcell's *Dido and Aeneas* was first performed. Amateur theatricals were already part of a girl's 'improving' education.

With the establishment of Roedean and Cheltenham Ladies' College, the girls' public school, it was hoped, would be put on the same footing as the boys'. Team games were encouraged and, as well as academic work, riding, dancing and deportment lessons were provided. The English girl's love of her pony is now so widespread, with pony clubs, riding schools and stables dotted throughout the countryside, that there were allegedly more horses in England in the 1990s than when they were still part of the urban workforce at the beginning of the twentieth century.

Many smaller boarding schools sprang up whose names are largely unknown to those outside the circle that provides their clientele. They were to spawn their own literature in the form of the girls' school story, avidly read by girls of all classes who had never been near such an institution, or indeed had any idea whether the life described was closer to fact or fiction. Authors like Elsie J. Oxenham, Elinor Brent-Dyer, Angela Brazil and later Enid Blyton turned out a book a year with a new adventure of their Abbey girls or Chalet school or Towers. They had their own jargon, a version of the hyperlect. A classic example is the opening to Angela Brazil's *The Madcap of the School*, largely incomprehensible except to aficionados.

'Here they are!'
    'Not really!'
    'It is, I tell you!'
    'Jubilate! You're right, old sport! Scooterons nous this very sec! Quick! Hurry! Stir your old bones can't you?'

The books embodied English middle-class public school virtues, which were carried over by their readers into grammar and other 'good schools'. Conformity is very important: what's done and not done. In *Varvara Comes to England*, a young Russian brought up in Paris who is to live in England with her elder sister and be educated there questions the value of uniform: 'What suits one suits not another perhaps?' only to be told, priggishly: 'In England we don't bother about suiting.' Of course, by the end of the book she learns to be a model English schoolgirl. That was what the schools specialized in.

The books also express the inevitable homoerotic element, indigenous to single-sex schools, certainly since Jane Eyre's Lowood. Girls have crushes or pashes on other girls, prefects or favoured teachers, reflecting the reality of the school system they are based on. They range from suppressed passion to the sentimentality of the late Abbey books of Elsie J. Oxenham. The heroines are embodiments of the English virtue of fairness, together with common sense. Whatever pranks they get up to or mistakes they may make, all will come right in the end. Bullies will be humiliated but not severely punished. Liars and cheats will be exposed, confess and reform. The worst that can happen is expulsion, to be cut off from the microcosmic society, the comradeship that the school provides, and cast into shameful darkness.

The strong pull of conformity for truly upper-class girls culminated until 1958 in their 'coming out'. This was their first 'season' of balls, cocktail parties, teas and dinners, Ascot, and the other ritualized occasions where they could be paraded and appraised, an ordeal for all concerned, before they were husbanded and had to put into practice the skills they had learnt. Against these conformists there have always been the exceptions, if not eccentrics: the Victorian women explorers and travellers giving us Marianne North's exquisite botanical paintings of tropical plants, Julia Cameron's photographs, Gertrude Jekyll's gardens. These stand out from the thousands of ex-public school women running their homes efficiently, being pillars of the local community, the Lady Bountiful, whether the locals wanted them to or not. Resisting change, maintaining tradition as E.M. Delafield noted, they at least went along with her further observation that it's 'a firm belief of Englishmen that all good women are naturally frigid'.

Katharine Whitehorn famously described Roedean as 'that potting shed of the English rose'. Linda Blandford, a product of the system herself, contributing 'The Making of a Lady' to *The World of the Public School* in the late seventies, asks four young matrons in a Knightsbridge flat: ' "Can a state-school girl pass herself off as The Real Thing?" There's a moment of embarrassed surprise. "When she's young," says Sal in a slightly strained voice, "any pretty woman with a good figure can dress herself up and pass herself off as anything. But when she gets older she inevitably reverts to type." Nicki describes a well-turned-out, well-educated and ambitious state-school girl as "a cultured pearl, not a real pearl".'

What opinion polls and the women's magazines show is how many of us still aspire to that culturing, that emulation, unaware that in the eyes of the Real Thing our efforts are doomed from the start. Still we go on trying, determined that, if we can't be Naomi Campbell, we can at least aspire to be a long-stemmed English rose: blonde, peach-complexioned, 'with legs that start

under her armpits', even against the looking-glass reality that the
average Englishwoman's height is five feet five inches and her
average clothes size is fourteen.

14

Come the Revolution

TWO EVENTS, STILL part of our political mythology, are rooted in the period known as the slump, although one of them occurred five years before the official start of the hungry thirties. The first, the General Strike of 1926, so belongs with the second, the Jarrow March of ten years later, that in the public mind they are, as indeed they were, part of the same process that coloured English politics for the rest of the century.

In 1919, after the threat of a miners' strike, the Sankey Commission accepted the principle of nationalization in the mining industry, but the principle was rejected by the Lloyd George government, which had won the so-called 'coupon' election at the end of the war, and, not surprisingly, by the mine owners. A series of strikes by railwaymen, dockers and miners followed, including the symbolic blacking of the *Jolly George*, loaded with munitions for the British troops who had been sent to Russia to fight the communist revolution. Meanwhile the trade unions were consolidating their organization, amalgamating into the familiar names of the next half-century: the Amalgamated Engineering Union (AEU), the Transport and General Workers (TGWU) and the National Union of General and Municipal Workers.

The TUC itself was restructured as a national, centralized body under Walter Citrine, its general secretary whose rules still govern the conduct of trade union meetings. Many middle-class left-wing radicals saw this as the bureaucratization of socialism and were as critical of the growing Labour Party, and organized labour, as of the Conservatives and what they called the 'Money Men', international capital. Writers like Goldring and Rathbone believed that these were the people responsible for the war and the lost peace. In the final chapter of Rathbone's *We That Were Young*, *'Nineteen Twenty-Eight'*, Philip Nichol, ex-officer who had become a schoolmaster after the war, kills himself with his service revolver, leaving a suicide note to 'All Whom It May Concern':

Ten years after the Armistice I find that the world is not worth living in, and that I, personally, have failed to make it better. I cannot face another celebration of that day which seemed to many of us such a radiant dawn. Nowhere have responsibilities been shouldered or promises been fulfilled; everywhere is an undercurrent of despair and shame. I prefer to be with those who died before they knew.

Britain had returned to the Gold Standard in 1925, following what many on the left saw as an outdated financial concept of 'sound money'. The immediate result was an even greater fall in British exports, especially coal, which meant that the mine owners were unable to pay the wage rises agreed in 1924 and began to demand longer working hours for shorter pay. Exports had declined from a pre-war peak of twenty-three per cent to twenty per cent, the beginning of the long road to the miners' strike under the Thatcher government. The miners were locked out in May and the TUC agreed to support them. The General Strike lasted nine days in which thousands of workers' families pawned their few valuables for money to eat and pay the rent. It was broken by the equal thousands of volunteers from all strata of the middle classes who took over transport and food distribution.

The government had used the pre-strike period of a Royal Commission, and a temporary subsidy to keep up the miners' wages, to organize the newly purged police and troops, along with the volunteers to maintain essential services and to take out 'agitators'. Four thousand strikers were prosecuted and a thousand imprisoned. Labour was weakened by internal divisions, with the Independent Labour Party, supported by radicals like Hannah Mitchell and intellectuals like Douglas Goldring, taking a much more revolutionary line, which alarmed the TUC and the official Labour Party. A TUC negotiating committee was set up, which accepted a Cabinet offer to end the General Strike. The miners held on for another six months but in the end were forced to accept longer hours and wage cuts. The following year general strikes and sympathetic strikes were outlawed.

Two years later the Labour Party won two hundred and eighty-eight seats in the general election against the Conservatives' two hundred and sixty. With the support of the Liberals it formed the government, only for the Cabinet to be split two years later by the onset of the slump and what some of the Cabinet saw as the need to reduce unemployment benefit in the face of the mounting numbers of unemployed. In October 1929 came the Wall Street crash, when the boom in the American share market collapsed, with disastrous knock-on effects on the European economies, dependent on US loans and credits. Britain was forced off the Gold Standard. Our trade balance went into the red. The numbers of identifiable unemployed rose towards three million. Finally, under Ramsay Macdonald's National Government, the hated means test was introduced, which meant that those applying for benefit not only had any savings taken into account but could be forced to sell even their furniture if it was judged unnecessary by the new Public Assistance Boards.

The National Unemployed Workers Movement was set up,

seen by many as a communist front to incite and exploit social unrest, and bring about a revolution through a series of hunger marches that often ended in violence and riot as the police tried to disperse them, or prevent the marchers reaching their goal. As John Stevenson and Chris Cook point out in *The Slump*, far more demonstrators were injured than police in the hundreds of baton charges over the next few years.

In response to the supposed Bolshevik threat, Sir Oswald Mosley formed his New Party as a breakaway from Labour in 1931, which became the British Union of Fascists after Mosley's visit to Mussolini in Italy. The lines were drawn for the street battles between left and right, which culminated in the most famous of them all, in the East End of London at Cable Street, in 1936. By then the adoption of the Blackshirt uniform, the drilled marches on the lines of continental models with massed uniform banners and the systematic roughing up of hecklers at the Olympia rally of 1934 had begun to lose Mosley the support of those like Lord Rothermere, owner of the *Daily Mail*, the Labour MP John Strachey and even Harold Nicolson, who had at first been inclined to follow him.

Even so, by its peak in 1934, the BUF had forty thousand members and was able to mount increasingly provocative anti-Semitic marches. Like Hitler, Mosley used the spectre of communism to justify a violent response: 'When we are confronted by red terror, we are certainly organised to meet force by force, and will always do our utmost to smash it,' he wrote in his 1932 manifesto *The Greater Britain*. Two years later the tone was unmistakably anti-Jewish. Aliens were to be barred from British jobs and the 'unwelcome' deported. Already refugees were starting to arrive from Hitler's Germany. 'For the first time I openly and publicly challenge the Jewish interest in this country commanding commerce, commanding the press, commanding the cinema, dominating the City of London, killing industry with the sweatshops.' The East End of London was home to many small tailoring businesses run by Jews, some of whom had been there since the nineteenth century and provided variety of employment, especially for women, in an area dominated by dock work.

At Cable Street Mosley's three thousand Blackshirts were faced by a hundred thousand anti-fascists. Asked by the police to call off his march, and perhaps daunted by the sheer size of the opposition, he led his followers away westward along the embankment. Eighty-two London anti-fascists out of a total of eighty-eight people were arrested; seventy people, including police, were treated for injuries. A Public Order Act followed, prohibiting military-style uniforms and giving the police the power to ban processions. The police in their report pointed the finger at the role of communists in the Cable Street action, but the total membership of the party was only eleven and half thousand at the time and, although they often provided the leaders in direct action, the rank and file of the Cable Street demonstration must have been made up of tens of thousands of ordinary members of other parties, or none, to whom the open manifestation of fascism, and particularly anti-Semitism, was repugnant. Some of those of the far left, like the Labour League of Youth and, ultimately, Young Communist organizer Ted Willis, would become dedicated traditional Labour supporters. The anti-fascists now adopted a strategy of staging more meetings than the fascists in London, and in the London County Council elections of 1937 the BUF failed to gain a single seat, even in those areas of the East End where their support had seemed strongest.

Stevenson and Cook have analysed the political and economic reasons for 'the Revolution that never was' in the thirties when it seemed most ripe. They point out that once the first traumatic years of the slump were over the British economy began to recover as a whole, leaving pockets of high unemployment and poverty, isolated principally in the areas of the old industries of coalmining, steel production and shipbuilding. The last of these included Jarrow, *The Town that Was Murdered* in the words of its MP, Ellen

Wilkinson, who led the march to London, which is also part of our mythology of the period and that ends the decade of protest that had begun with the General Strike.

The march to bring back employment to a shipbuilding town whose industry had died, leaving eighty per cent of the workforce without a job and with no prospect of any improvement, was carefully planned. It was to be non-political and orderly. Two hundred men were chosen out of many more volunteers, the fittest for the three-hundred-mile march, and supplied with leather and nails to mend their own boots. They were supported by the mayor and council, and by the local churches. The Boy Scouts lent field kitchens, carried in a second-hand bus, to provide food. The marchers set off on 4 October after a service and blessing by the Suffragan Bishop of Jarrow. They were led by a brass band, at the start of a walk that would take a month, in a column four abreast with banners proclaiming the *Jarrow Crusade*, and with Ellen Wilkinson at the head.

Special Branch, who followed the march closely as it moved south, reported that 'the demonstrators were warmly welcomed by the inhabitants of the places through which they passed, and no untoward incident calling for police action occurred'. Mostly they were provided with church halls, schools and similar places to sleep in overnight by local sympathizers. Only York turned them away. In London they held a rally in Hyde Park, refusing a share in a simultaneous communist-led rally, afraid that their specific cause would be swamped or tainted by association. They had wanted to make the case for Jarrow and present their own petition to Parliament. They were entertained to tea in the House of Commons by sympathetic MPs but it was only while they were on a sightseeing trip on the river that Ellen Wilkinson was able to present their petition. The next day they took the train back to Jarrow.

They had been fobbed off with tea and sympathy, the climax of their protest denied them, and there was bitterness among the marchers. Nothing was done for the town until rearmament gave shipbuilding new impetus, but they had created one of the abiding icons of the Left. The NUWM's near simultaneous march of one thousand four hundred men and women from all parts of depressed Britain, organized into ten contingents, this time had the broad support of a united platform of the Labour movement including Ellen Wilkinson, Nye Bevan, George Strauss, Edith Summerskill, Clement Attlee and J. Jagger, which could serve as a roll-call of the first post-Second World War Labour Cabinet. Twelve thousand people attended the Hyde Park rally, according to police estimates, which always tend to be on the low side. It was the last big march of the hungry thirties and passed not only without incident but also hardly noticed, except by the *Daily Herald* and the *Daily Worker*.

The Jarrow March, which attracted enormous sympathy and publicity, if very little hard result, succeeded in becoming part of the myth for very English reasons. It was orderly and we could exercise our charity. No one was asking for revolution, only, pragmatically, for jobs. The dignified column of men in their uniform caps posed no threat to the status quo. They represented not foreign socialism but English labour as old as *Piers Plowman*. Their caps became part of the imagery of the English left in their own right, only expiring with the death of the cartoon figure Andy Capp of the *Daily Mirror* who had, by the time of his demise, with bitter irony become a vehicle for cherished English bigotry and misogyny.

In emphasizing the political and economic aspects of the revolution that never was − the strength of the traditional parties and their members' loyalty, and the new manufacturing jobs in the art-deco factories lining the arterial roads of the Midlands and south-east − Stevenson and Cook are inclined to leave out or downgrade the merely cultural. By 1936 unemployment had fallen from its peak to a million and three quarters. Long hours and overtime provided a wage equal to food and rent, and with a very little left over. More than a million and a half houses were built over the next four years, enabling the middle class to move to the Betjemanian suburbs, the worst slums in the capital to be cleared and working-class families to take over the better terraces previously occupied by white-collar workers, although they were usually two families to a house, there were still no bathrooms and often only outside lavatories.

The spread of electricity began to oust gas lighting in the towns and cities, although electrical domestic appliances were slow to appear. Even by the late forties, in a typical East London home there was no fridge, telephone, bathroom, indoor lavatory or washing machine. The first machines to be bought were a vacuum cleaner and spin dryer. But there was radio by the mid-twenties and talking pictures by the beginning of the thirties, and these provided the twin diversions that kept revolution at bay by distracting thousands of people from their immediate problems and surroundings, and from politics. Some commentators have pointed to more frequent holidays and better transport for day trips as signs of increased affluence, but these were usually only once-a-year palliatives, compared with the daily diversion of the BBC or the often twice-weekly visit to the pictures with their double bills, news and shorts that made up several hours of entertainment, of imaginative nourishment in the comforting dark.

The first easily available radios in the twenties had been crystal sets with a 'cat's whisker', that could be assembled from a kit. The great advance in quality came about through the spread of sets using the valve and the accumulator which, with several yards of aerial strung round the sitting-room picture rail, provided better reception for millions. Often home-made by a skilled member of the family or workmate for the cost of the materials, their characteristic brown wooden cases, with brown cloth infill backing to the cut-out front, brought now despised as 'nannyish' Reithian programmes like the *Brains Trust*, *Children's Hour* and the *Man in Black* into the home, reinforcing solidarity as families gathered round the set and keeping men out of the pub for most of the week.

Granted a Royal Charter in 1927, the new British Broadcasting Company was made responsible to Parliament and moved into Broadcasting House in 1932. Schools broadcasting began in 1927 and was soon followed by broadcasts to Europe and America, and in the early thirties by *Empire News*, soon replaced by *Empire Service*. Although there was no explicit intention to govern the policy or output of the BBC, the fact that it had a government-appointed board of governors and was answerable to Parliament inevitably coloured its whole tone and ethos. For the first time we could hear ourselves as some of us wished us to be heard, and in the movies we could see ourselves as others saw us through the filter of Hollywood. In both cases the result was to codify the myth of England in a form that wouldn't be seriously threatened until the sixties and is still with us.

The Hollywood version of England, whose own embryonic film industry had been destroyed by the First World War and has never recovered, was largely historical throughout the thirties. Adaptations of the classics, now the staple of our native television, Dickens, Shakespeare, Shaw's *Pygmalion*, Coward's *Cavalcade* and historical romances, *Robin Hood*, *Queen Elizabeth I*, *The Charge of the Light Brigade*, *Mutiny on the Bounty* and *The Scarlet Pimpernel*, showed an England living on the past, whose time had gone while America forged its modern image.

The BBC taught traditional English values of reticence and conformity, what was 'done' in speech and action, through the medium of popular entertainment to a captive audience whose eagerness to absorb the message was reinforced by a hierarchical class system which extended to the empire. Never had England been more conscious of its Englishness; never had it seemed more palpable, encapsulated in the 1939 song by Ross Parker and Hugh Charles:

There'll always be an England
While there's a country lane,
Wherever there's a cottage small
Beside a field of grain.

There'll always be an England
And England shall be free,
If England means as much to you
As England means to me.

Agriculture had collapsed again between the wars and there were miles of country lanes for cyclists like the writer Denton Welsh to explore, though the fields of grain had shrunk and the import of cheap wheat reached its highest during the thirties. Wildlife flourished and, although the number of cars produced doubled every decade, it had still only reached half a million by 1939. Cycling and hiking, going for walks were the major and hallowed form of exercise for those who could get beyond the towns and cities.

The charm of 'unspoilt' countryside was reinforced by nature programmes like *Out With Romany* and by music. Beginning at the end of the nineteenth century, under the influence of continental folk music and story collectors, an attempt had been made by English musicians and folklorists to gather up the remnants of such English rural heritage as had survived the industrial revolution and the contempt of the sophisticated for anything that smacked of the English peasantry. Sabine Baring Gould, Violet Alford, Cecil Sharp and their followers succeeded in taking down and later recording the songs remembered mainly by country people, and in some cases re-establishing festivals and folk customs that had almost died out. These included the despised morris dancing that can always be relied on for a mocking laugh and the more respected, perhaps because less widespread, English sword dances.

The body of music itself, with its characteristic use of the modes instead of the classic scales and of the diminished seventh that gives such a plaintive, dying fall to our folk tunes, became a seedbed for a generation of English composers who took this material, arranged and adapted it. George Butterworth, who was killed in the First World War, John Ireland, Vaughan Williams, Frank Bridge, Benjamin Britten and even the Australo-American, Percy Grainger, were all affected by it. Forming an important and popular part of the repertoire of English vocalists like Heddle Nash and Kathleen Ferrier, it was extensively broadcast and became funda-mental to the music curriculum of English state schools. Folk clubs sprang up across the country, particularly in girls' schools and later universities, many of them affiliated to the English Folk Dance and Song Society with its headquarters at the custom-built Cecil Sharp House in London. The canon included many of the most popular and haunting carols and ballads, as well as love and work songs, and dance tunes. Vaughan Williams's orchestral version of 'Greensleeves' was a persistent top favourite of radio request programmes for many years. After three centuries of foreign domi-nation, and with the earlier example of Elgar showing us that it was possible to be a respected English composer, we had a musical identity of our own again. This coincided with, or encouraged, a renewed interest in Elizabethan madrigal, Purcell and his contem-poraries, English choirs and choral music, both sacred and secular and, eventually, the counter-tenor voice. From their first broadcast the BBC's promenade concerts furthered a knowledge of English music among thousands who had never attended a concert.

As well as books about native wildlife, travel guides to parts of the country that could be reached by bicycle or train, like H.V. Morton's *In Search of* series, or Arthur Mee's *Companion* books on each of the English counties, made record sales. Flora Thompson's *Lark Rise* was published in the last year before the war as an apex to this renaissance of the English countryside, the repository of a fading dream that drew together so many strands of the myth. Even the railway companies, realizing the commercial importance of this green bandwagon, commissioned English artists to produce original posters that cast the landscape into a series of idealized scenes as seemingly immortal as Keats's Grecian urn. The peculiarly English genius of Stanley Spencer turned a village into the place where Francis Thompson's ladder 'pitched betwixt Heaven and Charing Cross' came down on Cookham Moor, where angels walked as in the imaginings of William Blake and the dead resurrected in their Sunday best.

The long tradition of English landscape painting was reanimated with what the art critic Edward Lucie Smith has dubbed 'neo-Romanticism with a dash of surrealism'. Paul Nash, Graham Sutherland, John Piper and to a lesser extent Ben Nicholson, together with the primitivists Alfred Wallis and L.S. Lowry, or George Chapman and the Great Bardfield group, found a typically English compromise in face of the also typical English hostility to the intellectual and the avant garde. St Ives and Manchester as centres for English artists in their different ways, were also caught up in the visionary tradition of Blake and Samuel Palmer.

With the bulk of the population still only educated to the age of fourteen, with our fear of pretentiousness, of being thought a 'show-off', and our anti-intellectualism, we managed for a while in England in the thirties if not to hold back modernism, at least to provide an acceptable popular alternative. Intellectuals might rage at the dumbing down of art and discourse but the newly literate public, now supplied by both public and circulating libraries, were ready to consume quantities of undemanding middle-brow pulp fiction. Tarzan had made a first appearance in 1917, followed two years later by Edgar Rice Burroughs's science fiction series, set on Mars. Westerns and every variety of crime novel were extremely popular during these inter-war years, as were humour and children's books, read by all ages. Wodehouse and *Winnie the Pooh*, selections from *Punch*, fairy books, *The Wind in the Willows*, together with the appetite for genre fiction, all suggest a society in retreat from reality, while authors like Graham Greene, D.H.

Lawrence and Virginia Woolf vainly tried to rub our noses in it.

These classic children's and cartoon books now seem to us quintessentially English. We pride ourselves on our nostalgia for our lost innocence, that's as old as Wordsworth's 'shades of the prison' that close about the growing child, and on our sense of humour that constantly tries to defuse life, rather than attempt to solve its problems, and is so much a product of the early twentieth century of war and depression. *Vile Bodies*, Evelyn Waugh's evocation of the twenties, published at the beginning of the thirties, ends with the hero lost on a battlefield not of the war just ended but that to come. Irene Rathbone's *They Call It Peace*, published in 1936, ends with the protagonist Lorna describing the next war:

'Slaughter on a scale beyond the dreams of the men who lived through the Somme and Passchendaele. Gases for burning and tearing the lungs – for flaying you alive slowly, for sending you mad. Poison-clouds on you from the air, without warning, children and babies, as well as women, as well as men, dying in torture . . . Seas of flame in the cities. And, for protection, a few useless gas-shelters, a few useless gas-masks, a few courageous fire-brigades.' She paused. 'Right.'

'Right . . .'

'And the certain knowledge of all this by governments, and the vague knowledge of it by peoples, and the memory – still quick – of the last war, no deterrent?'

'None.'

'And goodwill, and aversion to world massacre, and *ordinary* efforts at peace, so much futility.'

'So much futility.'

'Now, then. You've a pretty large acquaintance, David, haven't you, among all sorts of people. Know any chemistry research men?'

'Ye-es . . .'

'You must get me an effective poison.'

223

This was the mood of the thirties, a decade Rathbone earlier in the book described as 'night' coloured, amorphous, bewilderedly unselfconscious, and headed by a thing called 'the Slump'. Confronted by the inevitability of the next war, suicide seems the only appropriate response. Others took refuge in religious revival or in the occult with the antics of Aleister Crowley or the spiritualism of Radclyffe Hall. Roman Catholicism claimed Evelyn Waugh, Hilaire Belloc, G.K. Chesterton and Graham Greene, while T. S. Eliot and Evelyn Underhill fostered their own brands of Anglican mysticism. Eastern religions, Confucianism, Buddhism had their adherents. Politics also assumed the mantle of religion, as communism and fascism slugged it out in the minds of many rationalists.

Communism had the greater idealistic appeal, which was perhaps why it appeared such a threat to the Establishment of financiers and property owners. It's easy with hindsight to say that these 'finest minds of their generation' were deceived. Ted Willis, in the first part of his autobiography *Whatever Happened to Tom Mix*, describes the dilemma that faced European socialists for most of the decade.

There was an anger in the atmosphere, born out of the memories of the slaughter of the First World War, of decades of poverty and unemployment, of the cynical policies of Tory and so-called National Governments, of the failure of our own leaders to lead. Something of the heroic spirit of the Russian Revolution lingered in the back of men's minds, and the Soviet Union still seemed to be the star by which they could steer their hopes. Men like John Cornford, the young poet, and Ralph Fox, the novelist, who died on the battlefield in Spain, seemed to have a vision, the communism they believed in had a human face . . . It was easy and natural to see such men as allies in a common struggle.

The bitterness of revelation was still hidden below the horizon, still to come.

Another quirk of our ambiguous history is that one of its most mythologically charged episodes should have taken place not here but abroad, in Europe. We had had such foreign episodes before in the Black Hole of Calcutta, the siege of Ladysmith during the Boer War, even the battle of Agincourt, but our involvement in the Spanish Civil War was quite different. As England we had nothing to gain from it: not territory, not trade. Our own rulers stood back from the conflict while thousands of their subjects set out to fight against fascism, not as mercenaries, but in support of a foreign government. At home, thousands more threw themselves into relief work, even though we too were only just emerging from the slump. The Spanish Civil War, especially in its impact on civilians – a thousand people were killed in the first raid on Madrid – prefigured the Holocaust. The two were in any case linked by Hitler's insistence that Jews and Bolsheviks were two parts of an international conspiracy. In supporting Franco against the legitimate Republican government, he was striking his first blow against this alliance outside his own country.

Writing of the end of the war and its effect on English socialists, Ted Willis says: 'The thirties still had a year to run, but this extraordinary decade really came to an end with the fall of Spain. Certainly something of the spirit and heart seemed to go out of the movement. We argued that we had lost a battle and not the war, but the defeat was there for all that and it was a bitter one to take.' To read through the contents list of Valentine Cunningham's *Penguin Book of Spanish Civil War Verse* is to hear a roll-call of the great and the good, as well as the forgotten, among the poets of the thirties: Auden, Spender, Day Lewis, MacNeice of course, but also Sylvia Townsend Warner, Ewart Milne, George Barker, H. B. Mallalieu, Jack Lindsay, Miles Tomalin . . .

Franco's victory emboldened Hitler. Those who came back from fighting with the International Brigade to an England of bicycle clips, long shadows across the village cricket green and warm beer had a sense of shame and unreality. They had failed to halt fascism in Spain and now it would trample all over Europe. When Ted Willis, invited to lunch at the Savoy by Winston Churchill in early 1939, put forward the view that Hitler might still be checked by an alliance of Britain, France and Russia,

> Churchill shook his heavy head, and thrust out his chin.
> 'Too late,' he said.
> 'Why?' we asked.
> 'Herr Hitler must go to war. He can't pull back now. The only question to be decided is this – will he move against the East or the West?'
> He went on to foretell the Russo-German pact, brushing aside any youthful protests. 'Stalin is a realist. We are not talking of betrayal. We are talking of practical politics. We are speaking of survival.'

The revolution was over. Our central myth of 'There'll always be an England' was about to be put to the test. We had hoped for an end to war but it would be war that would now again reinforce while it fed upon our sense of 'the island race'.

MacNeice had written the decade's epitaph in 1938, encapsulating the sense of futility in his 'Bagpipe Music' as Dryden had done at the end of the seventeenth century:

> *The glass is falling hour by hour, the glass will fall for ever,*
> *But if you break the bloody glass you won't hold up the weather.*

15

The Bulldog Breed and After

Sixty years on we're still fighting the Second World War, as our fellow Europeans remark from time to time. Partly perhaps because Churchill told us so in our darkest moment on the 18 June 1940, after the retreat from Dunkirk, with the Battle of Britain about to begin and invasion expected daily, we believe that that was our 'finest hour'. Everything since must therefore, against all the evidence of improved health and living conditions for most of us, be downhill. We had an empire and a purpose. We thought we knew who we were. Our allies had been overrun. America looked on in splendid isolation. Russia had a pact with the enemy. Dictators and their armies ruled in the oldest centres of European civilization. We were alone. But that is actually how we like it. We like to 'do our own thing'; to be in control, which is what we have been used to as governors of an empire. Our island xenophobia makes it hard for us to accept genuine co-operation, except from our former colonies. They, of course, are expected to come to our aid, even America, which shook us off a century and half ago but with whom we keep up an ambiguous interdependence of love and hate. Our need to be in control, which we express as a concern for our national sovereignty, makes it hard for us to accept the equal triumvirate of us, France and Germany as the leaders of Europe. Rather like children in the playground, if we can't get our own way we are easily persuaded to go away and sulk.

The war that began in 1939 was one that, for once, we truly hadn't wanted. Even as it was beginning with the fall of Czechoslovakia and Poland, many on the left saw it as another capitalist war instigated by the bankers and arms manufacturers. The bankers had refused to let England and France intervene in the Spanish Civil War, while being unable to prevent Hitler doing so, because their fear of Bolshevism was as great as his. Even after the declaration, or rather the ultimatum that began the war, against Hitler's expressed wish that he had no desire to bring down the British Empire (when anyone who has read *Mein Kampf* knows that he would have had to do so, that the new German empire and the old British couldn't have co-existed even if America had kept to her isolation), even at that moment there were members of the British Establishment, Lord Halifax, the Foreign Secretary chief among them, willing to try appeasement.

Rose Macaulay wrote to her sister that she had heard that some people were saying they would be no worse off under Hitler, so why not let him come without bombing us first. On the other hand those who, like Virginia Woolf and her husband Leonard, had Jewish and left-wing connections, knew that if the country were occupied they would be imprisoned and deported or murdered. A black list did indeed exist among the German invasion plans of those to be liquidated, among whom was the young Ted Willis, all of nineteen, as a socialist youth organizer.

Churchill was determined not to negotiate, rightly understanding what was at stake politically for Hitler. The German army seemed to have raced through Europe, it couldn't stop now without unconditional surrender by Britain. Hitler's mistake was to believe that he needed to destroy the RAF and achieve air supremacy before he could invade, as his army and naval commanders told him. He also believed Goering when he said he could deliver the required defeat. It was a close-run thing, a battle of nerve as much as of armies. It was Alfred in retreat in the Somerset Levels, or Hereward holding out in the Isle of Ely.

The invasion fleet and supplies began to assemble in June. On the 1 August Hitler ordered the *Luftwaffe* to overpower the 'English' Air Force by Eagle Day, 13 August. By the 20th the RAF was still fighting back and received Churchill's recognition as 'the Few', but by 6 September both men and planes were dangerously weakened. Hitler made his last threat of invasion two days before, at the Berlin Palace of Sport. 'In England they keep asking, why doesn't he come? Calm down, calm down. He's coming. He's coming.' He promised: 'We will raze their cities to the ground.'

Richard Hillary, in his autobiography *The Last Enemy*, recounts an argument between two pilots, one himself, the anarchist, and the other Peter Pease, the traditionalist who expresses the concepts of England and Englishness as it was still possible to hold them at the beginning of the war. 'He hoped that his role would consist in . . . keeping alive that ancient, sturdy self-reliance of the true born Englishman that had made England what she was . . . What he said was, if you like, stupidly English. But what he would do, the lengths to which he would go, the probity and clarity with which he would live that extinct form of existence, would also be English; and magnificently English.'

On 7 September, as the second part of the invasion threat, wave after wave of German bombers attacked London, but they were easier targets for the Spitfires and Hurricanes than the German fighters, and the bombers suffered heavy losses. The raid began seventy-two nights of continuous attacks on London, extended by November to many other major towns and cities, and continued until May 1941, when Hitler's bombers were withdrawn east for the invasion of Russia. In spite of the deaths and devastation there had been no overall collapse of public morale, although there had been inevitable pockets of terror and near hysteria, especially in the beginning. Forty thousand people were killed, fifty thousand injured and two million made homeless, in a country that already had a serious housing shortage. The Blitz made it the people's war; that, and rationing, and general conscription. We believed we were all in it together.

The icons of that belief are still with us in anthologies of songs of the forties, films, television series, books. Some of us still treasure ration coupons and Home Guard manuals. After our long history of class division, of the extremes of poverty and wealth, we were at last united again by a common enemy as we had united before against Spain under Elizabeth I, then against France and Napoleon, then in the trenches against Germany. This time it was against a Germany that would have imposed an alien way of life on the majority of us who had spent the thirties rejecting, and some actively fighting, fascism. Our dependence on the pragmatic makes us inimical to theories of the extreme right or left. Our eccentricity in conformity and tendency to muddle through rather than plan protect us from political militarism, while of course making us less than efficient in many spheres. We admired the autobahns while mocking them and the organized work gangs that created them.

The efforts of the Home Guard, at least in the beginning, and the civil defence apart from the professionals, were often improvised and Heath Robinson. Drilling with broomhandles wasn't a myth but a reality that has become mythical. That part of our culture which loves DIY and gardening could be called on to make us all believe we were contributing to the war effort and admire, modestly, our own ingenuity. Reared on *Robinson Crusoe*, *The Swiss Family Robinson* and *Children of the New Forest*, we could take in the survival skills that still find expression in the continuing popularity of *Dad's Army* and even *Desert Island Discs*, with its final questions about the competence of the distinguished castaway to survive, build a hut, a boat, find food with, as their only comforts,

Shakespeare and the Bible, the two literary mainstays of the English.

It was the traditional perception of the myth expressed by Peter Pease, and rejected by the anarchic Hillary who would nevertheless 'do his duty', be horribly burnt and return again to fly and be killed, that Churchill was able to call on in his series of rallying speeches at this early and crucial stage of the war, speeches in which he showed no public doubt of the outcome, even though he was later to confess to it. He was consciously following in the tradition of Henry V, as written up by Shakespeare, and of Queen Elizabeth I at Tilbury. These speeches were a deliberate counter-poise to Hitler's own, couched not in modern English but in the vocabulary, rhythms and periods of the previous century, carefully archaic constructions that transcended time and class.

In their turn, the complement to Churchill's oratory were the cartoonists like Pont in his collection *The British Carry On* of 1940, reproduced from *Punch*. The ability of the English to laugh at themselves even *in extremis* may, of course, hide the most acute form of arrogance but it still wins points from others. The French Eurostar magazine contributor notes it approvingly, though the example he gives is more appropriate to the English dislike of confrontation: telling the waiter that a disgusting cup of chocolate was 'perfect' but not leaving a tip, an instance of never complain, never explain, which he notes, as also the corollary that it isn't 'understood by strangers working in London'. Carrying on is itself a basic English stratagem, translated into wartime cliché as 'press-ing on regardless' and with the additional innuendo of having sex.

This tradition of what can't be cured must be endured contrib-uted to the ability of the English to endure the Blitz, at that time the most intense and prolonged aerial bombardment that any civilian population had been subjected to. Later, when matters were reversed and German cities were under even more devastating attack, Goebbels was to call on German civilians to show the courage and stamina of the English, pointing out that they too were a Teutonic people. Mostly, Pont's cartoons show the upper classes 'carrying on', with affectionate digs at their arrogance and incomprehension. In one example among many, the elderly Englishwoman seated in her armchair reading the newspaper, cigarette clenched in her thin lips, exclaims: 'War of nerves! War of Nerves! I haven't the slightest idea what they mean.' Another cartoon, which shows the complementary working-class reaction, has two capped beer drinkers in a country pub slumped in their chairs in attitudes of total indifference, with the landlord behind the bar between them, and the radio relaying one of Lord Haw-Haw's speeches. 'Meanwhile in Britain, the entire population faced by the threat of invasion, has been flung into a state of complete panic . . . etc., etc., etc.' Two other cartoons in the series *Popular Misconceptions* depict the German view of themselves as heroic characters from Teutonic mythology in a Wagner opera, and of the English as a collection of mad eccentrics, men, women and children in tweeds, leaping in the air, firing off ancient popguns and brandishing cutlasses.

When Hitler turned his attention away from the invasion of England to Russia with the launch of Barbarossa, it gave back to the British Left what it saw as its natural ally. The pact with Germany had been Uncle Joe buying time, not the great betrayal it seemed, just as Churchill had perceived. The ferocity and inhumanity of the German invasion supported this view. Stalin had been right to protect his people as long as possible. And there was relief that the fire had been withdrawn from us. Now we could pour out all our sympathy on the Russian people in their heroic struggle, supporting them practically with everything we could spare, for if they went down we would be alone again, still waiting on the Americans to come to the aid of the party.

Children were encouraged to clean their plates of food, by the image of the starving Russians holding out in the besieged cities of Stalingrad and Leningrad. We cheered when the BBC told us of a successful run to Archangel by our merchant ships, through freezing waters with food and armaments. Munitions factories held 'tanks for Russia' weeks when the whole output was to be dedicated to the cause; there were Anglo-Soviet committees everywhere. Eight million pounds of aid to Russia was raised by a fund under the patronage of Clementine Churchill, and Red Army Day was celebrated in the Royal Albert Hall. Churchill was worried that the British people might 'forget the dangers of Communism in their enthusiasm over the resistance of Russia'. Membership of the Communist Party did rise to sixty-five thousand at its height but fell back as the war went on.

Disaster followed disaster for the British, with the fall of Hong Kong, Singapore, Burma and Tobruk. Japan had entered the war with the attack on Pearl Harbor, the American naval base in Hawaii, in December 1941. This brought in the United States so that the war was now indeed global. But the British failure on every front almost caused Churchill's resignation. A motion of censure in the House of Commons on his handling of the war was only lost because no one could suggest a credible alternative leader. We had been at war for three years before Montgomery achieved a land victory at El Alamein and began to roll back the German and Italian armies in North Africa.

By 1943, saturation bombing of German cities was bringing the reality of war home to their citizens. Germany retaliated in 1944 with the doodlebugs and flying bombs that spared the *Luftwaffe* some of the terrible losses suffered by RAF bomber command and once again brought the Blitz to London. Eight thousand people were killed and twenty-four thousand injured. A further one and a half million houses were damaged before the launch sites in the Pas de Calais were overrun by Montgomery's advancing army after D-Day. There was some sympathy for the similar suffering of German civilians, but mostly, British people, sampled by a Mass Observation study in 1943, were able to tell themselves either that mainly military targets were aimed at and that it would end the war sooner, or that the Germans were only getting a taste of their own medicine.

The British and Americans invaded Italy in 1943 and had forced its surrender by the end of the year, but it was another six months before the D-Day landings in Normandy opened up the real second front Stalin had been asking for for two years. It still took the best part of another year for the Allied armies to grind their way towards Berlin from east and west, uncovering the horrors of the concentration camps as they went.

A million American soldiers had peacefully invaded Britain in preparation for D-Day. Our attitude towards them was much more equivocal than towards the Russian people, our other allies, who had been in the war with us for longer, had suffered in their homeland, as we had by the Blitz, and whose standard of living was even worse than ours.

Many of the American GIs were seen as boastful, oversexed, overbearing and overpaid. They brought a taste of consumer plenty with their gifts of food, cigarettes, clothes and cosmetics, the coveted nylons and Max Factor pancake make-up, the tins of jam and ham, and the ubiquitous gum. But their higher pay compared with British troops, smooth uniforms, jitterbugging while we still quickstepped and foxtrotted, the inevitable sexual rapacity of the soldier in a foreign country, seemed alien, exaggerating the differences in a language that was basically the same. We were used to images of Americans from the movies where they seemed modern and glamorous. The real thing, in a country straitened by war, was different. Only the black troops seemed to behave with courtesy. For many of them, being invited into English homes and dancing openly with white girls was their first taste of equality. The civil rights movement may be said to have begun in an English sitting room.

D-Day relieved the social pressure from this army of occupation. We went back to the slog of carrying on, now with images from our own revived film industry to sustain us. *Henry V* with Laurence

Olivier as the king was a reminder of another invasion that had been successful. Noël Coward's *In Which We Serve*, *The Way Ahead*, *Target for Tonight*, and the documentary on the battle of El Alamein, *Desert Victory*, presented the British at war to counter the many filmic American battle hymns, pointing up the traditional English virtues of doggedness and phlegm, the stiffest of upper lips.

When the war in Europe was finally over and Hitler had killed himself in his bunker like a rat in a drain, there was at first a sense of numbness followed by wild relief. It was hard to take in; what would we do now without the barbarians? The celebrations were the last of pre-war England: street parties as there had been for jubilees and coronations, sing-songs, 'Knees up Mother Brown', the Conga and the Hokey Cokey. Flags and bunting were brought out, lights turned full on, the blackout finally thrown away. Our best utility clothes came out to dance in the streets. We didn't know it was a wake as well as a celebration, that the virtues of wartime would have only a limited application in peace.

There was still Japan to be defeated, knocked out in the end by the atomic bomb on Hiroshima and its Nagasaki cousin. It also began the era of stress and fear known as the Cold War, during which we would wonder whether we would see the end of another year and reflect that if the 'atom bomb' hadn't been tested on Japanese cities we might all have been destroyed by ignorance. For the moment, though, we could relax and attend to the home front, that had finally been turned into a respectable war support machine by Ernest Bevin, the minister in charge, and that now had somehow to begin on the unfamiliar craft of beating swords into ploughshares. We understood that the world had changed, but we had to make sure that it didn't return to the hungry thirties. Sir William Beveridge had produced his report on his vision of the way forward just before the victory by the Desert Rats at Alamein, when for the first time it looked as if there might be a future to fight for and win.

Beveridge advocated a comprehensive National Insurance scheme, a National Health Service, full employment, the redistribution of 'national income to put first things first, to ensure the abolition of want before the enjoyment of comforts'. The report sold six hundred and thirty-five thousand copies. Beveridge was a pragmatic Liberal proposing a third way between laissez-faire and state capitalism, an English compromise that now again, because of political shift, seems almost revolutionary. The concepts of fairness we still cling to, that some call sacred cows, are enshrined in Beveridge's vision of the Welfare State and especially in the National Health Service. It seems to most of us 'unfair' that access to health care should be conditioned by income as it largely was until 1945. In the end even Mrs Thatcher couldn't knock them off the pedestal that had been built by 'the people's war', Beveridge's own phrase. A landslide victory for the Labour Party in 1945 was a way to ensure a 'people's peace'; Beveridge again.

We had in effect had five years of state capitalism in the guise of the 'war effort'. Conscription, censorship, rationing, direction of labour, requisitioning, evacuation, restrictions on travel, identity papers, all accepted for the duration, 'until Jerry was beaten'. Taking the lid off was to let a genie out of the bottle. We wanted the things Beveridge proposed and in the main we got them, but at the price of continued austerity, made publicly manifest in some of the sourer faces of the Labour hierarchy, in particular Clement Attlee, Sir Stafford Cripps and Dr Edith Summerskill who were perceived as joyless and repressive. The country was bankrupt and exhausted, with millions of broken homes and soldiers to be reintegrated into civilian life. The effective withdrawal of American aid, diverted to rebuilding Europe as a bastion against Bolshevism, while it reversed the mistakes of Versailles after the First World War, left us abandoned. At the same time we were negotiating our withdrawal from the last outposts of that empire that had been the admiration and provocation of Hitler. Now we were alone again. Our attempt at a welfare state under a pinko government was inimical to a newly naked capitalism, undisguised by the need for co-operation against a common enemy.

Now we lost even our other allies in the truly Orwellian volte-face of the Cold War. From Jerry's face under his spiked Prussian helmet, the enemy features had suddenly become those of 'the Soviets' in their fur hats. It's still too soon to disentangle the realities of the terror time of the fifties, when the people marched in their thousands not against the supposed enemy but against the world's leaders who had, as they told us, their fingers on the red button. To many of the British people the attempt to present the Russians, our allies we had empathized with and sustained for five years, as some kind of reincarnation of the Asiatic horde, bred only cynicism: 'a plague on both your houses', as the English might have thought with some justification, and as Shakespeare has Mercutio say when he receives his death wound in *Romeo and Juliet* in the struggle between the Montagues and Capulets. Mercutio is a very English creation in his rejection of both sides. We were forced to watch, powerless, while our two former allies threatened to destroy the world in the name of ideology.

Our sense of purpose and our identity were deeply eroded. We were being made by circumstances to recognize that we were no longer a world power. Yet hadn't we won the war as we saw it, as the Russians believed that it was their war and their victory, and the Americans that they had as usual come to Europe's rescue? Because of our lack of money to buy foreign wheat, bread, which had escaped rationing during the war, now had to be restricted by a coupon system. This, although no doubt making economic sense, was a bad psychological error, for bread, 'the staff of life', carries with it an historical and cultural baggage second to none. Marshall Aid, which gave us a share of American aid to Europe, made it possible for the government to end bread rationing by July 1948 but the damage to our hopes had been done. Desperately the government tried to give us back a sense of identity and of a better future with the 1951 Festival of Britain, meant to echo the confident Great Exhibition of a hundred years before at the height of empire. Only hold on and it will all come right. But we were sick of holding on. What was the good of winning the war and losing the peace to become the 'sick man of Europe'? The Labour government had made many of the changes we wanted. We believed the clock couldn't be put back, that we could never return to the bad old days of the thirties. Perhaps the old Tory Establishment, with its links to America, trade and finance, could make us great again, give us back our sense of identity.

Our cities were still gap-toothed with the ghosts of houses, shored up and marked dangerous. Returning soldiers in their utility demob suits found it hard to settle in civvy street. This time they got their jobs back and women retreated to their homes, to have the children postponed by the war. There was suddenly a shortage of labour in key industries, in the expanding National Health Service and in public transport where wages were low. The English seemed not to want these jobs. Not only were they badly paid and highly regulated, they smacked of wartime. We wanted nationalization of essentials, yet groused at the restricted conditions, wages and the ethos of a nanny state, all elements of discontent that the rejuvenated Tory Party could exploit. The reopening of the London Foreign Exchange Market followed two months after the narrow Conservative victory.

The new government soon moved to reverse the nationalization of the steel and road haulage industries, and end the rationing of sugar. Its popularity was helped by the outburst of pageantry that attended the death of George VI and the coronation of the young Queen Elizabeth. These were both recorded on television, which really took off as the nation's favourite medium of entertainment after the second event when people clustered around the still relatively few sets in search of glamour and a sense of belonging. It was to be a new Elizabethan age that would bring back our days of glory.

We became instead the sick man of Europe, our best brains

drained away to America. The British workman, who had so lately been the admired British Tommy, was reviled as work-shy, incompetent, interested only in his right to tea breaks. Workers were recruited in the Caribbean for the jobs he and she didn't want to do. By 1955 unemployment was at its lowest ever and two years later Macmillan ushered in the age of consumerism with the slogan: 'You've never had it so good.' The year before, independent television had brought advertising to the small screen.

In spite of all the apparent changes, we remained rigidly class structured. Nancy Mitford's *Noblesse Oblige* and the discussion of 'U and non-U' belongs not to the mid-thirties but the mid-fifties. Working-class students, probably the first from their families to reach university, were advised to lose their regional accents if they wanted to 'get on', even in the non-Oxbridge colleges where they mostly ended up. Attempts were made throughout the fifties to hold on to the status quo, the version of the myth known from British war films which we had inherited from the thirties and fought the war with. Debutantes still came out. Workers still wore cloth caps, and city gents the bowler and rolled umbrella. But if the forties had been our 'finest hour' this must be a dying fall.

The island race, which Churchill had so relied on as an image of invincibility, looking back to Shakespeare's John of Gaunt, and his 'scepter'd isle', could be obliterated in an instant by a couple of well-placed nuclear bombs, leaving a few sheep and hill farmers on the fringes of Wales and Scotland. In a desperate effort to keep our ability to defend ourselves against all the evidence of Hiroshima and Nagasaki, we embarked on our own last-ditch programme of nuclear missiles and submarines, adding to atomic waste, destroying our own servicemen and polluting distant islands. The jury is still out on whether the tit-for-tat power of nuclear deterrence really deterred, as it is still on whether the Aldermaston marches, which began in 1958, had any influence on events.

The Campaign for Nuclear Disarmament was a movement in

the tradition of the Peasants' Revolt, the Chartist gatherings and, more recently, of Jarrow and the hunger marches of the thirties, born out of the people's impotence and frustration, and forerunner of the anti-Vietnam war protests. The great powers had locked themselves into a nuclear arms race that was translated into space with the Russian sputnik and Gagarin's first manned flight. In a limited nuclear war our little island was most vulnerable to a weapon dropping from space. As so often in wartime, for this was at least a war of nerves and resources, we turned to the opposite of death.

The sexual revolution of the sixties, while it depended on the scientific breakthrough of the contraceptive pill for women and the economic liberation of cheaper, easy-care clothes and consumer goods, especially the washing machine that did away with centuries of female drudgery, was epitomized by the ubiquitous jeans for all nations and sexes. Sexual liberation was also a reaction to half a century of war, actual or feared, with its attendant emotional rollercoaster. At the same time other cultural movements, that can be seen as reactionary or liberating depending on the viewpoint, manifested themselves in the drama and fiction of the 'kitchen sink' that brought working-class venues and characters to the forefront of critical attention.

We already knew that *Fings Ain't Wot They Used T'Be*. The two dramatic poles of East and West London theatre, Joan Littlewood's Theatre Royal, Stratford and George Devine's Royal Court, English Stage Company, now showed us to ourselves, as some wartime and post-war British films, and Noël Coward's *This Happy Breed*, had already begun to mirror us. At the same time the English novel moved out from Hampstead to the kind of territory Robert Tressell, Graham Greene and Walter Greenwood in *Love on the Dole* had pioneered in the thirties. The neo-realist dramatists and novelists, Arnold Wesker, John Osborne, Shelagh Delaney, Alan Sillitoe, Stan Barstow and Nell Dunn, show a class in transition whose demand for equality of attention continues in television soaps and that strand of the British film industry that runs from *Kes* to *Brassed Off.*

The act of artistic re-creation is both a celebration and a death. Even as writers were portraying the kind of lives that had largely been absent from English literature except as peripheral comic relief, so those lives were being set in aspic or amber, fossilized because the way of life itself was passing. We still had heavy industries but they had been in decline since the turn of the century. Global trade provided us with cheaper alternatives to our own goods that we had to acquiesce in by the terms of the first GATT world trade treaty of 1947 and the even earlier establishment of the International Monetary Fund. Already we relied on invisible exports of banking and finance to achieve anywhere near a balance of trade. The colour of successive governments mattered less and less as we struggled to maintain a national identity, the myth of England as an independent power against the increasing homogenization in every area of our daily lives.

Immigration has always been part of our culture; indeed, we're all immigrants, apart from a few Welsh and Scots whom we can't trace much further back than Stonehenge. Taking England as in truth the land of the English also makes immigrants of any newcomer since the Norse invasions, including the Norman (French–Danish) ancestors of Lord Tebbit, who in a recent television programme claimed to be 'English'. But in the past the migrants have been largely pale-skinned: Huguenots, European Jews, Poles and Italians between the wars. There has always been a smattering of brown skins: Roman legionaries, Asian and African servants, many of whom, as parish registers show, married natives and disappeared into the national mix. The arrival of Caribbean workers, on the *Windrush*, and then of Asian entrepreneurs expelled from Kenya and Uganda, has added a recognizable strand to the population that's still being assimilated. Many Jewish settlers, faced with the problem of a possibly hostile reaction, anglicized their names to be less conspicuous or to remove the linguistic traces of the cultures

241

of persecution. Such an option isn't open to most post-war immigrants although as the pace of miscegenation quickens, the perceived differences will be so common as to be merely interesting rather than threatening.

Enoch Powell's infamous 'rivers of blood' speech in 1968 on the dangers of allowing further immigration, although arguably not intended as racist, carried the dangerous implication of racism in the very violence of its language to a culture whose identity has so often been expressed in language and imagery. To the English ear and inner eye it isn't necessary to advocate; it's enough to depict. Because our sense of ourselves has been mythically constructed element by element over the centuries and is now seen to be receding further from our present, we are susceptible to even suggestions that seem to threaten its fragile image further. English is a language of understatement that mirrors our dislike of confrontation. We rarely give direct commands, preferring to ask 'Could you . . . ?' rather than say 'Do such and such'. Powell's speech merely described a possible scenario of rivers of blood, but its violence of language was enough. The current xenophobia of the tabloid press against both Europe and foreign asylum seekers sounds grotesque to the traditional English ear, used to gentlemanly understatement. In Powell's case, while he denied any underlying xenophobia, he must be presumed to have been, however unconsciously, in pursuit of political advancement, playing to the gallery. In the case of our tabloid press it's simply the cut-throat competition to sell more papers and for a dominant place in the global media markets. The campaign of 'naming and shaming' by the *News of the World* against paederasts shows how easily violence can be aroused against 'the other', how quickly that evil genie can be let out of the bottle.

As Europe stabilized and reconstructed itself, not only economically but politically, into a union where no one member would ever be able to put the others at risk again, we found our traditional suppliers and markets, the old colonies, increasingly going their own way and building economic relationships in the developing countries closest to them. Constantly in hock to the International Monetary Fund, we turned to the special relationship with America to bail us out, forgetting that the nature of the American economy is expansionist while its politics are isolationist.

With an American mother, Churchill felt no misgivings about what he saw, even in 1940, as a greater intermingling with the United States. 'These two great organisations of the English-speaking democracies', as he described them, 'will have to be somewhat mixed up together in some of their affairs for mutual and general advantage.' The process he saw as unstoppable. 'Let it roll on full flood, inexorable, irresistible, benignant to broader lands and better days.' The better days, however, brought the Cold War, the Space Race, the competition for minds and markets which the USA, with its head start from an industrially rich, homogenized, domestic base, almost limitless natural resources, and an agriculture and industry which had been expanding for a century, providing a classic surplus for export, was bound to win. Britain was of interest to America only as an easy market, especially for the entertainment industry whose products needed no translation, not even in cultural terms since our long exposure to Hollywood had made them the instantly recognizable fairy tale, alternative to our own.

For a time in the sixties, much maligned by conservative politicians, we seemed to be redefining ourselves. Our inventive pop music brought in revenue from sales around the world. Even our film industry was able to produce a string of hits in the early sixties that are now recognized as classics. Many of them were adaptations of the new novels or plays: *The Entertainer, Saturday Night and Sunday Morning, A Taste of Honey*. Hollywood in turn drew on the talents of English writers and actors to produce its own classics: *Tom Jones, My Fair Lady, Accident*. Even where we weren't making the films in British studios and reaping the box office benefit, we were at least seeing ourselves, our culture, our myth reflected back.

Swinging London, with the lid taken off our sexual repression and our native tweedy dowdiness banished, burgeoned still under the influence of transatlantic flower power but without losing its own identity. The question posed by David Lodge's novel, which accurately portrays the sexual dilemmas of the fifties, *How Far Can You Go?*, was answered with: 'As far you like.' Committees under the unlikely chairmanship of the ex-headmaster Sir John Wolfenden, came out with sensible recommendations, for the time, on prostitution and homosexuality. Englishwomen were seen to have been not frigid but merely frightened of unwanted, socially stigmatized pregnancy. Divorce on grounds of 'irretrievable break-down' ended the domestic misery of many. Family planning could be provided by the Local Authority. The Abortion Act replaced centuries of botched backstreet abortions with legal terminations.

A weight of censure and misery was lifted from thousands, even millions. The miniskirt, the Beatle suit, the bird's-nest hairdo, Biba and Mary Quant, flowers and bright-coloured man-made silks and satins gave us a new, liberating image that repelled our island fogs and damps. We were banishing the priests in black gowns who had bound Blake's 'joys and desires' with briars. The emphasis under Harold Wilson's premiership was to be on science and technology to replace the traditional industries now in sharp decline.

France and Germany, determined that Europe should never be plunged into total war again, had established the European Economic Community. Under the prime ministership of Harold Macmillan, Britain had joined the European Free Trade Association in 1959, beginning our hesitant move towards Europe, realizing at least that that was where our future markets lay. Then in 1973 Edward Heath took us into the European Economic Community itself. He seemed to have no fear that we would lose our identity. We could salvage the best of the myth and blend it into a new Britain that was also European.

16

If England Were . . .

If England were what England seems
An' not the England of our dreams
But only putty, brass an' paint
How quick we'd drop her. But she ain't.

THE SEVENTIES WERE a struggle to maintain the modernizing momentum of the sixties against increasing external and domestic pressures. The world fuel crisis meant that our enhanced expectations couldn't be fulfilled. Any attempt by Labour governments to manage the economy brought conflict with unions in traditional industries already in decline, while public sector employees chafed at low wages and high interest rates. It's the function of unions and their leaders to safeguard and improve the pay and conditions of their members, which they tried to do, but in the changing economic conditions they were forced in the process into a position of attempting to hold the country to ransom by strikes that brought essential services to a standstill. Eventually, white-collar voters, including those in many of the service industries, with secure jobs and prospects, brought in a right-wing government to impose economic and political order, however harshly. Fortunately for them, their election coincided with an international upturn in trade, especially financial. The free play of market forces was the new dogma, now seen as an exercise of English pragmatism and our traditional freedoms. Under its umbrella the government was able to sell off many of the nationalized industries and thereby reduce taxes. Individual responsibility was to replace the 'nanny state'. Tough, no-nonsense policies must be made acceptable.

To do this the government had to create the necessary culture. It turned to the myth of England, ready-made and easily reanimated. The myth has always flourished best when we're threatened and this was no exception. If the threats didn't exist they could be created. There were still the commies, though the sting had rather gone out of the Cold War, even if President Reagan and Margaret Thatcher did their best to keep it and the special relationship alive. However, there was Europe, which we signed up to but whose embrace we continued to resist, and then the bonus of the Falklands War, with our brave boys yomping to victory over the 'Argies' in an extension of a World Cup match in which some of the players were brutally murdered or hideously mutilated. We went

> to gain a little patch of ground
> That hath in it no profit but the name.

The rhetoric of Tilbury was brought into play and for a time we knew who we were.

There was to be a return to 'Victorian values', the sixties were vilified and the family was exalted. Society was abolished. 'There is no such thing as Society. There are individual men and women and there are families,' Margaret Thatcher was able to say in *Woman's Own* in 1987. Her struggle with the miners' leader, Arthur Scargill, and eventual victory, set the end seal on the death of the British mining industry. Scargill was right in his analysis of the situation: its threat of pit closures, the death of the nationalized industry and the government's ultimate intentions. Economic reality and the expansion of global capitalism gave the government the opportunity to destroy not only what was labelled 'the power of the unions' but also, as the Prime Minister intended, the British version of socialism, which forced the Labour Party to set about reinventing itself.

The yearning to return to a traditional concept of England, which immediately preceded the eighteen years of Conservative government, can be seen in a curious publication of 1978, Douglas Sutherland's *The English Gentleman*, an affectionately satirical look at 'that apparently vanishing species', as Sir Iain Moncreiffe describes it in his introduction, before going on to explain that 'the species is not really vanishing . . . the coming generation of English leopards are, as usual and with long practice in camouflage, quietly engaged in adjusting their spots'.

The adjustment to the leopard's spots was made easier by the glorification of the individual and the family, of the new conservatism, helped along by a boom in house prices and consumer spending. Making money, the rise of the City yuppies and of London as the financial capital of the world, while the country's manufacturing base declined, appealed to an old instinct in the nation of shopkeepers.

Bulwer Lytton, in *England and the English*, first published in 1833, as part of our long literary line of navel gazing, wrote of us: 'The first thing that strikes the moral enquirer into our social system, is the respect in which wealth is held: in some countries Pleasure is the idol; in others, Glory, and the prouder desires of the world; but with us, Money is the mightiest of all deities. . . . In England . . . on one side, you see the respect for wealth – on the other side disdain.' An early-2000 piece of research shows us to be the most discontented nation in Europe and to believe that more money would make us happier. Yet we still hanker after a mythical time of cottage and village, when we also believe we were poorer yet happier. Bulwer Lytton's culture of co-existent respect and disdain still operates.

Sutherland's English gentleman lives 'in the country, and then only in a selected part of it'. The new conservatism elevated the country house to a renewed importance in the myth. Through the medium of Laura Ashley and similar designs, any suburban semi could be turned into the Englishman's rustic manor, disguising the pursuit of money with the innocence of cotton prints and flowered wallpaper.

Private schools flourished to give a gentlemanly gloss to the children of the newly affluent, while state education was derided in the persons of its teachers and neglected in its materials and buildings. Even fashion was gentrified in the long-skirted discreet print dresses and new country casuals for both sexes. The doctrine of the supremacy of the individual, the family and the nation state, the particular manifestation of Thatcherite England, required an enemy to focus it. A top Nazi, Walter Schellenberg, once commented on our tendency to ambiguity, describing us as 'contradictory and arbitrary' and both at the same time. Margaret Thatcher, while realizing that from an economic point of view we had to be part of Europe, nevertheless cast the European Union and its institutions, especially its civil service, the Commission, in the role of the enemy, and conducted our relations with it like an extension of the Falklands War. Alternatively derided and attacked they, 'Brussels', were to be outwitted and whenever possible defeated for our supposed benefit. Our identity seemed to her so frail that there could be no question of co-operation for fear of being subsumed into some federal Europe based on federal America, which she continued to court in her close relationship with the American president, Ronald Reagan.

While endorsing Darwinian economics, the survival of the fittest in a free market, with its concomitants of mergers and globalization, she was unremittingly interventionist in Europe, refusing to allow any natural progression of it or its institutions that would make it a real counterpoise to the United States. Those who should be our partners were still seen as rivals in some mythical struggle. The pound is advanced as a manifestation of our nationhood that must be preserved at all cost, when it's only one in a long line of coins or monetary symbols that have served their purpose for different monarchs and epochs, and then been taken out of circulation: the noble, the angel, the crown, which survived until decimalization in the form of the half-crown, the guinea, florin and shilling. The pound was originally the weight of twenty silver shillings or two hundred and forty silver pennies. As a measure of weight it has already been metrically replaced. Logically we should now be dealing in the kilo sterling. Only the Anglo-Saxon penny has any real claim to English authenticity.

This late-twentieth-century attempt to reinvent the stereotypical English myth, John Major's warm beer and cricket as a follow-up to Thatcher's Victorian values, only emphasizes how weak that image has grown and how badly we need to turn to what isn't new but has always existed alongside, or as part of, our myth. The version that denies community and even the existence of society as if there could be a nation without it, like a brain without the concept of mind, makes us into a state of line dancers, dressed in the clothes of another culture, dancing to the called-out orders of a master of ceremonies, in step but never touching.

That part of the myth which Matthew Parris has wittily dubbed in *The Spectator* of February 2000, 'PS', 'politically sound', as against the left-wing US-derived PC, 'politically correct', he characterizes as xenophobic, misogynist and homophobic. Fear of change, of loss of privilege, are its chief emotions. The PS still base themselves on the country lifestyle of Sutherland's English gentleman and, as Sir Iain Moncreiffe foretold, are very much alive over two decades later and able to organize massive demonstrations and petitions in favour of a way of life that goes under the guise of preserving the countryside and 'country ways', while vigorously opposing the right to roam, which would open up their enclosures to the descendants of the people who once enjoyed them as common land.

While inveighing against all things Brussels, the English gentleman was able to take the fullest advantage of the Common Agricultural Policy, developing the agribusiness of the seventies and eighties, expanding subsidized yields by grubbing up hedges and copses, ploughing up verges and making vast stretches of monoculture kept sterile by aerial doses of pesticide. As a result, millions who grew up before this onslaught mourn the loss of grasshoppers, skylarks, the songthrush, even the common sparrow, and many unseen others, which their children will never know. The countryside of Shakespeare and his successors in all the arts, Vaughan Williams's 'The Lark Ascending', for instance, no longer has a true point of reference. Nature will indeed have to learn to imitate art if our landscape is to be restored as part of the benign myth that we must recreate for ourselves as Anglo-Europeans, if we're to keep a viable identity that will satisfy our need to respect our self-image.

Another Eurostar magazine contributor instanced as two of her reasons why England had grown on her, the observation that perfect strangers may share a taxi in London and expect an honest contribution to the fare, and not be assaulted or mugged, and the regular appearance on television of newscasters from ethnic minorities. The newscaster, of course, is the modern authority role, a pillar of the Establishment, as the respect accorded to Sir Trevor Macdonald by the public and even by the television companies makes clear. Though racism is far from dead in many quarters of our society, the population as a whole dislikes and despises it. Where a newspaper tries to whip up a hate campaign against a particular ethnic group, as distinct from the perpetual Aunt Sally of Brussels, it has to focus on some aspect of behaviour, on begging or benefit scrounging, rather than on the mere fact of 'foreigners'. We can simultaneously support the Romanian orphans and revile the Romanian squeegee windscreen cleaners. In rebuilding the myth we need to be able to see ourselves in a good light, as personally generous in contributing to disaster funds and good causes, against the official, institutionalized slowness to react of ministries and organizations.

In the global economy no man, and certainly no small nation state, can afford to be an island. We are now reattached to our continent by the umbilical cord of the Channel tunnel and we have to acknowledge that that is where our future, and indeed our interests, lie if we aren't to be merely an offshore bankers' paradise. Already there are more foreign banks in the City than natives. We need the invisible exports this brings us but increasingly, with mergers, the Internet and globalization, this won't continue to provide sufficient employment for a population of forty-eight million, concentrating in the south-east. The problem is most acute for Englishmen who, under the influence of one aspect of the myth, traditionally reject the service industries as 'women's work'. They will find some employment as e-commerce develops, as warehousemen and errand boys, further crowding the roads with traffic as people stop fetching and carrying themselves, in favour of home ordering. A recent piece of research shows most of us rejecting the label 'working class' in favour of 'middle class', since we're no longer employed in heavy industry. However the statisticians try to stratify us by income, we believe it isn't what we earn but the nature of the job that defines our class, and we're mostly no longer labourers, 'workers'.

But will e-commerce catch on in a country where people are used to going out not merely to shop but to meet others, either by accident or design? Our perceived discontent will be greater if we become a nation of fearful stay-at-homes. This loss of community brought down the Ronan Points that isolated women high up above their children's playgrounds and necessary shops. Though the idea that our shopping would be delivered in a pre-World War Two way might be superficially attractive, it only addresses the symptoms rather than the complex causes of overstressed lives.

Although we are the least touchy-feely of people, we still need social intercourse, we need to feel the village beyond our front door, even where we construct a horizontal village of friends tied together by schooling and class.

We have a lot to contribute to Europe; there is nothing America wants from us except as a secondary market. Increasingly, as Latinos and Amerindians move north, it will become clear that America as a social model, polarized between haves and have nots, isn't for us or for Europe. Our admired stability, which contains of course the danger of atrophy, depends on consensus, not on the naked survival of the fittest of laissez-faire capitalism. From mediaeval times we have seen it as part of our duty to provide for the whole of society, including its so-called weakest members, through Church or state, the monasteries or the secular Poor Laws, rather than merely through private charity. The concept of 'fairness' is still part of our ethical fabric even if at times it fails or is overlain. We have massively rejected the eighties' attempt to abolish society and if New Labour fails, or even appears to fail, it will be punished electorally. We are dealing with aspects of the myth, that must satisfy our idea of fairness and our perception of ourselves as fair. The National Health Service is dear to us as our flagship not only because of fears for our personal health and access to treatment, but because of a deep-rooted belief that the poor shouldn't suffer more than the rich when ill. As the oldest among the industrialized nations, however, we also have the greatest residue of ill health linked to poverty from low wages and a rigid class structure.

The benign myth that we must create now, leaving behind the darkly ingrained strand of xenophobia, will encompass fairness and tolerance and courtesy. It won't need an enemy to define it, for there are enemies enough in poverty and disease. It will expand our concern for animals and landscape into making Europe a green lung of the globe rather than a dark satanic mill. Under the banner of John Ball and the freeborn Englishman, rather than the caricature John Bull, our myth will mitigate and if necessary oppose the excesses of naked capitalism and, out of a very English tolerance of eccentricity, will respect the cultural rainforest of diversity that is the European ideal, against the homogenizing impetus of Macsumerism.

Credits

Select Bibliography

Anglo Saxon Chronicle, The, translated M. J. Swanton, London 1997

Asser, *Alfred the Great*, translated S. Keynes and M. Lapidge, London 1983

Auchmuty, R., *A World of Girls*, London 1992

Barrow, J. A., *A Book of Middle English*, Oxford 1996

Bede, *A History of the English Church and People*, translated L. Sherley-Price, London 1968

Caesar, Julius, *The Conquest of Gaul*, translated S.A. Handforth, London 1982

Colibri, Stefan, *English Pasts*, Oxford 1999

Contemporary Chronicles of the Middle Ages, translated Joseph Stevenson, Felinfach, 1988

Davies, R. T., *Mediaeval English Lyrics*, London 1963

Farmer, D. H., *The Age of Bede*, London 1986

Fisher, John H., *The Emergence of Standard English*, Kentucky 1996

Florence of Worcester, *A History of the Kings of England*, translated Joseph Stevenson, Felinfach 1996

Fraser, George Macdonald, *The World of the Public School*, London 1977

Geoffrey of Monmouth, *The History of the Kings of Britain*, translated L. Thorpe, London 1966

Gildas, *The Ruin of Britain and Other Works*, translated M. Winterbottom, London 1978

Godman, Peter, Alcuin, *The Bishops, Kings and Saints of York*, Oxford 1982

Goldring, Douglas, *The Nineteen Twenties*, London 1945

Gregory of Tours, *The History of the Franks*, translated L. Thorpe, London 1979

Hillary, Richard, *The Last Enemy*, London 1942

Hilton, Rodney, *Class Conflict and the Crisis of Feudalism*, London 1985

Honan, Park, *Shakespeare, A Life*, Oxford 1998

Honey, John, *Language Is Power*, London 1997

Hughes, Kathleen, *The Church in Early Irish Society*, London 1966

Hughes, Robert, *The Fatal Shore*, London 1986

Hunter Blair, Peter, *Northumbria In the Days of Bede*, London 1976

Lapidge, M. and Dumville, D., eds, *Gildas: New Approaches*, Suffolk 1984

Layomon's Brut, translated W.R.T. Barron and S.C. Weinberg, Harlow 1995

Le Saux, Françoise M., *Layomon's Brut, The Poem and Its Sources*, Cambridge 1989

Lewis, Peter, *A People's War*, London 1986

Longman Handbook of Modern British History 1714–1980, The, ed. C. Cook and J. Stevenson, London 1983

Miall, Antony and Milsted, David, *The Xenophobe's Guide to the English*, London 1998

Montgomery, Bernard, *A History of Warfare*, London 1968

Nennius, *British History and the Welsh Annals*, translated J. Morris, London 1980

Parker, Peter, *The Old Lie*, London 1987

Porter, Roy, *London*, London 1994

Rumble, A. R., *The Reign of Cnut*, London 1994

Simeon of Durham, translated Joseph Stevenson, Felinfach 1987

Stenton, Sir Frank, *Anglo Saxon England*, Oxford 1998

Stevenson, John and Cook, Chris, *The Slump*, London 1977

Sturdy, David, *Alfred the Great*, London 1995

Sutherland, Douglas, *The English Gentleman*, London 1978

Tacitus, *The Agricola and the Germania*, translated H Mattingly, London 1970

Thomas, Hugh, *The Spanish Civil War*, London 1990

Thompson, E. P., *The Making of the English Working Class*, London 1963

Thompson, Flora, *Lark Rise to Candleford*, Oxford 1945

Trevelyan, G. M., *A Shortened History of England*, London 1959

Whitelock, Dorothy, *The Beginnings of English Society*, London 1968

William of Malmesbury, *Gesta Regum Anglorum*, translated R.A.B. Mynors, R. M. Thomson and M. Winterbottom, Oxford 1998

Willis, Ted, *Whatever Happened to Tom Mix?*, London 1970

Index

shipbuilding, 182, 215–17
Sidney, Sir Philip, 140
Simnel, Lambert, 88
Sinn Fein, 202
slave trade, 129
slump, 88, 189, 202, 211, 213–17, 224
Smith, Adam, 117, 126–7
soap operas, 163–4, 173, 241
socialism, 133, 212, 224, 247
soldiers, 178–9, 183–5, 187–91, 192, 193–4
Somerset, Duke of, 94
songs, 30–1, 136–7, 199–200, 219–20, 230
South Africa, 180–1
sovereignty, 227–8
Spain, 95–6, 104, 106, 107
Spanish Armada, 96, 98, 99, 102
Spanish Civil War, 225–6, 228
Speenhamland system, 146
Spencer, Stanley, 222
Spender, Stephen, 172
sport, 120, 149, 161–3, 172
Stalin, Joseph, 226, 232
Star Chamber, 111
steam power, 130
steel industry, 120, 158
Stephen, King, 60–1, 69
Stevenson, John, 214, 215, 217
Stevenson, Robert Louis, ix
Stewart, Frances, 11
'stiff upper lip', 188, 235
Stock Exchange, 119
Stonehenge, 2–3
Strachey, John, 214
Strafford, Thomas Wentworth, Earl of, 112

Street Porter, Janet, 174
strikes, 134, 192, 211, 212–13, 245
Stuart, James, Old Pretender, 118
Stuart dynasty, 49, 62, 105–17, 118, 128
Stubbs, George, 124, 141
suburbs, 160, 169, 218
Suetonius Paulinus, 10, 11
suffragettes, 80, 193, 201–2
Sutherland, Douglas, 247, 248, 249
Swein (son of Godwine), 45, 46
Swein Forkbeard, King of Denmark, 41–2

Tacitus, 3–4, 10, 11, 23
taxation, 54, 58, 62, 76, 79, 127, 246
Tebbit, Lord, 241
television, 149, 162–3, 173, 176–7, 198, 219, 238, 239, 240–1, 250
tennis, 162
Tennyson, Alfred, Lord, 10, 11, 155
Tertullian of Carthage, 13, 14
Thanet, Isle of, 21, 34
Thatcher, Margaret, 11, 121, 212, 236, 246–7, 248–9
theatre, 97–104, 167, 240–1
Theodosius, Emperor, 17, 18
Thompson, E.P., 133
Thompson, Flora, 175–6, 185, 186, 197, 198–9, 206, 221
Thorkell the Tall, 41
Tolpuddle Martyrs, 133, 137
Tostig, Earl of Northumbria, 46–8, 49, 50
Tower of London, 53–4, 104, 109–10
trade, 119–20, 121, 157, 212, 241, 246

William Rufus, King, 57–9
Willis, Ted, 215, 224, 225, 226, 228
Wilson, Harold, 244
Winchester, 17, 53, 59, 115
Windsor Castle, 82
woad, 8
Wodehouse, P.G., 222
Wolfe, James, 126
Wolfenden, Sir John, 244
Wolsey, Thomas, 91
women, 195–210; 'English rose', 25, 204; language, 61, 67–8, 169; male hostility to, 80; growing freedoms, 114, 115, 195–6; prostitutes, 122; industrial revolution, 130; in paintings, 155; First World War, 184–5; in the home, 185, 186–7; voting rights, 193, 201–2; stereotypes, 195, 205; appearance, 195, 206–7, 209–10; marriage, 195, 200, 207; employment, 196–9, 200, 203; sexuality, 199–201, 203–4; pregnancy,

200–1, 244; flappers, 203, 204, 205; homosexuality, 204–5, 208; education, 207–8, 209
Woolf, Virginia, 204–5, 223, 228
Wordsworth, William, 131, 223
work ethic, 135
working classes, 81–2, 83, 119, 120, 131–3, 135–7, 171, 172, 175, 182–3, 186–7, 251
Wren, Sir Christopher, 121
Wulfstan, Archbishop of York, 42–3, 48
Wycliffe, John, 76, 80, 81

xenophobia, 123, 182, 227–8, 242, 249, 252

Yeamcs, W.Г., 112–13
Yearsley, Anne, 140
York, 32–3, 35, 216
Yorkists, 85–6, 88

Zulu Wars, 180